MINISTRY

MINISTRY

by

ROBERT S. PAUL

Waldo Professor of Church History
Hartford Theological Seminary
Hartford, Connecticut

WILLIAM B. EERDMANS PUBLISHING COMPANY
GRAND RAPIDS, MICHIGAN

Dedicated with Affection
to
Robert James Kingsbury Paul
and
to the Memory of
Florence Eliza Paul

Preface

It will not sound very clever if I say that this book has been written because no one else looked as if he were going to do it, but in a most profound sense that is where we begin. I would have been well content if some writer more competent to write on the Ministry, more authentically "American" if you will, had set his pen to paper, but if we have waited in vain for that, this is offered in the hope that it will stimulate more earnest and thorough study of the Church and its Ministry.

This book is concerned not with the technicalities of being a Minister or with becoming an effective preacher, but with the meaning of ordination itself. It has arisen out of the prevailing mood of anxiety and doubt described in the first chapter — the contemporary uncertainty of many clergymen and theological students about the validity and nature of their own calling in the Church. If you detect a note of urgency in the writing, you will not be mistaken. I write only because I know there are young men on the threshold of the Christian Ministry who have been half convinced by much that suggests that the ordained Ministry is outmoded, and who are genuinely asking themselves whether such a profession in the Church of this century can be considered "Christian." The thoughts set down here may not be very learned or original, but they are an attempt to grapple with this problem from the standpoint of biblical theology, and if the book solves no problems, I hope it will at least provoke others to do better. The nature of the Ministry has become one of the vital pressure points in our contemporary Church.

7

From time to time you may detect a distinctly British accent in the writing. The most obvious reason for this I can do little about, but there are other reasons which make it relevant to our subject. In the first place, as you will notice in Chapter II, the continuing discussion between the Anglican Church and the other churches in Britain has meant that the Ministry has received much more attention from British scholars than it has either in continental Europe or in America. Moreover, I suggest that a more profound knowledge in America of the British literature on the nature of the Ministry would clear away some of the cobwebs on the subject. There is a further sense, too, in which the Free Church situation in Britain, for all its obvious national characteristics, is very closely related to the church situation in America, and I am reckless enough to suggest that we could learn from each other. This should remind us that, if the concept of Ministry is derived from the gospel itself, we are not to look for any specifically "American" or "British" view of Ministry, for only if the office is functional and man-made should it reflect a predominantly national coloring. We are concerned with *Ministry,* which to be valid should arise from the gospel itself and be of universal application in the Church.

Since a word of encouragement to the reader might be considered out of place, perhaps I may offer a few words of guidance. Chapter I says something concerning the modern perplexity about the ordained Ministry and describes some causes of this perplexity. Chapter II briefly reviews the historical debate on the nature of the Ministry, and considers several views in the contemporary discussion that may help us in our own search for meaning. In Chapter III and IV my own basic approach to the theology of Ministry is developed with reference first to the ministry of our Lord, and then to the ministry of the whole Church; and in the light of this, Chapter V discusses the extremely important but disputed question of ordination. The final three chapters branch out from this point to discuss the implications of the concept of Ministry that we have set forth within various crucial areas of the Church's life and thought — the problem of ecclesiastical and Ministerial authority, the difficult questions surrounding "apostolic succession," and lastly, the relationship of the Minister to the "secular."

That is the book. It will not help anyone become a more

efficient church administrator, a more insightful counselor, a more persuasive preacher or a more competent pastor. It may — it just *may* — help him to become a more reconciled administrator, a more understanding counselor, a more zealous preacher and a more committed pastor, even though none of these subjects is treated directly. For we are concerned with the *meaning* of Ministry, and that begins with Jesus Christ.

My thanks are due to many who by their teaching, preaching, and pastoral example have illumined the meaning of Ministry to me, but in particular I must thank my colleagues on the faculty at the Hartford Seminary Foundation who have stimulated my thinking and offered their wisdom at the places where I threatened to reveal my ignorance. I am especially grateful to those who read the book in typescript and who helped by their advice and encouragement: Dr. James N. Gettemy, President of the Hartford Seminary Foundation; Dr. Frederick Alden, Professor of Pastoral Theology; and my friend and present Minister, the Reverend Robert L. Edwards. Mrs. Bernice Sebold typed most of the manuscript, and in addition deserves my thanks for the very many valuable criticisms she made along the way. Similarly I must thank Dr. Charles T. Russ for undertaking the ungrateful task of compiling the index.

I dedicate the book to a layman whose ministry will always stand first in my life, my father, and to the cherished memory of my dear mother.

Robert S. Paul.

Hartford, Connecticut

Contents

chapter one

A Ministry Perplexed

I

INTRODUCTION

It has been called "the Perplexed Profession."[1] The Protestant Ministry* is perplexed, and it does not quite know why. In Britain or Europe one might be able to understand this, but in America the churches have enjoyed a religious boom the like of which has been rarely seen in history. Figures for membership and church extension have reached unparallelled heights, the churches administer an unprecedented amount of money not only for their own programs but also for charitable causes, and religion appears to have reached a new high tide of popularity as a constituent element in the American Way of Life.

The Minister shares in the evident success of the Church; he has a recognized even if diminished place in society, and, despite

---

[1] H. Richard Niebuhr, *The Purpose of the Church and its Ministry* (New York & Evanston: Harper & Row, 1956), pp. 48f., 65f., 72f.

* It is evident that the word 'ministry' can be used in two different ways. In its most popular usage it represents the ordained officers of the Church — the "Ministers." We have capitalized these forms to distinguish them from the other use of the word, i.e., ministry when it represents "the act of ministering," although in quotations the original capitalization of the author has been maintained.

13

the separation of Church and State, it would be almost unthinkable not to invite his invocation of the Deity at public functions.

No Minister would admit any desire to be complacent, but he senses that he ought to be reasonably satisfied with the way things have been going. In particular he would like to feel sure that the signs of "success" that are lauded in his profession really represent success in terms of the gospel that he preaches. He would like to be sure that the job in which he has been spending his time and energy is the one to which God called him when he entered the ministry.

The evidence suggests that many students in our seminaries and clergymen in our parishes are not so sure: there are many "uncertain servants in seminary and ministry."[2] That in itself might not be too much to worry about, but the disquieting fact is that often the degree of their uncertainty seems to be in direct proportion to their spiritual sensitivity.

This provides us with a hint that the causes are likely to be complex. Some of the anxiety may be due to the general confusion and universal threat we all inherit in this mid-twentieth century, for a person does not cease to live in the world or experience its tensions when he becomes ordained. But in itself it is not sufficient to explain the present malaise, if malaise it be, for many have lived with the tensions of the nuclear age since childhood. In any case a Minister is one who by accepting that vocation proclaims his conviction that God has spoken a Word to just such a situation as the one which our race faces. The uncertainty lies at deeper levels — it arises primarily, not from perplexity about the world, but from perplexity about the Faith and the institutions entrusted with its proclamation. Perhaps Ministers are especially anxious about those institutions that are entrusted with its proclamation.

We have said that the causes are complex, and one could very well compound the complexity by discoursing at length on the many revolutionary ideas that threaten to undermine the Christian Faith. But I suspect that ever since the breakdown of the traditional systems of orthodoxy in the middle of the last century, the exhilarating study of theology has been nearer the danger and thrill of uncharted space flight than to the safety and certainty of the scheduled airlines. "A hundred years ago, fifty years ago, thirty

[2] The subtitle to Walter D. Wagoner's book *Bachelor of Divinity* (New York: Association Press, 1963).

years ago," declares a scholarly British Minister, "our fathers were in possession of exact definitions of all the great truths of the Christian Faith. Immense provinces of Christian doctrine were laid down in their theological schemes with all the definiteness and clearness of an Ordinance Survey." The preacher's task was not too difficult because "definitions of every doctrine were under his hand . . . . He was travelling in a country in which the roads were all made, and in which it was impossible for him to go wrong." The same writer goes on to declare, "Now all this has passed away . . . . The substance of the ancient faith remains, but people find it hard to give their faith a definite expression and on many questions that seem to be remote from the central truths of the Christian revelation there is the greatest indecision and uncertainty."[3]

True enough. That is exactly the case. But it may put the matter into clearer perspective to know that these words to theological students were uttered by R. W. Dale in 1880. We suspect that some of our theological uncertainties are not so modern, and that an innocent paradise of theological certainty has existed only in our romantic imaginings about the past. The Church has always been engaged in a life and death struggle to make its faith intelligible and relevant to the emerging new age.

Nevertheless, let us hope that Dr. Dale from his present point of vantage would be prepared to concede that there are factors in our twentieth-century situation that make the problems faced by nineteenth-century theology look like the "two-times table" in comparison with modern binary mathematics. It is not simply, as it was in his day, that science, historical criticism, and philosophy arouse indecision about many areas that are "remote from the great centralities of the Christian revelation." Now they raise fundamental questions about the central truths themselves. The modern student of theology in the classroom or the parish, if he is to keep abreast of the latest thinking in his subject, has to face "existentialism on all sides, Tillichian ontology above, Bultmannian hermeneutics below," and "the surgical analysis of the church from all quarters."[4]

Present indications are that the Church is probably better pre-

[3] As quoted by George Jackson, *The Preacher and the Modern Mind* (London: Charles H. Kelley, 1912), p. 3.

[4] Wagoner, *Bachelor of Divinity,* p. 12.

pared and equipped to answer the threat to her faith than she is able to meet the attack on herself or to justify her official Ministry. After all, she has been engaged in answering threats to the Faith for a long time, whereas more often than not she has been prepared to leave the defence and prestige of her clergy and institutions to the partisan favor of the State. To her shame, we admit it.

Therefore we leave the defence of the Faith to the scholars and theologians who are competent to deal with it. We turn our attention to the place of the Minister in the Church itself, for this is where the problem has become suddenly acute: this is where, as the paid servant of an institution whose magnificent claims appear tawdry beside its shabby imperfections, he feels himself to be most vulnerable.

The immediate problem has undoubtedly arisen from the criticism launched by two complementary but unrelated disciplines which have become insistently vocal during the postwar years — sociology's critique of American denominationalism, and the restructuring of Church and Ministry that has been implicit in ecumenical thinking on "the theology of the laity."

We would entirely mis-state the case, however, if we were to suggest that what we need is an ingenious defence or justification for the conventional pattern of the Church and the traditional functions of clergymen. That would be irrelevant. Most Ministers recognize that it would be a basic betrayal of the gospel. But the acuteness of their genuine perplexity is sharpened by the fact that although Protestant churches in America have inherited traditional positions from former centuries, they lack a clear definition of the Church in terms of Christian doctrine and in relation to its task in this century. The Minister lacks a theological position from which he can assess the truth or falsity of the criticisms to be faced. The fundamental cause of his perplexity is not what sociology or any other discipline has to say about the Church, but his own lack of a clear view of what the Christian gospel itself wants the Church and its Ministry to be in the twentieth century. His unease centers not simply in misgivings about the present structure of the Church, but even more in uncertainty about the structure that Jesus Christ wants; not only in doubts whether the traditional function and image of a clergyman can be justified, but still more in what is truly involved in being a Minister of the gospel.

Therefore the Minister shares with his own church members

in "the prevailing mistiness" about the nature of the Church and
its Ministry. Fundamentally he does not doubt that God has called
him — few men who have been humbled by the hand of God could
do that — but he senses a certain indefiniteness, a lack of clarity
in himself and his colleagues about the nature and function of
Ministry within the Church of this century. His uncertainty
comes to its focus in the meaning of 'ministry' and particularly
in the way in which he thinks of his own ordination. Does ordination mean what it has meant to the Church traditionally, or
can it be justified within the new forms of the Church which
should be emerging within our own nuclear age? Faced with a
theology of the Church that stresses the responsibility of every
member of the Church, is there any place left for certain Christians who are set apart and "ordained" to the special tasks of the
full-time Ministry?

This drives us back to the doctrine of the Church, for ultimately
the question mark encompasses the very nature of the Church itself.
Uncertainty about the ministerial vocation would not be likely if
'Ministry' were conceived as existing in its own inalienable right
apart from the Church. In denominations where the doctrine of
the Church is constituted upon a particular form of the Ministry
or clerical hierarchy, there is not likely to be much need for
self-justification among the clergy. But for the Protestant the
Ministry does not exist by independent right, nor can it ever. The
very perplexity that a Protestant Minister may feel about the
nature of his office is a witness to the fact that in Protestant
theology the Ministry belongs to Christ *in His Church*: he receives
his call from Jesus Christ, but he exercises his office and functions
through, within, and in relation to the Church. The inter-relation-
ship between the Community of Faith and those within its
ordained Ministry is bound to be basic to any true understanding
of the problems that are being raised. On the basis of Protestant
theology it could not be otherwise.

These are the basic areas for study. But before we can approach
them, we had better take an honest look at the criticisms of
Church and Ministry as they have been developed in our day.
We shall also turn in this chapter to the late H. Richard Niebuhr's
The Purpose of the Church and its Ministry, which has been the
only serious attempt in America to reconstruct an adequate view
of the Church and the Ministry in our generation.

II

CRITICISM FROM WITHOUT

This heading refers to criticism that comes not necessarily from outside the ranks of the Church, but from outside the theological disciplines and the ranks of those who are professionally engaged in maintaining the churches' life and work. It is essentially the criticism of those who profess to take an "objective" position, particularly that of the sociologist as he seeks to apply the critical tools of his own discipline to the Church in relation to its prevailing culture.

Why does the Church need to listen to such criticism? The Christian Church has been criticized in the past. It has been accused of being unrealistic, inefficient, and otherworldly, but it has not always developed an oversensitive conscience about these strictures, whether offered in the name of science, business, or so-called "common sense." Criticisms from the time of Nero to the present day have created storms of prejudice against the Christian Church, but more often than not they have failed to cause the slightest ripple on the Church's own thinking because the standards of judgment of the World were so radically different from those which Christians recognized as absolute. Then why should the disrespect of a few twentieth-century sceptics or sociologists be a valid reason for Ministers to become anxious or doubtful about their work? — especially at a time when (to a European observer) their work in America seems to receive more popular acclaim than it has done since the Puritans applauded their Ministers in the holy Commonwealth.

It is because these critics from the outside seem to be echoing the moral terms of the gospel itself. The Church might very well ignore charges motivated by ethical standards different from those of the New Testament, but it cannot ignore the judgment of its own gospel. It can ignore a pagan society that criticizes its New Testament ethic or racial brotherhood for being unpractical, but it cannot ignore the pagan when he castigates the Church for its support of those very elements which prevent social justice. It can ignore the practical scientist when he charges the Church with subjecting scientific programs to the overriding concern of humanity, but it cannot ignore his charge of inequality and prejudice. When the judgment of the gospel itself is uttered, whether it is voiced by churchman or by pagan, by preacher or by sociologist, the Church cannot remain deaf.

The charge is that the churches today are concerned less with proclaiming the gospel of Jesus Christ than they are with supporting the *status quo* and with putting their *imprimatur* on the aims and mores of a prevailing middle-class culture. Ministers are uneasy because they see the force of this charge in the apparent irrelevance of a great deal of the activity that occupies their time and the time of their congregations. The Minister accepted his vocation, recognizing something of the truth in George Macleod's statement that "the supremely important sermon only the Christian fellowship can preach," but this corporate sermon seems to have lost its text, or at least to have turned for inspiration to sources far removed from Jesus Christ.

It is true that the charge of irrelevance against the Church has been around for a long time, and not always with justification; but now many Ministers have a shrewd suspicion that there is something in it, because they themselves are the ones who are forced to maintain the eternal round of busyness. A major part of a Minister's misgivings about the frenetic circuit of his own functions may be centered in the Church's failure to utter and embody the Word that Christ has committed to it. This failure is manifested in so many significant characteristics of the institution which he serves. It is reflected in the amount of time that he knows he must spend to maintain a happy program of extraneous, less-than-important social organizations, while the world is burning. It is illustrated in the fact that the high task of evangelism is often reduced to a neatly calculated marketing operation — not so very different from that of any business enterprise — a matter of suave public relations, improved sales techniques, exploitable markets, and careful social surveys: "This is the place for our new church: these are 'our' kind of people, who will be looking for the degree of acceptance and prestige that membership in *our* church can give them." Even the competition among denominations is not so very different from that among rival television networks, and the same bitter rivalry is carried through all the echelons down to the local parish, where hypocritical talk about "common goals" and "essential unity" casts only a thin veil over pious dog eating pious dog.

There is an element of tragedy in this system because it has been so successful. Yet the Minister, in the brief quietness of the moment as he threads his way through the traffic from one committee to another, may wonder what it all has to do with the gospel of Jesus Christ to which he gave his life. It is hard to convince one's self that the time taken in running the administrative structure, paying social calls, and delivering invocations at service club luncheons, is essential to the work of the Church. If it is, then it is even harder to justify the kind of churches it reflects.

The sociologist offers a plausible but acid reason for the pattern. The Minister has become the priest and executive of a new form of culture religion, in which the Christian Faith is a comparatively innocuous ingredient that can be used to undergird the dominant culture and its secular value system. Faith in God may be the public confession of the church, and therefore expected of its members, but beyond a superficial religious intent the act of joining a church carries important social implications, for it "manifests publicly the adherence to this value system and to the majority of the nation which embraces it."[5] The church becomes part of the same socio-religious structure by which "religion becomes an essential element of what we might call the 'O.K. world,' and membership in a church "becomes an act of allegiance to the 'O.K. world,' to normalcy, to the *status quo*."[6]

I do not believe we can wave aside this criticism on the grounds that it is unfair and that it does not give a carefully balanced account of the Church pro and con. In any case, I doubt very much whether such an omnibus, not to say Olympian impartiality, is possible in this life, and if we are going to face bias anyway, let it be that of the prophetic voice.[7] For that is the authentic note which we catch in many of the writings of the sociologists, and it is for this reason that the Church has to listen respectfully to their utterances. The charge is that in joining the rush to become part of the "Established Church" of American free church cul-

---

[5] Peter L. Berger, *The Noise of Solemn Assemblies* (Garden City, N.Y.,: Doubleday, 1961), p. 89.

[6] *Ibid.,* p. 93. The critique of a sociologist like Peter Berger, who writes from within the Church, is particularly significant, because, as he shows very well, the questions levelled at the Church by sociology are ultimately parallelled by those which the gospel raises itself. Cf. also *The Precarious Vision* (Doubleday, 1961).

[7] Cf. Wagoner, *op. cit.,* p. 21.

ture, the major denominations are well on the way to relinquishing their claim to represent the Church of Jesus Christ.[8]

It should be made clear that the danger is no more particularly American than it is British, or Swiss, or for that matter Fijian.[9] Wherever the Church begins to feel at home in the dominant culture, the danger is present, and it is complicated by the fact that there are many basic liberties and laudable objectives in Western democratic society that the Church feels impelled to support. But although we believe in the basic decency of our own culture over against the various forms of political or social totalitarianism, only a starry-eyed romantic from Wall Street (New York) or Transport House (London) would attempt to identify Western democratic culture with the Kingdom of God. Yet that is precisely what most people expect the churches to do. Perhaps it is difficult for those who were born in it and have grown up in it to realize how much our churches actually promote a national "way of life" rather than the gospel of Jesus Christ; how much they offer "peace of mind" and social adjustment rather than prophetic nonconformity and the lonely scandal of the cross: soporifics rather than salvation. It was exactly their proneness to this danger that led H. F. Lovell Cocks to call the Free churches of Victorian England "the Established Church of the Middle Classes," and to ask the pertinent question whether the overt pressures exerted by pew rents and freewill offerings in English Nonconformity had managed "to tune the pulpit note no less effectively than patronage."[10]

The criticism becomes far more devastating when it is backed

---

[8] One senses this tension very much in the last two chapters of Sidney E. Mead's book on the place of the denominations in the development of American consciousness. *The Lively Experiment: The Shaping of Christianity in America* (New York, Evanston and London: Harper and Row, 1963), chaps. vii and viii. The sociologists who are particularly pertinent on this subject are, of course, in addition to Peter Berger, such writers as Will Herberg and Gibson Winter, to which we might add the criticism of suburbia itself in the books of Vance Packard.

[9] In an occasional newsletter, the *Mansfield College News* (1962), the Reverend T. Hawthorn, a former classmate of mine and now a missionary in the Niué Islands, described a situation among the churches of the older missions remarkably similar to that of the "privileged" churches in America or Europe.

[10] H. F. Lovell Cocks, *The Noncomformist Conscience* (London: Independent Press, 1943), p. 80.

by modern sociological analysis, and it is not quite honest to
brush it aside because a sociologist may not be an active churchman and may be unacquainted with the details of ecclesiastical
administration. He does not need to be either a professing Christian or a church administrator to apply the insights of his own
discipline, nor do we need to listen if those insights are based
upon judgments unrelated to the gospel. But the sensitive parish
Minister probably realizes better than any one else how near the
criticism comes to that of the New Testament itself, how far his
church falls short of the gospel standard, and how much of its
life is geared to promote those very things that the sociologist
describes. However much a minister may be prepared to defend
the democratic way of life on political or ethical grounds, however convinced he may be of its fundamental decency, the whole
paraphernalia of religion becomes for him a blasphemy when its
main drive is directed towards a happy gregariousness that makes
people feel pleasantly contented with things as they are.

He begins to feel a fundamental uncertainty about his own
part. It is not that there has ceased to be a place for the Minister in the modern world. Quite the contrary – the secular
patrons of religion and the worldly churches are agreed on his
role, and it is by no means unimportant in producing the end
product; but he is like an actor who contracted to act a part in
the play and finds himself filling the post of business manager.
It is not that there has ceased to be any role for him, but that it
is a radically different role from the one for which he contracted.

As soon as a Minister starts raising questions like these, he
finds himself face to face with a whole series of problems. If he
had felt called to be a propagandist or a promotion executive, he
might have equipped himself differently, learned the most effective methods and sales techniques, and entered business where
he could employ them openly. Then again, since a good part
of his time will be spent in personal counselling (and many
find this one of the most satisfying aspects of their ministry) why
not concentrate on that, and be free of all the administrative
frustrations of the modern parish? To be a good professional
psychiatrist may not be quite the same as the call to the Ministry,
but it is surely far closer to Christ's call than to be a harrassed
and frustrated parish organizer. And there is a good deal to be
said for the rewards that come with it.

Or why not try politics? Here is a Minister who has his social conscience stabbed awake by Amos and the prophets, and who has been brought to his convictions by God's concern in Christ for the underprivileged. He knows that the Church should be without barrier of race or class, and he feels that the good news of the gospel should have something practical to say to the conditions in which men live and die. He recognizes that the Church is not perfect, and that it will take a long time and a great deal of patience to bring his congregation to the point where it recognizes its own social responsibility in the locality where it is placed. But after years of being blocked in any attempt at wider fellowship beyond the boundaries of race, or in evangelism because "they are not our sort of people," after becoming convinced that the apathy to other people's hunger is due to plain old-fashioned stinginess, it would be strange if such a man did not begin to wonder whether his ministry was being exercised in the right place.

Illustrations might be multiplied. The criticism of the Church from outside is only too well founded in fact, and the Ministry is caught in the down-draft. Now the results are beginning to be felt. Since the G.I. Bill has run out, many seminaries are facing a radical drop in the number of applicants; college educators tell us that in spite of a lively interest in religion on the campuses the Ministry as a career is ceasing to be a live option among good students; there is a constant drift of men out of the Ministry into other professions or from the pastoral ministry to less exacting forms of religious work. It is significant that when *The Saturday Evening Post* decided to run an article on "Why I Left the Ministry"[11] it aroused such public interest that denominational leaders were stirred to make strong public comment. Those who work among seminary students know that the men feel unsure about their vocation and that there is a deep questioning about the parish ministry. These may be only straws in the wind, but the wind is arctic.

So far the social aspects of church life have apparently been sufficient to maintain the membership rolls, but anything might change that, for culture is an arbitrary and fickle patron. I am reminded that the British Nonconformist churches, whose spiritual strengths and weaknesses are so parallel to those of American churches, were at the height of their prestige and power at the

[11] November 17, 1962.

beginning of this century; they also lost approximately thirty per-
cent of their membership from 1918 to 1954, and have not recovered. When the hurricane comes, it will not relent.

The Minister is *perplexed*. He is not cynically disillusioned.
We are set within a dilemma because he does not face such a
clear-cut issue as the foregoing would suggest. His dilemma lies
in the fact that the problem is not solved by giving up his vocation
and becoming an insurance agent or an advertising executive.
There are too many facts on the other side to allow so easy a
solution.

To those of us who are Ministers, the Church is still the Church
of Jesus Christ. Despite all that can be justly said about her
conformity to this world, it was through her imperfect but continuing witness that we too were first brought under commitment
to a God who redeems men by giving himself to them completely.
Through Word and Sacrament the miracle of God's incredible
grace was proclaimed to us and received by us in this context of
the Church, even though the Minister may have spent more time
on his sermon celebrating George Washington's birthday than he
did for the one he preached on Christmas Day. And through
this kind of faltering testimony we felt ourselves captivated and
called to serve Jesus Christ. We were inspired, not by the features
of culture-religion that were certainly there in the church, but by
the great acts of God, the humility of Bethlehem, the service of
Galilee, the sacrifice of Calvary, and the glorious promise of the
empty tomb. True, we have often fallen into the same mistakes
as our predecessors, and yet throughout our own ministries we
have had undeniable proof that despite the little prides and stub-
born prejudices of which we are all too conscious, the same
Christ has reached down to save men, the same miracle has happened. Indeed, when we have felt most near to Christ's own
work, we have seen the faults of the Church and our own mistrust
most clearly.

As long as the Church carries within her own life and witness
the gospel of Jesus Christ, she has all that is necessary for her
own repentance and reformation — even if it be as small as a
grain of mustard seed. No other institution contains at its heart
such devastating possibility for self-criticism. This is the other
side of the dilemma for the Minister, and one of the reasons why
he is perplexed; for when in the face of growing unpopularity

our Lord asked the disciples if they also wanted to leave him, Peter answered, "Lord, to whom shall I go? Your words are words of eternal life." We are perplexed but we cannot succumb to despair, for where else can we turn for ultimate truth?

III

CRITICISM FROM WITHIN

Recently the Protestant Minister has found his role in the Church open to an oblique attack from another quarter. It has come from the unlikely direction of Christian theology and from those ecumenical circles that have been most concerned with asserting the Church's divine vocation within the world. Far from sharing the quasi-iconoclastic features of the criticism from without, this critique is deeply and positively concerned about the Church's proper relationship to society. But insofar as it raises radical questions about the place of ordained Ministers in the structure of the Church, it is no less disturbing to the Minister.

Perhaps no subject has received more profound attention in ecumenical discussion since the foundation of the World Council of Churches in 1948 than the place of the laity in the Church. Out of it has developed a serious attempt to develop a "theology of the laity" which reflects some of the most original and exciting thinking in the continuing ecumenical debate. Moreover, few subjects touch Protestant ecclesiology in such sensitive areas, because, after nearly five hundred years of Protestant thought and many years of Reformation Day sermons, most Protestants are fully persuaded that the "priesthood of all believers" is a fundamental part of their heritage. We do not need to be convinced that Protestantism stands in defence of this principle.

The threat to the Minister is seen in the way in which the subject has tended to develop in Protestant thinking. We recognize that we are concerned here basically not with a "theology of laity" but with the doctrine of the Church. Ecclesiology is the center. Our difficulty, however, is with our tendency to one-sidedness, for a doctrine of the Church that concentrates all ministry in the hands of the total fellowship, the people of God, does not seem to leave much justification for the specific calling of an ordained clergy. If the original questions which stimulated the concern about the laity in the Church were "Is lay life an in-

ferior religious existence? — a concession to human frailty?"[12]
the end product of the present discussion would seem to be
couched in precisely opposite terms, "Is the ministerial vocation
an inferior religious existence? — a concession to human frailty?" The Minister seems to be left with a role that has no theological justification, but which is at best a concession to the
human weakness of church members and their reluctance to accept their own proper commitment.

Perhaps in the light of a thorough biblical review of the doctrine of the Church this is the view which we may reach — we
cannot presume on the result of the ecclesiological discussion or
foreclose on such an inquiry — but at the moment we should
simply understand how the trend of the theological debate today
affects the self-understanding of the Minister.

Possibly the direction of ecumenical thinking on this subject
can be explained in some measure by the fact that it has arisen,
at least in part, in reaction to recent Roman Catholic concern
about the laity. Therefore it may be of some value to look at
the discussion in the light of its antecedents.

It seems clear that the Roman Catholic interest in the subject
arose out of the call for a lay apostolate, and it has been stimulated by the writing of Yves Congar, Gérard Philips, J. M. Perrin
and others.[13] Yves Congar set the tone from the Roman Catholic
side when he declared that there could be only one valid theology
of the laity — a total ecclesiology (*une ecclésiologie totale*).[14] He
declared that the pastoral situation in the Church demands, and
will continue to demand that the work of evangelism must be
considered not as the responsibility of the clergy alone but of

[12] Joseph Duffey, "The Lay Movement — A Threat to the Pastor?"
[13] Yves Congar, *Jalons pour une Théologie du Laicat,* (translated by
Donald Attwater, and published as *Lay People in the Church,* London:
Geoffrey Chapman, 1959); *Si Vous êtes Mes Témoins,* (translated by
Donald Attwater, and published as *Laity, Church and World,* Baltimore,
Md., Helicon Press, 1960); Gérard Philips, *Le Rôle du Laicat dans l'Eglise,*
(translated by John R. Gilbert and James W. Moudry, and published as
The Role of the Laity in the Church, Chicago, Fides, 1955); J. M. Perrin,
"L'Heure des Laics, (translated by Katherine Gordon, and published as
Forward the Layman! Westminster, Md.: The Newman Press, 1956);
George Tavard, *The Church, the Layman and the Modern World* (New
York: Macmillan, 1959).
[14] Congar, *Lay People in the Church,* p. xviiii.

clergy and laity working together.[15] As he expressed it, "The full artificer of evangelism is neither simply the baptized person nor the priest alone, but the Christian community."[16] That is what he meant by a "total ecclesiology," a doctrine of the Church which views the work of the Church — particularly its evangelism — as a totality, and in which clergy and laity share the responsibility.

Other writers were prepared to extend the principle to other areas of church life. Gérard Philips, for example, bluntly charged the Roman Catholic laymen with their responsibility to speak out in the face of clerical error,[17] and J. M. Perrin attacked the whole idea of a double standard of ethics in which it was to be assumed that there was one standard for the clergy and the religious orders, and another standard for the layman. He too emphasized that priests and laymen are engaged in a single task. "We are brought back," he declared, "to the indissoluble wedding of laity and priesthood. Laymen, by being entirely lay, must provoke their priests to be fully priests."[18]

The ecumenical significance in this line of thinking is obvious. Msgr. Philips explicitly stated that the way for the Roman Catholic Church to review its attitude to the laity was being opened by its decreasing prejudices about Protestantism,[19] and the same point is made implicitly in the writings of George Tavard. It must be clearly recognized that these writers are devoted Roman Catholics and should not be regarded as crypto-Protestants: there is a good deal in their books with which a Protestant might seriously take issue. Furthermore, despite the welcome signs of church renewal in the Vatican Council, we must not claim too much for their views, for they do not necessarily represent the views generally accepted within the Roman Catholic Church or held by controlling influences within the Roman Curia. Congar and his associates are of French background, and we must note that ecumenical relations between Protestants and Catholics have progressed much further in France and Belgium than in some other countries. We shall really have to take notice when writings like these begin to appear in Dublin, Madrid, or Bogota.

---

[15] Congar, *op. cit.*, p. 257; also *Laity, Church and World,* pp. 57-58.
[16] *Lay People in the Church,* p. 358.
[17] *The Role of the Laity in the Church,* p. 33.
[18] *Forward the Layman!* p. 30.
[19] *The Role of the Laity in the Church,* p. 12.

The ecumenical movement rightly holds, however, that if it would be foolish to overstress the influence of such opinions, it would be an even greater folly to ignore them. There is a new spirit abroad within many parts of the Roman Catholic Church, and many Protestants have begun to be aware of it since the accession of Popes John XXIII and Paul VI and through many courtesies during the second Vatican Council. More fundamentally, however, Congar and his colleagues may not be ignored because they unconsciously recall Protestants to the Protestant heritage, and remind us of some of our deepest Reformation insights. The question they raise for all Protestants is this: if perceptive Roman Catholics can see a true doctrine of the Church in a *total* ministry within which both priests and laymen are joined for a common task, what possible justification can Protestants have for organizing their churches as ministerial monopolies? Seen in this light, the Roman Catholic writers' critique of their own church structure constitutes no occasion for Protestant self-congratulation, but rather the most pointed reason for humble penitence: we have been so often unfaithful to the light that has been entrusted to us. To give due credit, ecumenical theology has understood this.

Hendrik Kraemer may be regarded as the representative Protestant at this point, and in his book *A Theology of the Laity* we can trace the characteristic emphases of the thinking about the Church that has developed out of the concern for the laity. Kraemer eagerly accepts Congar's basic premise, that for a clear understanding of what it means to be a Christian layman we need an inclusive doctrine of the Church,[20] and we can appreciate that it would be a most promising augury for future Protestant-Catholic relations if such a common starting point for ecclesiology should prove possible. Kraemer also characteristically emphasizes the Church's mission; indeed, he maintains that this determines the very nature of the Church in the New Testament. The Church is not an end in itself: the Church is mission. If the missionary enterprise and expansion of the Church were only fulfillments of an obligation, "then," he declares, "Mission would be a mark of the Church but not its very essence. But Acts 1:8,"

---

[20] *A Theology of the Laity* (Philadelphia: Westminster, 1958), pp. 77, 91ff.

he affirms, "goes deeper."[21] He recognizes that the Church also represents ministry, from the biblical concept of *diakonia* (service), and he claims that the whole membership of the Church is involved both in the divine "sending" and in the divine service.

All this is close to what Congar and others would assert from the Roman Catholic standpoint, except that Kraemer does not go on to consider specific "ministries." He maintains that Protestantism is free from the hierarchical aspects of the Church, which he claims are bound to be an embarrassment to the Roman Catholic theologians in the review of the doctrine of the Church.[22] He is probably justified in this claim, but it is his reaction against what he feels is the unwarranted Roman Catholic accent on the clergy that leads to a possible imbalance.

Kraemer admits that any attempt to define a theology of the laity must try "to determine the place of the laity in the whole life expression of the Church,"[23] and that within this there must be "a mutual cooperation between theologians and lay people, in which both are teachers and taught."[24] This is fundamentally the Protestant position. But because it fails to deal with the specific contributions of 'theologians,' or with the nature of ministry and ordination, the total effect of Kraemer's book is to formulate a doctrine of the Church almost exclusively in terms of laymen who are also "ministers." This in *popular* thinking becomes not primarily a doctrine of the Church in terms of the biblical *laos tou theou* (people of God), but rather a doctrine in terms of laity as *we* know it. That is probably far from Hendrik Kraemer's intention, but the accent is there, and Congar's valid insistence on an inclusive doctrine of the Church thereby becomes changed: the ecclesiological problem virtually becomes resolved wholly in terms of the laity.

An example of the way in which this overemphasis could lead

---

21 *Ibid.,* p. 132.

22 *Ibid.,* pp. 77f. Congar points out that only one canon (No. 948) deals specifically with the laity in *Corpus Juris Canonici* (*Lay People in the Church,* p. xxvii); Gérard Philips says that forty-four canons out of a total of over 2,400 have something to do with the laity, but he points out that the *Dictionaire de Théologie Catholique* does not even include the word 'laity.' Philips, *The Role of the Laity in the Church,* p. 10.

23 Kraemer, *op. cit.,* p. 114.

24 *Ibid.,* p. 115.

to a "blind spot" is seen in Hendrik Kraemer's treatment of Ephesians 4. The RSV for vss. 11-12 reads:

> And his gifts were that some should be apostles, some prophets, some evangelists, some pastors and teachers, for the equipment of the saints, for the work of ministry, for building up the body of Christ. . . .

Kraemer rightly points out (as do others) that there is no justification for the comma which this and other versions use to separate 'for the equipment of the saints' and 'for the work of ministry.' He declares, "It is really startling to notice how radically the meaning of the text is altered by the removal of this comma. It restores to the text the meaning which fits in with the picture the New Testament gives of all the saints, i.e. *all* the members, being ministers, servants to the upbuilding of the Church."[25]

What Dr. Kraemer says about the unnecessary comma may be admitted — indeed, it is worth noting that the *New English Bible* brings the two thoughts together, "to equip God's people for work in his service" — but what he fails to point out is equally significant, namely, that *God* gave the Church apostles, prophets, evangelists, pastors and teachers in order *to equip the saints for their work of ministry.* Presumably these functions are themselves particular forms of ministry exercised on behalf of "the saints" to prepare them for *their* own distinctive ministry. To affirm that the members of the Church have their own ministry does not do away with the particular ministers who were called by God to prepare them for their task. It is not a question of one being more important than the other, but of both belonging to the Church.

One should emphasize that we are concerned here not with any conscious desire to disparage or get rid of the Ministry in Protestantism, but simply with a certain emphasis that has developed from the recent preoccupation with the laity which tends to explain the Church wholly in those terms. The views of Hendrik Kraemer are largely shared by those who have inspired the often exciting thinking that has come from the World Council of Churches' Department of the Laity in recent years, first H. H. Waltz and then H. R. Weber; and we are in the awkward situation

[25] *Ibid.,* p. 140.

that, although the thinking of the World Council of Churches may have moved on to pastures new, the ideas are only now beginning to percolate to the parishes. The general constituency of Protestant churches is only just recovering a concept of the laity's place in the Church, and by no means all understand what it is they are trying to recover. For all the genuine biblical insights and originality, the ideas which have often arrived from Geneva through the National Council of Churches have sometimes seemed to equate the laity with the whole Church too easily.

Those who have been responsible for keeping these concerns alive are not unaware of the need to think more deeply about the place of the Ministry in the Church. It is beginning to be realized that the New Testament says some very specific things about the tasks of apostles, prophets, evangelists, pastors, teachers and others within the ministry of the Church. The task of the Ministry has been likened to that of the Army commissariat in supplying nourishment to the "lay" troops of the "front line."[26] If it is a modest function it is at least necessary.

We are concerned positively with the comprehensive doctrine of the Church for which Yves Congar pleaded, and negatively with the results of our own Protestant lay emphasis upon the concept of the Christian Ministry. We do not need to be convinced that the apostolate of the laity is an essential part of the New Testament doctrine of the Church, but we do have to ask to what extent the concentration on this concern has contributed to the uncertainty of Ministers about their own place in the Church. It has been openly stated in some quarters that "the Church's recent emphasis on the ministry of the laity has backfired,"[27] and the issue has been raised acutely in reference to the recent falling off in the number of recruits for the Ministry. One of the leading educational administrators has asked very pertinently, "Has the emphasis on the ministry of the laity, one of the most important truths recovered by the Protestantism of our time, obscured the urgency of an ordained ministry?"[28] It is a good question. The material rewards of the Ministry have rarely

---

[26] Cf. Hans Reudi Weber, "Ministers of a Priestly People — Some Biblical Assertions," *Laity* (W.C.C., Geneva), No. 9, July, 1960, pp. 5-18.

[27] *New York Times,* quoted by Professor Herbert Farmer in a commencement address. *Hartford Quarterly,* II (Spring, 1962), 77.

[28] Charles L. Taylor, "Why Not The Ministry?" *The Interseminarian,* I (April, 1962), 13.

been exorbitant, and few people need much persuasion to seek more lucrative paths to modest success. If one can add to the financial enticement, the glamour of imagining oneself to be a "front line" fighter for the Cross behind a solid executive desk, the result can be predicted with reasonable certainty.

This is not intended to be sarcastic. Who could quarrel if we could be convinced that the Minister's present unease is simply due to a collapsed ego? The apostle reminds us that no man should think more highly of himself than he ought to think — we are each of us simply the unworthy recipient of God's continuing grace. If the apostolic mission were now to be accepted by Christian laymen everywhere with the preparation and commitment that the call demands, the future of the Church's witness would be bright with promise. Perhaps we *are* facing the necessity for a radical revision of the Church's structure in which the traditional concepts of priest, prophet, pastor, and minister must disappear, or at least be reborn in very different forms. This may well be so, but at the moment we seem to be fairly successful in pricking the Minister's bubble of self-esteem, without giving either him or his laymen the incentive to take up that apostleship to which all members of the Church are called. The ecumenical insights into biblical theology demand a radical review of church structures, and it is possible that in such a revision our former prejudices about the Ministry would be swept away; but perhaps we ought not to assume this too easily until we have applied the same biblical principles to the concept and function of ministry that we have applied to those of the laity.

Some of the perplexity among ministers may be due to a threatened self-image, but if I sense correctly the feelings of my more perceptive colleagues in the Ministry, their uneasiness is far less simple than this. Perplexity is the result of facing a genuine dilemma; and the Minister does face a genuine dilemma. On the one hand the questioning about the need for a distinctive ministry seems to come from important biblical insights: it appears to be uttered in the name of the gospel itself. On the other hand there is a Minister's compelling sense of his own call, there is his compassion as he sees people inside and outside the Church "as sheep not having a shepherd," and there is the privilege week by week of bringing to a particular congregation the means of grace in Word and Sacrament. Many men might be prepared to allow themselves to be argued out of this Ministry, were it not for the fact that in some way or other the service itself seems to go back to that of our Lord.

What has become very clear in the ecumenical discussion on the laity is that we cannot examine either Ministry or laity in isolation. However disunited and fragmented the Church is in fact, it must be considered as a unity, and we are defective in our understanding as soon as we treat the doctrine of the Church in any other way. We are concerned with the place of an ordained Ministry in the Church, but we are concerned with it because at a deeper level we are committed to understand the nature and mission of that ministry which the Church *herself* receives from her Lord.

IV

A TWENTIETH-CENTURY ANALYSIS

No more important or thorough survey of the Protestant Ministry in our century has been undertaken than that which was conducted by H. Richard Niebuhr, Daniel Day Williams, and James M. Gustafson in the course of their study of American theological education in the 1950's.[29] Although their critique was directed primarily to possible changes in the character of seminary training, it is clear that the most important factor in stimulating the study was the widespread uncertainty among Ministers about their proper role in a rapidly changing society. As H. Richard Niebuhr observed, "The contemporary Church is confused about the nature of the ministry. Neither ministers nor the schools that nurture them are guided today by a clear-cut, generally accepted conception of the ministry, though," he added, "such an idea may be emerging."[30]

Niebuhr reminded his readers that in previous ages the Minister had a very clear conception of his function which was generally accepted by the society in which he did his work — in me-

[29] The results of this study were presented in H. Richard Niebuhr's *The Purpose of the Church and Its Ministry* (New York and Evanston: Harper & Row, 1956), and in the book by H. Richard Niebuhr, Daniel Day Williams, and James M. Gustafson, *The Advancement of Theological Education,* (New York: Harper, 1957). It was supplemented by a series of historical essays edited by Niebuhr and Williams, *The Ministry in Historical Perspectives* (New York: Harper, 1957).

[30] *The Purpose of the Church and Its Ministry,* p. 50.

dieval times he was fundamentally the priest, in Reformation times he became principally the Preacher of the Word, while in the period of the great revivals he was primarily the Evangelist. In former ages there were also definite ideas about a Minister's authority and a clear understanding about whence it came, and Niebuhr ventured the suggestion that the present-day confusion may be due to radical change in the view of man which occurred in the nineteenth and early twentieth centuries.[31] He claimed with some reason that the present vagueness about the ministerial vocation has been growing for several decades. It has not manifested itself suddenly, although our world is in such a rapid state of social turmoil that the problem may be becoming rapidly more acute.

Richard Niebuhr and his colleagues asked themselves whether amid the welter of conflicting views, or lack of any view, they could discern any emerging self-understanding of the office among Ministers and theological educators. Were there any signs of a growing consensus as to the true nature of the Ministry and its function within the modern world?

Niebuhr addressed himself particularly to this question in *The Purpose of the Church and its Ministry,* which presumably gives us the underlying philosophy. He maintained that after extensive discussion with Ministers and from surveys and conferences, the researchers were able to discern a pattern that was becoming generally accepted. There is, he suggested, a "theory which seems to be emerging out of contemporary study of the Bible, participation in the tradition of the Church, the experiences and reflections of ministers in our day, and the needs of the time."[32] He went on to say, "Our problem is to describe the theory that seems to be emerging and to be gaining ground in the thought as well as in the practice of ministers. For want of a better phrase we may name it the conception of the minister as a pastoral director, though" he added, "the name is of little importance."[33]

We must point out that the term 'pastoral director' is intended to be descriptive — it is the term that, in the view of Niebuhr and his colleagues, best fits the idea of the Ministry that has been gaining current acceptance "in the thought as well as in the practice of ministers," and one senses that the author introduces the

---

[31] *Ibid,* pp. 76f.
[32] *Ibid.,* p. 79.
[33] *Ibid.,* pp. 79f.

term "pastoral director" hesitantly, even diffidently, as one which may only approximate the actual role that Ministers play.

To gather some idea of what is implied in the term, he suggests that we should look at its perverted form, the "big operator," who is "active in many affairs, organizes many societies, advertises the increases in membership and budget achieved under his administration and, in general, manages church business as if it were akin to the activities of a chamber of commerce." Niebuhr observed, however, that this was a perversion of the Minister's true function, not because the "big operator" is an efficient executive, "but because he does not administer the *Church's* work."[34]

Another picture to which he directs the reader is the trend in modern church architecture, and because of the significance of this passage it is perhaps worth quoting it in a somewhat extended form:

> To be sure, contemporary church architecture continues to betray how uncertain and groping are the efforts of the Church to define the nature of its ministry. Some of it is symptomatic of an experimentation controlled by no leading idea but only by vagary and desire to please as many potential church visitors as possible. Yet there is a dominant movement, so that the modern Protestant church building, not to speak now of the Roman Catholic, becomes a sign of what is being done in it. What is being done is evidently a very complex thing, for these many rooms of the parish house or religious education building are designed for a great number of meetings besides those of Sunday School classes and official boards. But the manifoldness is not unorganized. The focal center of the complex building is a room for which no name has yet been found. To call it either auditorium or sanctuary seems false. It is a place of worship and of instruction. The prominence given to Holy Table or altar, to cross and candles, does not indicate so much that this is the place where the sacraments are celebrated as that it is the place of prayer. The pulpit, however, has not been relegated to a secondary place as though preaching were not now important. Another architectural feature is symptomatic. The minister now has an office from which he directs the

[34] *Ibid.,* p. 81.

activities of the Church, where also he studies and does some of his pastoral counseling.[35]

Of course, we are concerned here with no more than a trend. On the other hand, if Richard Niebuhr and his colleagues have correctly discerned the developing pattern in the self-understanding of the American Protestant Minister, it is an extremely significant trend.

There is, however, one point to which we must return in order to clarify our fundamental criticism of the concept of pastoral director itself. The task of Niebuhr and his colleagues was not to evaluate but to describe. It appears that they were expected not to formulate an *adequate* concept of the Ministry, but to describe the concept of the Ministry which might actually be taking shape in the minds and practices of Ministers. This should be clearly understood, because regardless of the criticisms we may offer to the idea of the pastoral director as an adequate picture of a Christian Minister, it appears to me that Dr. Niebuhr and his team achieved their primary object by distinguishing an important trend with considerable acuity and insight. As one who has shared some of the trials of a parish ministry, I also have found that side by side with all the traditional pastoral functions the modern Minister does perform an administrative role: "the work that lays the greatest claim to his time and thought is the care of a church, the administration of a community that is directed toward the whole purpose of the Church, namely, the increase among men of the love of God and neighbour; for the Church is becoming the minister and its 'minister' is its servant, directing it in its service."[36]

The question to which we must address ourselves, however, is not whether this is the kind of self-portrait that the modern Minister is beginning to paint of himself, but whether it is an *adequate* portrait when judged by the Christian gospel. One suspects that many pressures may have been laid up on the Minister in helping to evolve the idea of the pastoral director, and not all these pressures have been necessarily Scriptural or Christian. I am not at all convinced that the contemporary study of the Bible has had as much to do with the concept as Dr. Niebuhr seems to imply; but I do discern in it something like the shape of the

[35] *Ibid.*, pp. 80f.
[36] *Ibid.*, p. 83.

executive vice-president in American business, even in the acceptable cut and color of ministerial dress. Of course, this is not necessarily to condemn the secular pattern. If such a professional "image" helps a Minister to understand his own vocation better, we are not to reject it simply because it is secular — as long as we can see our Lord in the role.

One of the primary criticisms which I would raise against the idea of the pastoral director is that it is derived *more* from contemporary society than from the New Testament doctrine of the Church. I submit that where such a concept prevails it will almost inevitably degenerate into the "big operator," and insofar as it uses the insights of biblical theology at all, it will use only those which are congenial ("stewardship"? theology of the laity?) and which forward goals that are essentially secular — numerical bigness and efficient organization rather than spiritual growth in depth and the equipment of the saints for their own work in God's service.

An example of my fundamental criticism is to be seen in the architectural picture that is used to illustrate the emerging trend in the Ministry. A carefully planned and precisely articulated structure of rooms for multifarious activities has at its center a room, the true function of which seems to be in some doubt. It is a place where worship and instruction take place, "and yet to call it either an auditorium or a sanctuary seems false"; the centrality of its holy table and its equipment cross and candles does not mean what the presence of table and cross might seem to imply, but simply that we are in a place of prayer. Why? Is this evidence that our doubts focus at the very place where Christian Faith ought to be most sure? Or, more basically, is it evidence of an inner falsity which uses the mystery associated with certain symbols to foster religious feelings rather than to affirm our worship before God's mightiest act upon the cross? Yet this place of worship should provide the very *raison d'être* for all the other activity of the Church which goes on around it. If we are vague here, what does the rest of the activity mean? I say this not to criticize Richard Niebuhr; on the contrary, I think he has unwittingly illustrated our basic confusion about the nature and purpose of the Church.

I suggest, however, that Niebuhr is more culpable at another point. Although he intended the term 'pastoral director' to be descriptive, he went on to undergird it with his own doctrine of the Church, and I question whether the doctrine is adequate.

Niebuhr admitted that without a definition of the Church "it is impossible to define adequately the work of the ministry," and he acknowledged that there is a great deal of uncertainty today about that.[37] By the Church he understands "the subjective pole of the objective rule of God," and within the concept he said that there are certain polarities that must be maintained. So the Church is both "community" and "institutional," local and universal, Protestant and Catholic, and set between both God and the world.[38] Obviously these polarities are inherent in the nature of the Church and might be indefinitely expounded, but the crucial point in Niebuhr's definition is his understanding of the Church's goal as "the increase among men of the love of God and neighbour." It is this basic concept of the Church's purpose to which he constantly returns in the course of his book.

But is there anything specifically *Christian* in this definition, and if there is not, can it be an adequate definition of the purpose of the Christian Church? It was, of course, the summary of the Hebrew law as restated or at least approved by Jesus (Mark 12:28-34, Matt. 22:34-40, cf. Luke 10:24-8), but it was precisely this standard which men discovered it was impossible to fulfill, and which Jesus came to interpret. Increasing the love of God and neighbour among men is in fact a *Christian* goal only as we remember who it was who gave us that summary, and who illustrated its meaning and fulfillment in His life, death, and resurrection. This is where I see clearly spelled out what love to God and my neighbour means, and without that specifically Christian context the promotion of the love of God and neighbour will very easily degenerate into sentimentality or moralism.

Perhaps the most serious criticism one can offer to Richard Niebuhr's view of Church and its mission is at this point. One

---

[37] *Ibid.,* p. 18.

[38] *Ibid.,* p. 25. In this section Niebuhr seems to set the principle of universality as the distinctive Protestant concept over against that of incarnation as the distinctive Catholic concept. I question this. It would seem to me that the distinctive Protestant principle in theology to set over against the Catholic emphasis on God's presence in incarnation is that of God's action in redemption. It is expounded more fully in my book *The Atonement and the Sacraments,* (New York & Nashville: Abingdon, 1960), pp. 282ff., 297ff.

feels that it is due to a reluctance to face the uncompromising uniqueness of the New Testament record. In his fear of the kind of christocentricity that tends to equate "Jesus Christ is God" with the proposition "God is Jesus Christ," he shies away from the centrality that the Bible gives to the figure of Jesus Christ in relation to man's knowledge of God. In the New Testament it seems clear that Jesus Christ stood at the center of the gospel, because in the view of the writers we truly approach God by faith only as we come to him through Jesus Christ. To the New Testament writers Christ is at the center, whereas Richard Niebuhr speaks of "the great, nearly central figure of Christianity, the God-man."[39]

I think I understand Richard Niebuhr's reason for saying that, and appreciate his concern to safeguard the majesty of God — the fact that God is greater than the human manifestation of Jesus of Nazareth — but I think his fear of the error he sees in that kind of equation at this point leaves an impression that he has fallen back from the Christian view of God: it does not transcend the theology of formal Christian orthodoxy, but comes to rest somewhere short of it. If the New Testament asserts that we arrive at a true knowledge of the Eternal God through the revelation of the human Jesus, then there is an unavoidable centrality to Jesus in the Christian Faith, not because the figure of "Jesus" exhausts the concept of God, but because this is where God in his mercy reveals himself in unmistakable terms.

Presumably too, since in Jesus God reaches down to meet us, this is where Christian worship begins. Therefore I must maintain that Richard Niebuhr's view of the Church's purpose is valid for Christians only as it is given a clear reference to the One who gave us the summary of the Law, and whose life revealed its meaning and its dimensions.

This is related to a further criticism of the thesis. He has pointed out that ideas about man have been changing, and that whereas during the era of the "social gospel" it was the needs of man in society which were dominant in the concern of thinking people, "a view of man is emerging that sets in the forefront again his relation to God . . . ; man is seen as man engaged in conflict, conversation and reconciliation with God."[40]

[39] Niebuhr, *op. cit.,* p. 113, cf. pp. 44f.
[40] *Ibid.,* p. 78.

This is a true and valuable insight, but if it is true, I am bound to ask where this need is recognized in the concept of the pastoral director. To revert to the illustration that Dr. Niebuhr gave us, when Ministers thought of themselves primarily as priests, preachers, or evangelists, they recognized that at the very heart of their Ministry they were committed to the proclamation of reconciliation between God and man through the gospel of Jesus Christ. They might think of this reconciliation as being made available to men principally through the sacraments, the preached Word, or through the religious experience of conversion, but however they thought of it there was very little doubt in their minds that to proclaim and offer this in God's name was the prime duty of a Christian Minister. Where is this made clear in the concept of the pastoral director? Within the terms in which it is described a man may pass as a good pastoral director if he organizes his church simply as a lonely hearts society or a togetherness club, providing he sincerely believes that this is the best way to increase among men the love of God and neighbour. He can still perform the role of pastoral director adequately according to the terms of its description if he has a thoroughly mistaken view of the Church's mission or little idea at all about the historic Faith of the Church. The result of such a ministry would probably be all the more disastrous because it can be performed with complete "sincerity." What I criticize is that there is nothing in this office to remind a Minister that the prime concern of his Ministry (whatever the terms in which it is to be expressed) is the proclamation of God's redeeming love in Jesus Christ, and to keep this message ever before the Church as the center of its own corporate witness. Ministry at its heart is concerned with God's grace and man's need, and *Christian Ministry* relates these two things as good news about Jesus Christ. At this point we must be explicit.

One of Richard Niebuhr's finest insights about the Ministry is his suggestion that the work of the Minister is to direct the total activity of the Church so that it fulfills its corporate mission: "for the Church is becoming the minister and its 'minister' is its servant directing it in its service." This is an excellent statement of the position that biblical theology has been reaching with regard to the Ministry during the last few decades. It truly reflects a relationship between the Minister and his church that can be justified by the New Testament. Even the implicit paradox which is contained in the thought of the "servant" *directing* is justified if we remember that all true ministry within the Church is derived ultimately from the ministry of our Lord and exercised in his Spirit.

Unfortunately, however, this statement does not stand alone as an example of what Niebuhr understands by the pastoral director. As we have seen, it is related to what the present writer would claim is a totally inadequate statement of the Church's purpose that removes the work of Christ from the center of Christian witness.

Furthermore, we have to ask *how* the Minister "directs" the church. If he were essentially a *pastoral* director in the sense of concentrating upon the spiritual cure of souls, there would be a good deal to be said for the term, but the impression we gain is that the directing is principally organizational. He is to engage in the "counselling of counsellors," the "teaching of teachers," but we are reminded that "the work that lays the greatest claim to his time and thought is the care of a church, the administration of a community that is directed toward the whole purpose of the Church, namely, the increase among men of the love of God and neighbour."[41]

Yet this same man in the midst of all this organizational activity is supposed to be leading the church to an understanding of its own *ministry*. How can he do this, if his own ministry is not essentially the example of what true ministry is? Surely the essence of pastoral care is in deep person-to-person relationship, in which the individual as an individual is of prime concern to the pastor. What will happen to a Minister's own basic ministry if this takes second or third place to the counselling of counsellors, the teaching of teachers, and most of all to administering the church in all its multifarious but often secondary activities? Possibly if real pastoral care could be exercised by the total Christian community itself, by those who are taught to counsel and teach, the community itself would not suffer. In fact, I would wholeheartedly agree that a great deal of a Minister's time ought to be spent in training people who will carry the concern of the community to individuals in the community; but not to the extent of removing the Minister himself from actual concern and involvement in the lives and problems of individual people. For his own spiritual health he needs that. Ask yourself, what happens to your *own* pastoral vocation when you are prepared to spend the

[41] *Ibid.*, p. 83.

greatest part of your time in the affairs of administration? In the long pull, what will it mean to a local church to have as its Minister (and therefore, to some extent as its example) a person who allows ecclesiastical administration to take priority over the pastoral care of souls?

One has no quarrel at all with the necessary administrative aspects of the Church's life. They *are* necessary, they are to be accepted in a spirit of humility and we hope efficient service, and they had better be exercised in terms of pastoral concern than any other: the "pastoral director" aspect of the Ministry *does* exist within every Ministry, as it has done from the time of the Apostle Paul to that of the twentieth-century city Minister. No one questions that rulership was a very important aspect in the life and organization of the early Church, and that it continues to be so today. But what we do question in the name of the gospel is that this can ever be allowed to become the primary or dominant aspect of a Minister's work.

Again, we must be clear about what we mean when we speak of the Minister as the "servant" of the church. The Minister is the servant of the church in the same sense as the Church is the servant of the world that Christ came to redeem; but neither the Minister nor the Church can fulfill the vocation to service unless they are first of all the servants of Jesus Christ. There is a danger when we use the word 'servant' loosely; it is a danger which is parallel to that which appears over the horizon when we speak of the Minister as exercising the "communal authority," which might very well imply a confusion between *vox populi* and *vox dei*.[42] I am reminded of some pertinent words uttered by a very wise Congregational layman at an ordination in a charge delivered to a local church:[43]

> In a way it is true that our brother is to be your minister, but in a far deeper and more important way he is a minister of the Word and Sacraments, a minister of the Gospel, a minister of Christ. From the Word that he preaches, from the Sacraments that he administers, from the Gospel that he sets forth, from the Christ whom he serves — from these first and most, from you in only a secondary way — he derives the

[42] *Ibid.*, p. 86, cf. p. 73.
[43] Bernard Lord Manning, *A Layman in the Ministry,* (London: Religious Book Club, 1944), pp. 152f.

power and the unction and the grace with which we pray today that his ministry is to be marked.

Do not flatter yourselves . . . . At your hands indeed he
receives his commission; but it is Christ's commission, not
yours; and it comes from Christ, not you. When your minister
speaks, mark whose word it is that he speaks. You do not
hear from him an echo of your own voice. It is the Word of
God that he proclaims, no word that you have committed to
him tonight.

This needs to be said, to be said very clearly and very often. To
be the church's servant is the Minister's vocation, but that will
sometimes mean speaking with an authority derived from a much
higher source than that of the "communal authority," and at times
it will cut across the "communal authority" that a local congregation imagines it has the right to claim as the body that pays his
salary. We need to be clear that no Minister can truly serve his
church unless he is first of all the servant of Jesus Christ and is
prepared to speak with the authority of the gospel delivered to us
in Jesus Christ. Nothing less than his vocation to *serve* the church
demands this.

In summary, then, our criticism of Richard Niebuhr's concept
of the Ministry centers in the question where the true pattern of
the Ministry is to be sought. If we start from the description of
what the Ministry has become within the pressures of a predominantly secular culture, we are liable to be misled and we must
not be surprised to discover patterns that bear unmistakable
imprints of the secular. This may be useful as a warning, but we
dare not try to build these patterns into a doctrine of the Church.
The definition and image of what a Christian Minister is called to
be is to be taken not from what he has become, nor even from the
ideas he may entertain about himself, but only from the ministry
of the One in whom all Christian Faith has its center.

chapter two

The Debate on the Ministry

I

THE CENTER OF DEBATE

Peter Ainslie once remarked that spiritual victories are not won by debates,[1] and if that is true we may wonder if the controversy over the nature of the Church during the past three hundred years has been pursued for spiritual objectives, for one has the impression it has certainly been marked more by the spirit of debate than of discussion. Nowhere has the subject of the Ministry received keener attention than in the Anglo-Saxon churches; and the interest is probably due in large measure to the particular place of the episcopacy in the history of the Established Church of England and to the relationship between the Ministry and the distinctive forms of polity which rival denominations developed in their doctrines of the Church. Episcopacy, Presbyterianism, and Congregationalism began their struggle for supremacy on the mainland of Britain, but they soon succeeded in transferring their ancient rivalries to daughter churches through a good part of the English-speaking world.

[1] P. Ainslie, *Some Experiments in Living* (New York: Association Press, 1933), p. 111.

During the greatest part of its history the Church of England has been episcopal in form, and because of this fact episcopacy has tended to become the focus of the debate, either to support or refute, and one of the most characteristic features of English church history has been the tenacity and infinite resource with which "High Church" Episcopalians have sought to justify theologically the essentially political form of the episcopate that they inherited from Henry VIII and the English Reformation. It is equalled only by the tenacity and resource with which, apart from the brief years of the Interregnum, the Bishops maintained their control of the Establishment.

It would be tempting at this point to introduce a survey of the debates on the Ministry in the Anglo-Saxon churches since the time of the Reformation, but it has been done more competently, and I have a sad feeling that it might prevent many readers from pursuing the discussion into its more relevant contemporary setting. So we must eschew the temptation, because it is in the modern world that the problem of the Ministry becomes acute for us; the Church needs the goodwill of all Christians who are prepared to think clearly and seriously on this subject, and so assist in redefining for the Church its own essential task and that of its servants. Of the debates in the more distant past it is perhaps enough to observe that they were often extremely dull and more than a little frustrating because they sooner or later reverted to the old game of providing scriptural proof texts to support a particular form of church polity (and hence Ministry), and we suspect that no one was much concerned to find anything in the Bible other than what he expected to find there. On this kind of debate Canon Streeter produced a commentary that is in danger of becoming hackneyed because nobody can better it, "in the classic words of *Alice in Wonderland,* 'Everyone has won, and all shall have prizes.' "[2] Just as one can find proof in Scripture for every theory of the atonement — the other pole in the Anglo-Saxon theological axis — so one can find evidence for all the classic polities of the Church. At the same time, in spite of the aridity of these debates, it is worth recognizing that the discussion did emphasize that the Ministry must be seen as part of the doctrine of the Church: it was not simply an item in the Church's practical

[2] Streeter, *The Primitive Church* (New York and London: Macmillan, 1929), p. ix.

organization. Our forefathers may have had a dull theology, but they at least had a theology. It is evident that for the past hundred years the Anglo-Catholic conception of the Ministry has set the pace for our thinking. A change came over the debates with the advent of the Oxford Movement, and by the development within the Anglican Communion of a theory of apostolic succession that Protestants regarded as essentially Roman Catholic. Whatever the reason for their success, the Anglo-Catholic first succeeded in winning the support of a large and influential part of their own Church, and in large measure they succeeded in getting the ecumenical debate about the Church reduced to their terms: the Church would be discussed *via* the Ministry, and the Ministry would be measured by its apostolic succession. This was increasingly true during the nineteenth century, and as Dr. J.A.T. Robinson, the Bishop of Woolwich, has pointed out, it was overwhelmingly true in the debate with liberalism in this century.[3] Whether the Anglo-Catholic success is due to the firmness of their principles, the weight of their scholarship, the persistence of their advocacy, or to the astuteness of their political management of the English Establishment, or whether it is due to a mixture of all these things, the Anglo-Catholics have so far "sold" their position to the Protestant world that the Ministry has become the central ecumenical problem in Protestantism. "Apostolic succession" is always in the spotlight when reunion is on the stage, and the fourth point of the Chicago-Lambeth Quadrilateral has a permanent position as prompter in the wings.[4]

[3] J. A. T. Robinson in *The Historic Episcopate — in the Fullness of the Church* (Westminster: Dacre Press, 1954), ed. Kenneth M. Carrey. The reference is to the 2nd edition of 1960, pp. 12f.

[4] Cf. J. A. T. Robinson's remarks, *ibid.* There has been widespread acceptance of the 'historic episcopate' as a constituent part of any comprehensive church union by responsible Free Church leaders, of which Eugene Carson Blake's recent proposals provide an excellent illustration. (Cf. "A Proposal Toward the Reunion of Christ's Church," *The Christian Century*, LXXVII, Dec. 21, 1960, p. 1509). It would be difficult indeed to say how far the Free Church opinion that is ready to accept episcopacy in this form is based upon (a) a genuine conviction that it should be part of the Church, (b) a political conviction that it will have to be conceded in order to include the Episcopalians, (c) non-theological factors, including (please, let us face it frankly) the attractiveness to some of the style and title. My feeling is (and it would be hard to substantiate it with exact figures) that study of the Bible and involvement in the ecumenical movement has brought about a genuine theological

Traditionally the "Catholic" view of the Ministry has depended on arguments from history rather than simply on scriptural "proofs," but its Anglican exponents have not been unhopeful that new methods in the study of the Bible or in biblical theology would eventually open an avenue for their justification in the Scriptures. They recognized that if they were to hope to draw closer to the Evangelicals within the Church of England, or to enter into any fruitful conversation with the non-Episcopal Free Churches, they would have to clarify their link with the New Testament. In any case, the theory of "development" as a justification for episcopacy could sometimes prove dangerous.[5]

This desire to find fresh scriptural warrant for the concept of apostolic succession is somewhat dramatically illustrated by the publication in 1946 of a book that was clearly expected to end all books on the subject, *The Apostolic Ministry*.[6] It represented the best in Anglo-Catholic thinking at that time and was edited by Dr. Kenneth Kirk, then Bishop of Oxford. Furthermore, it is clear that it was addressed particularly to the debate between Anglicans and Protestants, and was especially concerned with the position of the Church of England vis-à-vis English Protestant Dissent and the plans that were maturing in South India.

The authors recognized that the traditional basis for the Anglican position on apostolic succession had been in the appeal to history,

---

conviction among many, which is based upon the kind of conclusion that Canon Streeter expressed on this matter when he declared that "in the Primitive Church there was no system of Church Order laid down by the Apostles. During the first hundred years of Christianity, the Church was an organism alive and growing — changing its organization to meet changing needs." *Op. cit.*, p. 261. If this is a valid conclusion from the study of New Testament *history*, this leaves the question of church order to be discussed either on the basis of practical efficiency and/or on that of biblical theology. While there might be a good deal of sympathy among some Free Churchmen for the first of these alternatives, it could never be normative for the Church. Ultimately the character of the Church takes its form from the character of its Lord.

5 The danger of the theory of development was foreseen by the distinguished Danish churchman Nikolai Grundtvig, in his contacts with the early Tractarians J. H. Newman, E. B. Pusey, William Palmer of Magdalen College, *et al.*, some of whom became Roman Catholics as he predicted. P. G. Lindhardt, *Grundtvig: An Introduction*, (London: S.P.C.K., 1951), pp. 67ff., cf. p. 68, n. 5.

6 Edited and prepared under the direction of Kenneth E. Kirk, Bishop of Oxford (London: Hodder & Stoughton, 1946).

but it was now admitted that Free Churchmen had been right in demanding that "we must go back behind the apostles and sub-apostolic age to Jesus and the Gospels."[7] To anyone at all *au courant* with the history of church relationships in England this represented an important shift in position. Obviously the authors were experiencing a new confidence, which made them willing and even eager to transfer the battle to the most strongly fortified terrain of their opponents, the somewhat shadowy period (from the point of view of church organization) covered by the Gospels themselves, and to the ecclesiology that might be implied by the relationship between our Lord and the apostles' Ministry. So it was now agreed by the Anglican authors that "the ministry must be not only *representative of the Church to the people,* but also *representative of Christ to the Church.* The ministry is set in the power of His Spirit to take the things of Jesus and show them to the Church."[8]

Stated in this way the thesis is biblically impeccable, but when the epitome of this Ministry, the "essential ministry," was traced solely to the historic episcopate and all other forms of Ministry were considered subordinate and derivative, it appeared to be much more open to question, and particularly with reference to the last set of italics above. How could it be proved historically that this form of the episcopate was the one essential ministry which was "representative of Christ to the Church"?

The new evidence was provided by the hypothesis about the function of the *shaliach* in Hebrew society and law, which was taken out of storage by Dom Gregory Dix and forged into a crucial link in the chain of succession.[9] It had been pointed out that in Hebrew law a *shaliach* was the personal agent or plenipotentiary of the one who had appointed him, and it was argued that the apostles were the *shaliachs* of Christ, that they in turn had handed on the apostolic tradition and powers to the first bishops; and so on to the present day in unbroken succession. Dr. Kirk in describing succinctly the "Catholic" view indicated the

---

[7] Canon F. W. Green, *ibid.,* p. 545. Canon Green was citing the English Baptist scholar Dr. T. R. Glover in *The Free Churches and Re-union* (1921).

[8] F. W. Green in *The Apostolic Ministry,* pp. 545f.

[9] The reference is to K. Rengsdorf's article on 'Apostle' in Kittel's *Theologische Wörterbuch zum N.T.* Cf. Dix in *The Apostolic Ministry,* pp. 228-32, also K. E. Kirk, *ibid.,* pp. 9f.

importance of the *shaliach* to the whole structure. He affirmed that "the apostle, as later chapters will show, is the plenipotentiary (the *shaliach*) of his Master — the accredited representative of the ascended Lord. He is therefore the guardian of the faith, the source of the teaching, the minister of the sacraments . . . . The *shaliach* duties of the apostles must have been handed on, deliberately and with the full consent of the Church, to the resident bishops throughout the area where the Gospel had been preached. Thus the retention of an apostolic ministry must be regarded as of the essence of early Christianity. Everything else is of the nature of accident. It might have happened otherwise. But the continuance of the Essential Ministry was fundamental." He continued confidently, that hence "we are left no doubt with many gaps in our knowledge, but with few puzzles to be explained."[10] The case appeared to be proved — bishops who have received episcopal consecration in this apostolic succession are the plenipotentiaries of Jesus Christ and carry on the power and authority that he gave to his apostles, *quod erat demonstrandum.*

There is no doubt that the writers had complete faith in their production, and fully expected that it would irrefutably demonstrate that the Protestant position with regard to the Ministry is both irregular and untenable. As the Presbyterian scholar, Professor T.W. Manson, remarked, "There is a certain tendency to think that the last word has now been spoken; and that all that remains to do is to sit back and wait for the logical sequel in a reunited Church, a Church united on the only possible basis — the Apostolic Ministry as here set forth."[11]

Manson himself contributed a good deal to the deflation of these expectations when he blandly pointed out that in Jewish law the one thing that the *shaliach* does not appear to have been able to do was to hand on his powers to anyone else. Further, it was shown that the powers of the *shaliach* were by no means infinite but were held strictly within the boundaries set by his commission, and that so far from the word *apostolos* being derived from *shaliach,* "our evidence suggests that the term *apostolos* was earlier than the term *shaliach.*"[12] The result of these studies has been a virtual

---

[10] *Ibid.,* p. 11.

[11] *The Church's Ministry.* p. 9.

[12] Arnold Ehrhardt, *The Apostolic Succession* (London: Lutterworth Press, 1953), p. 18. Cf. the remarks of the same writer in *The Apostolic Ministry* (Edinburgh and London: Oliver & Boyd, 1858), pp. 4f. This

débâcle of the hypothesis built upon the functions of the *shaliach*, in which Anglicans themselves have taken a leading part in reducing the theory to its proper proportions. As Dr. Arnold Ehrhardt said, "The *shaliach* had no successor. We are therefore forced to conclude that unless Dr. Kirk abandons Rengstorff's theory that the apostle was the *shaliach* of Christ he cannot very well maintain the doctrine of Apostolic succession."[13]

Actually Dr. Ehrhardt engages in a very interesting attempt to put the historical argument for apostolic succession on a surer foundation. He maintains that the claim of Dr. Kirk and his associates to link the earliest bishops of the Church to the authority and function of the apostles was unsound, for the period of the "apostolic ministry" began with the election of the seven "deacons" and was confirmed in the martyrdom of Stephen. He argues that the later development of apostolic succession was established in the Church at Rome for the sake of good order against the spiritual exclusiveness of the Gnostics, and was achieved by grafting into the ecclesiastical system at Rome the "high priestly" succession of the Church in Jerusalem that was derived from James, the Lord's brother.

As a historical explanation of the way in which the apostolic succession came into being Dr. Ehrhardt's thesis is interesting, and is backed by a considerable amount of evidence that will intrigue historians for some time to come. But even allowing for the possible truth of this historical evidence, one is left with serious questions about the theological inferences that are to be drawn from Dr. Ehrhardt's theory. In its dependence upon *how* the Church developed it seems to be simply a modification of the development theory that has been the bane of the Tractarian Movement. He rightly criticizes the Protestant appeal to the earliest form of church structure as manifesting "an unconscious doubt in the real presence of Christ," and over against churches that consider matters of church organization to be "merely matters of expediency" he asserts the basic Anglican contention that the form of the Church is directly related to the gospel: "we maintain the

---

latter work is Occasional Paper No. 7 of *The Scottish Journal of Theology,* and must not be confused with the larger work of the same title edited by Dr. Kirk.

[13] *The Apostolic Succession,* p. 20.

hierarchy of the Church is founded upon sound tradition in accordance with the Word of God."[14]

One could point out that the claim to get back to the earliest
form of the Church, which has been so characteristic of Protestantism, is certainly not an appeal to expediency, but if we take Dr.
Ehrhardt's appeal to "sound tradition" itself, it seems to be based
on a theory of the Church's Spirit-guided development. That is
certainly the question at issue. Did the Church develop her
structure in accordance with a sound tradition that was *always*
compatible with the Word of God? If so, then the onus of proof
is on Anglican historians to show why we should stop at monarchical episcopacy and not go on to the monarchical patriarchate
or papacy. Why should we consider the Church as it had developed by the year A.D. 100 the norm for church government,
rather than the Church as it was in 300 A.D., 1054 A.D., or for
that matter, A.D. 1517?

We are in an old historical dilemma which has always haunted
Protestant-Catholic relations. Is the organization and development
of the Church a story of steady degeneration from the charismatic

---

[14] Ehrhardt, *The Apostolic Ministry,* p. 48, cf. p. 46. It is not possible
in the scope of this book to do justice to Dr. Ehrhardt's thesis. In *The
Apostolic Succession* he traces the development of the idea in the early
Church, but it is in his much shorter book, *The Apostolic Ministry,*
that his positive view of the Ministry itself is developed. In this the
writer emphasizes an integral relationship between the Apostolic Creed,
the canonical Scriptures, together with the apostolic Ministry (pp. 6ff).
His view gives valuable insights into the early Church, but it seems to
alternate between a flexibility that can envisage changes in the Creed
or Canon, and extreme rigidity regarding the relationship itself — "you
cannot have one without the other two." At times, too, it is difficult
to follow his logical connections; i.e., he declares that "By the Apostolic
succession of its ministry all the members of the Church on earth are
given the task of being Christ's witnesses" (pp. 42f.). I fail to see how
the appearance of the martyrs and the succession lists of the bishops at
the same time proves this point. (Dr. Ehrhardt might have made more
of his significant insight that the laying on of hands is common to both
ordination and confirmation, but there is still no proof of a relationship
between apostolic succession in the *Ministry* and the apostolate of the
laity). Perhaps it is the same lacuna in my own understanding of his
thesis that prevents me from seeing any integral relationship in his theological construction on episcopacy (pp. 44-58) and the historical sections
preceding it.

period of the earliest preaching and mission, or was the Church obedient to the Holy Spirit in all things? Here is the classic Protestant-Roman Catholic difference in the interpretation of church history during the time of the Apostolic Fathers and their successors, and 'Catholics' who reject the Roman Catholic claim but select some period outside the time of the New Testament as normative for the organization of the Church must justify their historical reasons *for stopping at that point.*

Today Protestants are far less ready to be dogmatic in their interpretation of church history than they would have been even a few years ago. Many denominations in the course of church history from sixteenth-century Separatists to nineteenth-century Disciples have based their doctrine of the Church on Restoration-ism and appealed to the Church structure of the New Testament, but today most of us are far less ready to claim that the New Testament speaks with a united voice in support of our own church polity; we are far less certain that we alone know our Lord's will in this matter; we are far less ready to deny that the Holy Spirit did guide the Church during its early history and continued to guide the Church through the Middle Ages. We would still have to maintain in honesty, however, that there were other influences within the Church leading in a very different direction from that of the Holy Spirit; vestiges of the "old Adam" remained and continue to remain.

At what points, then, was the Church true to the Spirit of her risen and ever-present Lord, and at what points did she prostitute herself to the spirit of the world? We are all agreed that she is the Bride of Christ, but was her adoption of creeds, canon, liturgy, and hierarchy a fulfillment of the Spirit's prompting, or a denial of that Spirit? Are there even distinctions to be made within these institutional manifestations of the Church? Or is it possible that some of the forms which were a sign of obedience in one age could be a sign of apostasy in another? If you accept the validity of these questions at all, then these are the questions that church history sets; and they are questions which church history by its very nature cannot answer with absolute certainty. The answers can be sought only within the nature of the gospel which the Church is entrusted to proclaim, the revealed ministry of Jesus Christ, the Lord.

II

A QUESTION OF PRIORITIES

The most promising attempt to put the concept of the Ministry on a more solid theological basis comes from the side of recent "biblical theology." It is promising not only for the ecumenical reason that its appeal is to the source which all Christians must recognize as authoritative, but also because it reviews and judges the development of the Church in history in the light of the gospel itself.

Possibly because of the very intimate relationship between the concept of the Ministry and the Anglican doctrine of the Church, we must acknowledge that in this area Episcopalians have been making some of the most notable and perceptive contributions. An example of this is to be seen in the opening chapter of *The Historic Episcopate*,[15] which is a masterpiece of compression and insight by Dr. J.A.T. Robinson, the Bishop of Woolwich.

1. *The Historic Episcopate.*

In the name of biblical theology Dr. Robinson roundly criticizes the sequence of theological priorities on which the Anglo-Catholic doctrine of the Church appears to be based — a progression that emphasizes Christ's consecration of the apostles, the apostles' consecration of the earliest bishops, and thus through the episcopate to the Church and hence to the world. He bluntly declares that biblical theology inverts this hierarchical relationship between Ministry, Church, and World, for the aim of the gospel is the proclamation of the Kingdom of God to the world. Thus the order of priority should be Kingdom — Church — Ministry. The ordained Ministry belongs to Christ "only as it is the ministry of the Church" and "its authority and validity derive from Christ-in-His Body."

By the same token, Robinson declares, we must keep our doc-

---

[15] *The Historic Episcopate — in the Fullness of the Church.* The references to J. A. T. Robinson in this chapter are to his chapter, "Kingdom, Church and Ministry," pp. 11-12.

We should note, however, that the views of recent Anglican writers in this vein were to some extent forecast in the work of Canon W. J. Phythian-Adams, who seems to have been one of the first Anglicans to apply the modern ecumenical perspectives of biblical theology to these matters. Cf. *The Way of At-one-ment* (London: S.C.M., 1944).

trine of the Church in its proper place, for the Church exists in and for the Kingdom of God and is not an end in itself: "as the Ministry is a function of the Church, so the Church is a function of the Kingdom, of the universal Lordship of God in Christ." In other words, the only priority that Ministers can claim in respect of the Church, or that the Church can claim in respect of the World, is the priority of *service*.

Perhaps a Protestant can be forgiven for a certain feeling of relief when he receives these important biblical insights from such an impeccable Anglican source, for they underscore some of the things that Protestant theology has tried to say. There are echoes of T. W. Manson's vitally important but oft-neglected statement that the messianic ministry of Jesus Christ is the only "essential ministry" that the Church knows and that all other forms of ministry, whether of the Church itself as the Body of Christ or of its Ministers, are "derivative, dependent, and functional."[16] Manson also reminded us that this Messianic ministry of Jesus "is the Kingdom of God spelt out in human terms."[17] Moreover, Dr. Robinson understands that a biblical view of the Church and its Ministry should lead to a "high" view of both. "The New Testament," he declares, "bids us have as high a doctrine of the Ministry as we like, providing always our doctrine of the Church is higher."[18] To which statement those who have inherited the theology of Calvin, Wesley, Cotton, and Forsyth should be able to utter a hearty Amen.

On the other hand, our appeal is to the Bible and not to any interpretation of it, however attractive or congenial it may appear to be, and although within certain limits Dr. Robinson's understanding of the relationship between Ministry, Church, and Kingdom represents a true insight into the New Testament, I suggest that there is a sense in which it needs to be supplemented. Taken

[16] *The Church's Ministry,* p. 100.

[17] *Ibid.,* p. 18.

[18] Cf. *The Historic Episcopate,* p. 16. In America "high" and "low" in reference to the Church are almost entirely regarded as a matter of liturgical ritual, incense and candlesticks. In Britain the terms are used to distinguish those who hold a "high" view from those who would explain the Church primarily as a voluntary human society. 'High Church' is therefore a term which may quite respectably be given to a Presbyterian like T. W. Manson, a Congregationalist like P. T. Forsyth, a Methodist like R. Newton Flew, a Baptist like H. Wheeler Robinson, or a Disciple like William Robinson.

by itself, a view which reads the priorities as Kingdom, Church, and Ministry rather than Ministry, Church, and Kingdom still represents a far too linear understanding of the organic relationship in which they all stand to Jesus Christ. It is simply the exchange of one sequence of priorities for another, and although we may readily admit that it stands much closer to the New Testament than the view represented by Dr. Kirk and his colleagues, it still does not tell the whole story.

Christ does not come to his Church or his Ministry only at the end, as King of his Kingdom. He is also the great Apostle who was sent by God and who in turn sends his Ministers; he is also Head of the Body, governing the action of every part of the Church that is called to obedience in him. He is the "wholeness" within whom Kingdom, Church, and Ministry are held together. Certainly within that wholeness there is an inner dependence of the Ministry upon the Church, and of the Church upon its relation to the Kingdom, but we must remember that this progression of dependence moves from Christ the Apostle and Servant to Christ the King. Although the Minister will find fulfillment of his Ministry in the service of the Church and the Church will find its own fulfillment in service of the Kingdom, there is also an immediate relation of the servant to his Lord, of the Church to its Head, of the Kingdom to its King. To relate this more specifically to the Minister — he *is* the servant of the Church, but it is first of all because he is the servant of Jesus Christ. As he finds his place within the total ministry of the Church, he is subject to Christ, the Head of the Church, but he occupies this place of service because first of all he is subject to Jesus Christ, the Great Apostle, through whom he receives his call and by whom he is sent.

We may approach the same truth from a slightly different perspective by way of the eschatological dimension to which Dr. Robinson recalls us. He suggests that our failure to maintain a proper relationship between the biblical concept of the Church and the biblical motif of the Kingdom has had its inevitable consequence in our failure to relate the Church properly to the Ministry, and he goes on to say that the misunderstanding about the biblical sequence of these priorities leads to an inability to maintain the eschatological perspective of the New Testament: "We shall not get our theology of the Church and Ministry right until we get our eschatology right."

Far from being the "remote and windy statement" that Dr.

Robinson fears it may appear, it seems to the present writer that it hits the nail squarely on the head. We cannot avoid the eschatological dimension of the gospel, for all that relates to Ministry and Church must be seen within the context of the universal victory and reign of Christ, and everything that happens in the Church and for the Church is ultimately proved significant by the Church's essential task of proclaiming the Kingdom of God by its word, deed, and presence. The gospel promises echo a dominant note of futurity which is always present in the New Testament, and in this light we must always recognize the interim character of this age and the provisional nature of the Church and its institutions. "The Church stands between the Kingdom accomplished and the Kingdom acknowledged. Its task is tied to the proclamation of that Kingdom and its time to the consummation of the age in the manifest vindication of God in Christ."[19] In other words, the Church is the *pilgrim* people of God, a people in transit with its face firmly set towards the future Kingdom of God, and which lives in the expectation that, in the person of the Lord who will return, it will be reunited with the Lord who once came in the flesh. Daniel Jenkins shows us the practical implication of this for the Ministry when he declares that "Ministers need to see that it is one of their main functions to keep churches on the move."[20]

All this is true. There is a dominant note of looking forward in the gospel. Yet there is also a sense in which the Kingdom has already come. Professor C. H. Dodd's insight that the gospel proclaims a "realized eschatology" may not be all there is to say about the gospel of the Kingdom, but it cannot be ignored or waived in favor of a wholly future hope. The Church has the task of proclaiming the Kingdom of God by word, deed, and *presence,* as a people "on the move," and within the Christian community itself there should be the ever-living testimony to the victory that God has already accomplished in Jesus Christ, and to his continuing victories in the Holy Spirit as we press towards the full hope of the Kingdom.

It is when these biblical emphases on the theme of eschatology

---

[19] J. A. T. Robinson, *op. cit.,* p. 16.
[20] *The Protestant Ministry* (Garden City, N.Y.: Doubleday, 1958), p. 46. Cf. also Edmund Schlink, "The Pilgrim People of God," in *The Third World Conference of Faith and Order: Lund 1952* (London: S.C.M., 1953), ed. Oliver S. Tomkins, especially p. 161.

are brought into relation to our understanding of the Church and
its Ministry that they underline the same truths to which we have
referred above. Certainly a view of the Church and Ministry
that is wholly concentrated in the past will have the stamp of
death, and will reveal it as it looks for the evidences of the Holy
Spirit in terms of legitimacy or the historic probability of that
legitimacy rather than in the living fruits of the Spirit. Certainly
a view of the Church and Ministry that is centered in the present
may become separated from the historic events in which our
Christian Faith had its birth, and may become so frenetically
concerned with "doing good" in the present moment that it has
no time to consider the eternal nature of that Goodness that was
revealed in Jesus Christ. Nevertheless, the past and the present
are also a part of the gospel and have their place in the proclamation of the Kingdom, for our certainty about the future consummation of the Kingdom is based both upon certain events in
the historical past and upon our present apprehension and experience of their meaning in this present time. Our risen Lord is
neither simply the King at the head of a kind of social pyramid
that has reality only in some future time, nor is he simply the
foundation of a historical structure that sends its spire into the
present but which has fundamental reality only in the past. He
is All in All, the Alpha and the Omega, the historic Foundation
on whom our Faith rests, the victorious King in whom our hope
is centered at the end, and the present Lord who builds us as
living stones into the service of the Church and sustains us in
witness here and now. It is one of the paradoxes of the gospel
that the "fulness of Christ" of which the apostle writes is not
only a future hope, but by the activity of the Holy Spirit we have
a foretaste of it in the Church: historic past and future promise
are brought into living relationship as present experience. The
living Christ pervades all the agents in his regal service, Ministry, Church, and Kingdom, and relates them to each other
finally in their dependence not only upon each other but upon
him. It is not so much a progression or sequence of relationships
"downwards" or "upwards" into him as it is like an organism, in
which every part is related to every other part through the Life
that flows through them all and gives them meaning.

It is probably clear from this that we may extend J. A. T.
Robinson's thesis to include the immediacy and the all-inclusive-
ness of Christ towards his Ministry, his Church, and his King-

dom. At the same time we must admit that within the total organic relationship there is the kind of dependence to which Dr. Robinson refers. The particular Ministry of those who are ordained and set apart does find its center in the Church itself, becoming part of that total ministry and finding its own *raison d'être* within it. If we look back at Ephesians 4, we see that Christ's gifts to the Church in the Ministry of apostles, prophets, evangelists, pastors and teachers were offered for the purpose of equipping God's people for their own work of Christian service, and for the building up of the Body of Christ. The Church has to be prepared for its service, and Christ gives to the Church *servants* who are specially charged with this ministry of preparation and of raising the Church towards spiritual maturity. If we can believe the apostle, it seems that the Church as a fellowship needs to have such a ministry of service exercised on its behalf. Just as Peter found that he could not be spiritually independent of that menial service that was offered to him by his Lord (John 13:6ff.), so within the fellowship of the Church we receive grace by being ready to receive it, and only as we are prepared to receive it at the hand of another are we made ready to pass it on ourselves. The Ministries mentioned by the apostle were Christ's gifts to his Church — part of his gift of the Comforter which flowed from Pentecost. They were to be received not as an imposition and a burden (cf. I Cor. 9), not as little divinities (cf. Acts 14:8ff.), but as *gifts* in the Holy Spirit from Christ, the Lord of the Church.

We are not concerned at this point with questions such as whether ordination serves any useful purpose in the Church or whether the traditional forms of the clerical profession can still be justified in the modern world, but we are concerned simply with the necessity for training and leadership in the community of faith. There is a modern parallel in an institution like the Peace Corps. True, the Christian Church did not grow up with the backing of modern publicity and a powerful twentieth-century State, but even before a well-conceived and carefully organized movement like the Peace Corps could get off the ground, the first need was to provide adequate training for the volunteers and a leadership that would possess a recognizable kind of morale. The Church has similar needs, particularly for spiritual leadership, for if it is to comprehend its own corporate ministry it needs to see the pattern of it demonstrated in its own midst.

It may need several different kinds of "Ministers" — apostles, prophets, evangelists, pastors and teachers — people who exercise different and complementary functions within the fellowship, but who all demonstrate the quality of the one "essential ministry." And although the Church may not need precisely the same functions of Ministry in every age, the gifts which are represented in Ephesians must never be absent from her; they must be available as their need is felt and as we are led by the Holy Spirit.

This may appear to be a purely practical view of the Ministry, but it rests on a far deeper theological justification. The basic theological consideration is that if the Church is to be prepared and nourished for her own corporate ministry, it *needs a ministry* to be exercised within the fellowship. The figure of the ordained Minister as a kind of army cook or quartermaster may not be very flattering, but in one sense it gets very near to the role which the New Testament assigns to Ministers in the early church — they bring the Bread of Life to God's people on the march.

They bring it to God's people not only in Word and Sacrament but in their whole ministry to the Church. The incident of Peter and the washing of the disciples' feet provides us with an analogy which must not be pushed too far, but Ministers are called to represent Christ in his humility to the Church. That is surely what "ministry" is all about. If the Church needs the ministrations of those who are charged with these functions, it does not make Ministers any more important than the members whom they serve, but by their humility in service they should reveal the concern of all ministry and the meaning of that corporate ministry in which the whole community of faith is engaged. The Roman Catholic Church shows a true insight into this essential character of all ministry when on Maunday Thursday the Pope takes a bowl of water and a towel and washes the feet of some of his servants; but this action cannot be reduced to a ritual act, however symbolic and valuable, for that which it portrays is the "essential ministry" of the Church. But if the Church is to fulfill this kind of mission in the world, she needs to see it demonstrated in the midst of her fellowship, just as our Lord illustrated it when he set a little child in the midst of his disciples. The Church herself *needs* ministry, and our Lord gives her this gift through those who are charged with the task of representing the Church *to* the Church.

A true gift is an act of pure grace; and if we are to speak of theological priorities in understanding the meaning of ministry, we must return to that which is perhaps most fundamental to the Christian gospel — God's grace in response to man's need.

2. *The Pioneer Ministry*

Another illustration of the Anglican Church's serious concern with the concept of the Ministry is Canon Anthony Hanson's *The Pioneer Ministry*.[21] The writer approaches the subject directly from the basis of biblical theology, and this makes his work of very great importance for all those who look first to the scriptural norm.

Dr. Hanson takes up a suggestion which had been made by Professor T. W. Manson some time ago, namely that the New Testament doctrine of the Ministry is directly related to the Old Testament doctrine of the Remnant, and that in some sense the relationship of the Ministry to the Church is paralleled by the relationship of the Remnant to Israel. Manson suggested that Jesus gathered the disciples around him to embody the Remnant ideal, and he pointed out that the disciples were "not invited to create the Remnant but to join it; not to build or bring the Kingdom of God but to receive it and enter it."[22]

Anthony Hanson takes up this connection with the Remnant and in some detail shows that it was at the center of the way in which St. Paul understood his own ministry and that of his colleagues. "It seems therefore," he says, "a clear deduction from St. Paul's teaching that the first disciples *were* the faithful Remnant and that their apostolate sprang from this fact. In other words, the apostles were apostles because they were the first church."[23]

Here we have the apostolate of the whole Church implied and a stress upon the apostolic character of the whole people of God that is solidly biblical. The theme is followed through St. Paul's

---

[21] Anthony Tyrrel Hanson, *The Pioneer Ministry* (Philadelphia: Westminster, 1961).

[22] *The Church's Ministry*, p. 15. It should be noted that Manson regarded the Remnant idea as central in the teaching of Jesus regarding his own ministry, and discovered the *corporate* aspect of the messianic titles even in terms such as the 'Son of Man'. Cf. *The Teaching of Jesus*, (Cambridge: Cambridge University Press, 1931), pp. 227-234.

[23] Hanson, *op. cit.*, p. 45.

theology, particularly in the Corinthian epistles, and Hanson
pays special attention to the many indirect ways in which the
apostle referred to those who were associated with him in his
work, maintaining that what St. Paul says about these fellow-
workers "provides in fact at least a foundation for a doctrine of
the ministry." Hanson suggests that Paul constantly included his
fellow-workers in his exposition of the apostolic work in which
both he and they were engaged, and that from what the apostle
says about the actual work we can gather a good deal about what
he believed about the nature of the apostolate.[24]

If St. Paul thought of the particular Ministry as a continuation
of the function of the Remnant in relation to the New Israel, then
the Ministry "shows in miniature what the Church should be."[25]
It is to pioneer the Church. It does not represent a different
order from the Church, nor is it different in essence from what
the Church is intended to be, for it *is* the Church in its pioneering form. "The pattern is Christ — the ministry — the Church,"
declares Hanson, "and the task of the minister is, not to undertake some specialist activity from which the rest of the faithful
are excluded, but to pioneer in doing that which the whole
Church must do." And a little later he adds, "It [the Ministry]
does not carry out Christ's work instead of the Church; it rather
enables the Church to carry out that work in its (the Church's)
own life."[26]

Here we have a view of the Ministry which is related at every
point to the Church's corporate work and mission. Over against
any attempt to interpret the apostolic mission either exclusively
in clerical terms or implicitly in lay terms, it tries to understand
the Church's mission as a totality in which both Minister and
people are joined. This is possible because the Ministry is not
represented as something substantially different from the membership of the Church itself, but rather discovers its own essential
place in the life of the community as it represents the messianic
character and mission to the Church itself.

The center of Hanson's exposition of Ministry in the Bible is
its direct reference to the atoning and reconciling work of Christ.
The Ministry is subject to Christ so that it may show the Church

24 *Ibid.,* p. 56.
25 *Ibid.,* p. 60.
26 *Ibid.,* p. 76, cf. p. 72.

that the Church too is subject to Christ. But the Ministry of Paul and his colleagues pointed deeper, to the very nature and meaning of Christ's atoning act; it was a ministry of reconciliation that took upon itself something of the redemptive quality of the cross — into which ministry the whole Church of Christ is called. "The ordained ministry," writes Hanson, "carrying on the Messiah's ministry, passes on that ministry to the Church which it founds."[27]

This is an echo of Manson's contention that the only "essential ministry" in the Church is the messianic Ministry of Jesus Christ himself, and Dr. Hanson comes perhaps as near to a genuinely biblical concept of Ministry as any writer on the subject since T. W. Manson. One may wish to criticize details, (Hanson is far less successful when he tries to relate his view to the "historic episcopate") but in his fundamentally biblical approach and his insights into the nature of Ministry in the time of St. Paul there is little we can add but our thanks. Of St. Paul's position he says:[28]

> What he [Paul] tells us is that it is the task of the ministry to live out the life of Christ in the Church and to be pioneers of the Christian life for the sake of the Church. But this is done only in order to enable the Church in its turn to live that life. We thus find the pattern: Christ — the ministry — the Church. But this does not mean that the ministry does nothing that the Church does not do: on the contrary, the purpose of the ordained ministry is to induce the whole Church to do what it does, i.e. what Christ does. We find therefore an apostolic, representative pioneer ministry. The ministry does not come in between God and man, still less is it a substitute for the laity. It is rather what Christ is to us all, a pioneer, a leader, an exemplar. It must also be prepared to empty itself and efface itself as Christ did.

The obvious question that suggests itself to us is, "Who can fulfill such a Ministry?" And the answer must frankly be, "No one — not even St. Paul, is adequate for the task," any more than the Church itself is fully adequate for the task to which it is

---

[27] *Ibid.*, p. 63, cf. pp. 59-63.
[28] *Ibid.*, pp. 108-9.

called. But we need to remind ourselves that although we know well enough our own insufficiency as Ministers and as Christians, we are not asked to do this alone. Like the apostle we discover that Christ, "by the power at work within us is able to do far more abundantly than all that we ask or think" (Eph. 3:20). We also need to remind ourselves far more often than we do that this Ministry is not a one-way process — it is a *mutual* ministry, and if it is the Minister's job to point his flock to Christ, it is often his delighted but humbling discovery to find that this local Christian community constantly reveals and expounds the living Christ to him.

Although Protestants may not have expressed their view of the Ministry clearly or explicitly, and have repeatedly fallen into their own forms of sacerdotalism, I have a feeling that the view which is emerging from biblical theology is basically that which the churches of the Reformation have been haltingly trying to express. We can only thank Anglicans like Canon Hanson for reminding us again of the biblical priorities.

III

THE CHURCH'S MINISTRY

It seems clear from these studies that biblical theology offers our best hope of reaching a truly ecumenical doctrine of the Church and Ministry, because it cuts through the denominational myths with which we have surrounded our thinking about these things, and forces us to concentrate upon the total message of the Bible. As we try to reach the center of that message, we can no longer be concerned with justifying from Scripture this or that view of the Church or Ministry as we have accepted the legacy from history, or with marshalling a battery of carefully selected proof texts, or with explaining away the passages to which other denominations make their appeal. We are committed to the primary task of discerning and trying to understand God's plan of salvation for the human race.

When we do make this task central, however, we discover that far from discarding the Church in favor of a purely individual view of salvation, there is at the very heart of the Bible's message a redeemed and redeeming community — the people of God, Israel, the Church. And with the Church there is Ministry — a Remnant whose members throughout the biblical story have been called by God to serve the people of God, and who in that service are charged with keeping ever before the community of faith the special character that it bears and the priority of its mission. They are called to personify for the sake of Israel that which Israel itself is called to be. In this sense we must agree with Dr. J. A. T. Robinson when he claims that "it is impossible to be a biblical theologian without being a high Churchman."[29] Indeed, from a biblical perspective it is precisely those who would subordinate the doctrine of the Church to something else, whether to an inflated view of the Ministry or an individualist theology of salvation, who have a low view of the Church. Only a doctrine of the Church which tries to see the nature and purpose of the Church in its wholeness will begin to do justice to the biblical pattern. Neither 'Ministry' nor 'Laity' can be used exclusively to define the Church, but both must be given their proper place as equal partners in the mission and life of the Church. In fact, a doctrine of Ministry that is centered in the Bible will not detract from the task of the whole people of God but will enhance the corporate call, for it will emphasize the imperative claim of Jesus Christ upon the commitment of us all, and bring his call to us to its proper focus — service.

This underlines the fact that biblical theology offers not only new possibilities of ecumenical agreement, but what is far more important, it opens the door to a doctrine of the Church and its Ministry that will represent more adequately the fulness of Christ into which we are called. One of the most important insights of the ecumenical movement in our day has been the recognition that a sufficient doctrine is more important than an "ecumenical" doctrine. We are fundamentally concerned with the truth about Jesus Christ and the meaning of his redemptive incarnation, and insofar as this relates to the Church and Ministry, we are concerned with a doctrine of Church and Ministry that truly expresses this gospel.

But how does the Minister fit into the picture of a Church that would fufill this pattern? Since the mission of the whole Church is the necessary backdrop against which all our particular ministries are set, how does the figure who is so often in the spotlight relate to the rest of that scene? What follows is certainly

29 *The Historic Episcopate*, p. 16.

not adequate to this theme, but the following two main points may possibly be suggestive of others. This is where we need to exercise our thought.

(a) *The Church's mission is a claim upon the whole membership.* We have emphasized that the vocation of a Christian Minister must be understood within the context of God's call to His whole people, and that if there is any place for an ordained Minister in a biblical doctrine of the Church it is not to be asserted over against the "theology of the laity" but as complementary to it. The Bible seems to be telling us that what Yves Congar said about the theology of laity is equally or even more true of a theology that deals with Ministry — only a total doctrine of the Church can keep it in proper perspective, and only by such a doctrine can it finally be justified.

We should mark well what that implies, for if this means that *every* Christian has his or her part in the ministry and witness of the Church as a whole, then there can be no "second class citizens" in the Church on account of race, class, sex, education, or native ability — all are called to engage in this ministry to the fullest extent of their powers and gifts. It means the total commitment of the whole membership. The Protestant cannot evade this *total* claim upon his discipleship. But it includes the one who is called to be the Minister. We do not regard the figure of the Minister as an army cook or quartermaster, as one likely to excite the red corpuscles of promising students, but perhaps we should remind those who hanker after the front line that in these days of offensive-in-depth the commissariat and supply center are likely to be among the first strategic targets of the enemy. All Christians are in the front line together. The functions of the Ministry are directed towards nourishing and preparing the Church for its ministry of witness, but this corporate ministry is also one in which *the Minister takes his place as an enlisted man.* The call to witness is a call to the whole Church, exercised corporately.

(b) *The Church's total ministry implies the Church's unity.* We cannot avoid the ecumenical imperative raised by the present pluralism of Christianity, for insofar as the visible Church is broken and fragmented, the ministry of the total Church is broken and fragmented. Our witness is partial and divided, and to that extent it is a flat denial of the intent and spirit of the great "high priestly prayer" where the unity and mission of the Church are so clearly held together (John 17:20-23). It is said that, when Graham Taylor, the Christian social reformer, addressed the Liturgical Club of Hartford on "The Evangelism of the World" in 1883, one of his audience suggested that all missionary endeavour should be postponed for a hundred years until the churches could unite.[30] The suggestion may not have been made too seriously, but at any rate someone realized that however much our divided witness inflates denominational promotion, the logic of a divided Church is to kill its real witness. If the gospel of reconciliation is at the heart of the Christian message, then division in the Church is a visible denial of all the most important things that the Church exists to proclaim.

Professor O. C. Quick pointed out some time ago that in the present divided state of Christendom all ministries and all churches are in some measure defective.[31] We would maintain that they are defective not so much because one or another form of Ministry lacks certain elements in the ritual of ordination or because this or that denomination is not sufficiently careful about its doctrinal standards, but more particularly because Ministers, who by the very nature of their office should represent the universal unity of the Church within the local congregation, in fact represent but one denominational part of the Church. Omissions in ritual and laxity in doctrine exist and they are not unimportant, but the real sin of the churches is deeper — they are content to remain in separation and even rivalry while continuing to act as if they were the whole Church. By a kind of pious fraud, by which we delude ourselves, we continue to utter fine thoughts ecumenically while acting denominationally: we have not cared enough for the unity of Christ's body to prevent or to heal the scandal of our divisions.

The redemptive and ethical imperative at the heart of Christ's own ministry is at the heart of all ministry in the Church, but it often appears to be a forgotten factor when we begin to discuss such objects as the "validity" or "defectiveness" of Ministerial orders. We need to "ethicize" our concept of the Ministry in the same way that P. T. Forsyth suggested we should ethicize our

[30] I am indebted to the Reverend Charles Russ for this illustration.
[31] *The Christian Sacraments* (London: Nisbet, 1927), 2nd, ed. 1948 reprint, pp. 145ff.

conception of the Church and its sacraments, for any adequate theology of the Church and its institutions must focus in the righteous demands of incarnate and holy love. This is where we must begin, for the only historical roots worth owning are those which we trace from the holy ministry of our Lord himself.

chapter three

The Messianic Ministry

I

THE UNIQUENESS OF JESUS

The title of this chapter is taken from T. W. Manson. "There is," said Dr. Manson, "one 'essential' ministry, the only ministry that is unchallengeably essential. That is the ministry which our Lord Jesus Christ opened in Galilee after John the Baptist had been put in prison, the ministry which he continues to this day in and through the Church, which is His body. . . . The Church is the Body of Christ; and the life of the Church is the continuation of the messianic Ministry. It follows that the nature of the Church's task can be defined by reference to the records of the public career of Jesus, His teaching and His acts."[1] This chapter, and indeed, all that follows in the book, is written in the belief that this represents the fundamental basis of all Christian Ministry — the Church carries on the messianic Ministry of our Lord — and Manson at least carries this writer with him when he implies that, if this is true of the Church's corporate ministry, it must be true in some measure also of the derivative ministries within the Church. All ministry goes back to the same source, and all Ministries must reflect that Essential Ministry.

[1] *The Church's Ministry,* pp. 21, 24.

69

At this point, however, we must introduce a somewhat lengthy parenthesis, and ask ourselves what sure ground we can expect to find in the ministry of Jesus for developing a doctrine of the Church and its Ministry. After all, although New Testament studies have gone a long way since Streeter wrote *The Primitive Church* in 1929, they do not give us any more reason for dogmatism about the primitive Church and its structure, and very much the same is true about our exact knowledge regarding the course of our Lord's life. No book has been subjected to a more thorough scientific investigation than the New Testament, and the question that every B.D. student has to face sooner or later about the events of the life of Jesus is, "How much of this record is factually true, and how much of it is simply due to the development of a mythology within the early Church about Jesus?" If there is uncertainty among scholars about the course of our Lord's ministry in detail, about the sequence of events, about the harmony of the Gospels, and about the historicity of many of the incidents that have been recorded, what can we declare certainly about the ministry of Jesus, and what can we build on it?

Without entering into a long disquisition on a subject in which I do not regard myself competent, I think we can say with some assurance that these questions have not passed unnoticed by the New Testament scholars, and are receiving increasing attention. Following close upon the heels of Dr. Bultmann's radical conclusions about the need to "demythologize" the New Testament, there has arisen a new interest among New Testament scholars to review again the problem of historicity in relation to the life of Jesus — the new "quest for the historical Jesus."[2] The Christian Faith is not founded upon an Idea or an Ideal, however revealing it may happen to be, but it is founded upon certain historic events which the Church has accepted as historic. These events happened in Israel at a certain time in history, and were connected at every point to the life and death of a man, Jesus of Nazareth, and, although the sequence of the incidents in detail may not be too important, it is vitally important to the Christian

---

[2] The plea is made by W. D. Davies in his inaugural lecture, "A Quest to be Resumed in New Testament Studies," *Christian Origins and Judaism,* pp. 1-17, but the "quest" may be followed in its new form in such works as Gunther Bornkamm's *Jesus of Nazareth,* E. Stauffer's *Jesus and His Story,* James Robinson's *The New Quest of the Historical Jesus,* and Reginald Fuller's *The Mission and Achievement of Jesus.*

Faith that such a man lived, that he was *such* a man, and that what happened at the end of his life actually happened. At any rate, the earliest Church thought so, and these things brought the earliest Church into being.

The historical record of this life as it has come to us in the Gospels reaches its focus in the events of Holy Week, and more specifically in the events of the Easter weekend, but these happenings would not have made much sense to the early Church if they had not been related to the previous life of Jesus of Nazareth. The life of Jesus is literally of crucial importance to Christians, in that the events of the cross and resurrection are revealed to be significant by the kind of life in which these things happened. The New Testament writers saw the purpose of our Lord's ministry in terms of atonement, the redemption of man, and as Vincent Taylor has written, "There is no Atonement apart from the whole process by which sinners are reconciled to God; and this includes the passion of God expressed in the Cross, *the life and the death* of Christ Himself, and the relation of men to Him and His atoning work. All this, nothing less, is the Atonement."[3] The life is part of the passion, for it is only as we see the crucifixion happening to this *kind of Person* that the meaning is revealed to be infinitely deeper than that of another innocent man suffering unjustly, and, in effect, the writers maintain that it is only when we see the resurrection in terms of the life of Jesus that the miracle discloses something about the ethical heart of God.

The history of the birth and explosive development of the Christian Church is a testimony to the fact that those who knew Jesus best could not dismiss his life in the way another life might be dismissed, and their testimony carried enough conviction to convince the early converts and send them out with the same burning faith that this man was different, and that the difference was in his quality of goodness. We must therefore presume that apart from all questions of detail in the accounts of our Lord's life, when the Christian community wrote the record in the Gospels, it was the intention to present the kind of life that Jesus lived and the kind of Person he was. Indeed, it seems clear from the Gospel writers that they are not concerned with giving us an accurate biography of Jesus, but they give us simply enough

---

[3] *Jesus and His Sacrifice* (London: Macmillan, 1937), p. 304.

of that which was typical of what he said and what he did to help us understand the significance of his death and resurrection as they understood it.[4] They were concerned not that their account should be a detailed portrayal of our Lord's life but that the total impression of Jesus the Christ which they presented should be true. We are concerned here not with factuality of incidents, but with the over-all Truth that is presented to us in the Gospels, the characteristic quality of his words and deeds, the kind of Person who met death in this way, the quality of this man whom the disciples believed had arisen because death could not hold him.

Perhaps modern writers have not given due weight to a complementary truth, that the early Christian community is itself a witness — perhaps the most convincing witness — to the character of the One from whom it took its name. The kind of people Christians became, the ethical standards they adopted, the nature of the worshipping community within which the name of Jesus was honored, cannot be ignored as a testimony to the character of Jesus Christ. The doctrine of the Holy Spirit, which was to bind the Christian community together, was essentially the same Spirit manifested in Jesus. The primitive Church was a community that produced the ethics of Paul — "Finally, brethren, whatever is true, whatever is honorable, whatever is just, whatever is pure, whatever is lovely, whatever is gracious, if there is any excellence, if there is anything worthy of praise, think about these things" — and the kind of life that goes with it; for the apostle went on to charge his readers, "What you have learned and received and heard and seen in me, do" (Phil. 4: 8f.). It was the community which recognized not simply a Johannine reconstruction of the life of Jesus in the Fourth Gospel, but much more profoundly the Johannine *interpretation* of that life as essentially true, an indispensable commentary upon the facts presented by the Synoptists. It is the conviction of the Fourth Evangelist that Jesus is the Truth, the final and ultimate Truth, and this fidelity to the Truth is a liberating force to which

---

[4] The events immediately leading up to the crucifixion and resurrection occupy eight out of twenty-eight chapters in Matthew, six out of sixteen chapters in Mark, over five out of twenty-four chapters in Luke, and ten out of twenty-one chapters in John.

the disciples are committed.[5] The character of the early Church, which is derived from the One in whom the disciples believed, thus underwrites the basic veracity of its testimony to the ministry of Jesus, just as the character of Jesus guarantees and illumines their faith in his atoning work: truth cannot take seed from a lie.

So much for our parenthesis. The Church's testimony, as it stands in the Gospels and New Testament writings, is guaranteed by the kind of community that the early Church became in obedience to its Lord. We cannot say that Jesus was fundamentally different in *character* from the person who is presented to us without saying that his closest companions were either tragically deceived by him or were deliberate liars.

If, therefore, all Ministry in the Church goes back to the essential ministry of Jesus Christ, it must reflect that essential ministry as it has been given to us in the Gospel records — not in literal detail but in its redemptive character and its compassionate concern. For these reasons we must plead that the way forward to a deeper understanding of Ministry in the Church is by trying to understand the ministry of Jesus as the early Church understood it as a whole.

It has been recently fashionable to rely upon the study of certain key words in the New Testament — *diakonia, kerygma, marturia,* etc. — as ways of expounding the nature of the Church, but it is now time to comprehend the meaning of Church and Ministry in a somewhat broader context; and at this point, we would claim, for a more adequate study of 'ministry' we must return to the essential ministry of Jesus Christ himself.

Yet when we say that Ministry in the Church of the twentieth century should reflect the essential ministry of Jesus Christ, we can see the very obvious temptation to regard the identification between what our Lord did for mankind and what the Church tries to do for men as too close. There is no biblical warrant for failing to distinguish sharply between Christ's ministry and ours. We are not Jesus Christ, and although we may not be

---

[5] John 8:32; cf. 1:14-18, 5:30-36, 8:39-47, 14:6, 16:12-15, 17:17-19, 18:37f., 21:24. The rest of the Johannine literature, however, has the same emphasis upon true testimony to Jesus Christ — I John 1:1-5, II John vs. 4, III John vs. 3, Rev. 1:1f. — moreover, the relationship of true testimony to the ethics of the Church is very fully brought out in I John 3-5.

tempted to make the identification as baldly as that, we may be tempted to magnify our office and its authority to the point where we virtually put "the Ministry" in the place of the living Christ. We must try to preserve a proper distinction between our Lord's uniqueness and the ways in which we are identified with him.

After all, it is not so obvious that our Lord's ministry can be regarded as normative for our Ministries. We recognize that the human situation faced by Jesus of Nazareth was vastly different from that of a twentieth-century pastor in a settled parish, or, for that matter, from that of a twentieth-century missionary or evangelist. But at a deeper level, when we are most honest with ourselves, we recognize just how vast is the gap that separates him from us. Charles Haddon Spurgeon, the great Baptist preacher, reminded his students, "Measure yourself by the Cross, and see how high you stand!" And as we study the Gospels week by week in sermon preparation, we know that Christ shrinks our best efforts into insignificance. This seems to remove his ministry to an entirely different level from that of the most dedicated Christian servant. I cannot read the records of the early Church without realizing that what Christ did was cosmic, "once for all time," never to be repeated. Does not this make his ministry so unique that it is "wholly other" from *my* Ministry? Moreover, is it not basic disloyalty to suggest any diminution of that uniqueness of Christ?

Certainly it is. The New Testament is uncompromising about the uniqueness of Jesus Christ, but it insists with equal urgency that the uniqueness is that of degree, as that which is first is to that which follows. It is in the absoluteness of our Lord's obedience to the Father that we discern his "wholly otherness" from us, not because what he does is removed totally from our human situation. There is a sense in which, far from being essentially different from us, our Lord alone reveals the true nature of what it means to be human, and he shows it through service, through ministry. In the Church we *are* called to follow him, to be disciples, and we *are* called to be witnesses to him. Whatever else his uniqueness is, it does not remove him from our life and experience, it does not make him a docetic Christ, but one who is more completely and absolutely Man. "For we have not a high priest who is unable to sympathize with our weaknesses," declares the writer to the Hebrews, "but one who in every respect has been tempted as we are, yet without sinning"

(Heb. 4:15, cf. Matt. 8:17). That which he did *first* we cannot do for ourselves, but as we accept it we are called into *his* service.

The Church has sometimes so stressed its identity with Jesus Christ that it has virtually ignored the sin and fallibility that remain within it. St. Paul calls the Church the Body of Christ, and of all the metaphors used in the New Testament this probably expresses better than any other the essential relationship between the Church and Jesus Christ; but it holds grave dangers if it is used so literally that it obscures the fact that the Church remains a human institution. It dare not claim the perfection that belongs to its Lord without risking self-idolatry, without virtually regarding itself as divine. Its origin is divine, but that is God's gift *in* Jesus Christ, and to claim it as something to be grasped at is to be unworthy of it.

I hope I may be forgiven for repeating what was written elsewhere (in *The Atonement and the Sacraments*) on this subject. To claim part of his incarnation or glory *as a right,* far from being a manifestation or proof of the Church's purity and holiness, might become nothing less than the sin of Lucifer. The Church *is* part of his life, incarnate and glorified, but how that is so and why it should be so is a hidden mystery of grace that can be revealed by God alone and will probably not be revealed until the resurrection of all things. The Church has it as a gift, but she cannot claim it as a right. The one thing she can and must claim in order to reveal and fulfill her own vocation is her share in the atoning purpose of the incarnation. She can be his Body in that, and only as she is faithful in that will it be manifest to men that she is born "not of blood, nor of the will of the flesh, nor of the will of man, but of God."[6]

The same thing is true when we speak of the Church's ministry as a continuation of the messianic ministry of Jesus Christ. This atoning life and death and resurrection *is* the messianic ministry, and the Church is a continuation of that essential ministry. She fulfills that ministry through obedience to God in Christ and in service to man within this world. Insofar as Ministers have a part in that, they share in the one essential ministry.

We err gravely if we push this identity of our Lord with our dependent ministries so far that we forget that we still see only

---

[6] *The Atonement and the Sacraments,* pp. 286f.

as in a glass darkly. Only in him do we meet the essential ministry face to face. All other forms of ministry are derivative, they come from him and they reflect that which his ministry revealed. They are not the original, they are not the source. We do not go to the ministry of Jesus Christ to claim a spiritual inheritance of which we are the executors and sole legatees, but we go to receive an unmerited gift of grace which we are charged to share with others. As Ministers of the gospel we have very much the same function as the disciples in the feeding of the multitude — they received the loaves and the fishes from him so that they might distribute the food to needy people, and it became a miracle in their hands. It was his gift, not theirs; and as we go to the ministry of Jesus to seek the pattern for our own, we go in humility and in penitence.

II

Continuity and Discontinuity in the Ministry of Jesus

No Hebrew ever obeyed the spirit of the Law more faithfully or more willingly than Jesus of Nazareth, and yet no prophet made a clearer break with some of the most prominent institutional features of the Hebrew religion. There are, therefore, elements of continuity and of discontinuity in the relationship that Jesus bore to the people of Israel — elements of continuity that were essential to indicate or fulfill his messianic purpose, and also areas of Hebrew life and religion that he rejected as unessential and even as serious hindrances.

(a.) The identity of Jesus with the Hebrew people and with its messianic character is a primary fact in the New Testament. Jesus was born a Jew of the Davidic royal house, he was circumcised on the eighth day in accordance with the Law, and he made a point of attending the synagogue on the Sabbath day: the Gospel writers are insistent upon these details and clearly intend us to understand that Jesus of Nazareth identified himself fully with his nation and its faith. At a deeper level Jesus claimed simply to be fulfilling the Law and the prophets of Israel's heritage; he put his trust in the God who had revealed himself throughout Hebrew history; and he seems consciously to have identified himself with the messianic figures in the sacred literature. As far as the prophetic line of Israel's religion was concerned, he was within it — there are many indications that he considered himself fully at one with the work and witness of this prophetic tradition, as we see in the parable of the wicked husbandmen and in some of his recorded sayings.[7]

But he was not a priest. Nor did he ever claim to be a priest.[8] Indeed, some of his most pungent comments were criticisms of the religious professionals. His utterances affirming the authenticity of the prophetic tradition were not lost on the priestly rulers of Jewry and were interpreted as being specifically directed against them (e.g. Matt. 21:45, Luke 20:19). These were the men who were in the regular priestly succession, who could point to a historic lineal descent from the recognized priesthood of Israel, and the meaning that the Gospel writers understood in our Lord's birth and ministry was that God intended to make a clean break with this aspect of Jewish religion. Whatever the value of the sacrificial and teaching offices that the Jewish priesthood represented, in the person of Jesus we see the most radical break with those offices, because he believed that the priestly leaders of Israel had twisted and perverted the meaning of Israel's historic faith. This element of discontinuity in the relationship of our Lord's ministry to the official "Ministry" in Israel cannot be avoided in our own understanding of Ministry in his Church, for it emphasizes that fidelity to the Faith in word and *in life* takes priority over all claims to a legitimate descent. I cannot substantiate any other position from the New Testament.

Therefore we see our Lord, on the one hand, identifying himself fully with the covenant people, and especially with the spiritually perceptive minority within Israel represented by "the Remnant" and other figures, but on the other hand we see in his words and actions a virtual denial of the religion represented in the Scribes, the Pharisees, the priesthood.

This may have been something of a problem to the early Church as its own forms of Ministry became routinized, and particularly when it sought to describe the ministry of our Lord in terms of Prophet, Priest, and King. The first and the last of those offices presented no problem, but that of Priest certainly did, and we see the writer to the Hebrews explaining to his

---

[7] Cf. Mark 12:1ff., Matt. 21:33ff., Luke 20:9ff., Matt. 23:29-37, Luke 10:49-52.

[8] Cf. T. W. Manson, *Ministry and Priesthood,* p. 46.

readers why Jesus could not be considered as the 'ideal' Priest within Israel's priestly succession. Jesus was not a 'Priest' within any *historical* order of descent because he was High Priest of the order of Melchizedek (Heb. 6:20, *et seq.*). The essential point which the writer is making is that this order of Melchizedek is not a lineal succession of priesthood similar to the Levitical order, for Melchizedek was "without father or mother or genealogy, and has neither beginning of days nor end of life, but resembling the Son of God he continues a priest for ever." (Heb. 7:3). Jesus was not related to Melchizedek in any physical way, but by the very character of his being and his acts: he represents on the one side a radical break with the Levitical priesthood (7:11-13), and on the other side he affirms a new spiritual resurrection priesthood. The eternal character of Melchizedek's order "becomes even more evident," says the writer, "when another priest arises in the likeness of Melchizedek, who has become a priest, not according to a legal requirement concerning bodily descent but by the power of an indestructible life" (Heb. 7:15f.). These chapters in the Epistle to the Hebrews concerning our Lord as the High Priest of the New Covenant deserve careful reading, for they lead us into the center of the meaning of his ministry, and therefore to the meaning of all ministry that springs from him.

(b.) In obedience to God and in service to his fellows Jesus represented the "ideal" Israel, Israel as it should have been and was intended to be, Israel of "the Remnant," "the Servant of Yahweh," the "I" of the Psalms; and by infusing Hebrew religion's deepest insights about Israel's mission and ministry into messianic concepts such as "the Son of Man," our Lord demonstrated that it was only in obedience and in service that the people of God would discover their true glory. It was Israel of the faithful Remnant that he represented, Israel in its obedience and its service, and he tries to show us that there is no fundamental impediment apart from sin which prevented the whole people of God from entering into this vocation, because this *is* Israel's vocation. All through his life on earth he was inviting the disciples to follow him. T. W. Manson maintained that Jesus held the door open for his disciples to join him in his redemptive task. Writing of the Son of Man passages in the New Testament, Manson says they suggest that "what was in the mind of Jesus was that he and his followers *together* should share the destiny which he describes as the Passion of the Son of Man: that he and they *together* should be the Son of Man, the Remnant that saves by service and self-sacrifice, the organ of God's redemptive purpose in the world."[9] None of them could accept the invitation, not even the best of them, but I believe Manson was right in suggesting that the way was always open from our Lord's side. Step by step Jesus paced out the pathway of faith for the community of faith to follow, so that others might follow *them*: "Be imitators of me," declares St. Paul to the church members of Corinth, "as I am of Christ" (I Cor. 11:1).

It seems to me that Canon A. T. Hanson's concept of the "pioneer Ministry" springs directly out of this understanding of the New Testament, but if St. Paul and the apostolic band that worked with him represented a pioneering remnant in relation to the New Israel that was coming into being, it was only because Christ himself, the great Pioneer, had first trod that way. Christ "calls out" his servants that they in turn, through service of a like kind, may call forth the Church to exemplify and expound the ministry of Christ in the world: "The ministry itself is no originator, but receives its task from Christ. The ordained ministers only exercise the ministry which Christ himself has first exercised, and which he continues to exercise through them, and through their activity in the whole Church also."[10]

(c.) But we must pause to take a second look at some of the implications of this view of the Ministry. Far from making a clear distinction between the charismatic ministry of our Lord in the Gospel accounts and the later ministries of the institutional Church, as some would insist,[11] it emphasizes the closest and most direct continuity between Christ, his apostles, and the Church, even to the extent of affirming that one ministry is common to them all and that there is no other kind of ministry but that which Jesus came to reveal.

Such a view of the Ministry is obviously fraught with danger. It is a danger which is present whenever we emphasize the identity between Christ and his "body" to the point where the

---

[9] Manson, *The Teaching of Jesus,* p. 231.

[10] A. T. Hanson, *The Pioneer Ministry,* p. 72.

[11] Dr. Ehrhardt in his book, *The Apostolic Ministry,* seems to argue for such a clear break.

Church is tempted to put itself in his place and claim the perfection and infallibility that are his alone. Yet perhaps it is a
danger which we must acknowledge and live with, for in a sense
there *is* no essential difference between our Lord's ministry to
us while he was on earth, and that ministry into which he calls
the Church. Our Lord's ministry was unique, but that uniqueness was in the fact that in his own strength and by his own
volition he did something that we could not do for ourselves.
In *his* strength and through *his* Spirit the Church is called to
fulfill the same kind of ministry in the world as its Lord; the
body *is* expected to obey the purpose and direction of the Head;
Israel *does* take its character from that of its messianic King.

However, if the task of the Ministry is to lead the Church into
its own essential ministry, then what is true for the Church
cannot be less true for ministers. The task of the ordained
Ministry, we suggest, is to re-present Christ to the community
of faith, so that this same community of faith may re-present
Christ to the world — not by claiming to repeat his unique
sacrifice, but by manifesting its fruits. If we speak of the
Church and its Ministers having a "redemptive" or "redeeming"
ministry, it is because our own service should witness to our
Lord's redemptive ministry: we become agents of reconciliation
as we make manifest in the Church and in the world the
character and evidence of that divine redemption. In that sense,
and in that sense only, can we speak of the work of the Church
or of its ordained Ministry as redemptive.

We must expect to find a paradox in the nature of the Church
and its Ministry which springs directly from the paradox of
the human and the divine in the incarnation itself, and the
danger is always that of trying to get rid of the paradox by
stressing one to the exclusion of the other. We face a double
danger: either we claim a kind of divinity that sets the Minister
absolutely apart from the Church or the Church absolutely apart
from the world, or we refuse to recognize that our ministry is
justified only in terms of Jesus Christ's ministry — we *are*
called to do the humanly impossible. The only way in which
we can keep the two sides of the paradox in proper balance
is by recognizing that everything that we are and everything that
we are called to be comes from the grace which we receive in
Jesus Christ: our Ministry can neither be begun nor continued
for a moment without recourse to the living Christ, who calls

us and sustains us. Gratitude and penitence are at the heart of our worship, and without them neither our intercession nor our petitions will have much meaning; and adoration becomes a mockery.

St. Paul understood this. "I have been crucified with Christ," he declared, but "the life I now live is not my life, but the life which Christ lives in me; and my present bodily life is lived by faith in the Son of God, who loved me and sacrificed himself for me. I will not nullify the grace of God" (Gal. 2:20f., *NEB*). He knew the One on whom his ministry was founded; as for his own best efforts, he was forced to confess that "the good I want, but the evil I do not want is what I do . . . . Wretched man that I am! Who will deliver me from this body of death? Thanks be to God through Jesus Christ our Lord!" (Rom. 7:19, 24f.). Here one of the clearest exponents of Christian Ministry recognizes the truth about himself, and if the Ministry is neither to deify itself nor shirk its essential ministry, it must keep the same perspective.

"The Ministry of the Church is to re-present Christ to the whole community of faith, so that the total membership of the Church may corporately re-present Christ to the world." If that were not substantiated within the Bible itself, it would be colossal presumption, but the danger lies in the temptation to ignore that ministers have part in the *Church's* ministry, or in the temptation to forget the final clause in that sentence. The Ministry is one of the gifts of the Spirit to the Church, and it is characteristic of the Holy Spirit that he always points away from himself to Jesus Christ (John 16:13f.). Presumably those whom he uses as vehicles of his grace should share a similar humility. The ministry of our Lord himself found its center not in status or in material authority but in the service of becoming identified with us and in complete self-giving.

This Spirit is characteristic of the "apostolic succession" which is blessed by the presence of the Holy Spirit, to which the New Testament bears witness. This is the spiritual continuity in Christ which links both the visible Church and a physical Ministry to him, and through him it links both to the messianic Ministry of historic Israel. Indeed, if there is any violent disjunction between our Lord's ministry and ours, the Church virtually proclaims a docetic Christ. Whatever the dangers inherent in a "high" doctrine of the Ministry, we must declare that all Ministry is derived from the messianic Ministry of Jesus Christ. This is of the *esse* of the Church, the one form of apostolic succession that must be maintained if the Church is to be the Church of Jesus Christ.

(d.) Church and Ministry have their common source in the ministry of Jesus Christ. Each helps us to understand the other, for the Ministry always points to the witnessing ministry of the whole people of God, and the Church stands as Minister to its own servants.

The witness of the "new" Israel was to reflect the same kind of continuity and discontinuity with the "old" Israel that may be seen in the life of our Lord himself. The function of the Church as witness to the saving acts of God is essentially the same as that of Israel through the ages, so that in a sense there is no such thing as a new Israel, but only Israel, *one* people of God in history. As Professor G. W. H. Lampe of Cambridge observed during one of the sessions in the Faith and Order Conference at Montreal, it is not so much a question of the "new" Israel, or the "renewed" Israel, but of the *true* Israel. On the other hand, the Church does represent a radical break with the institutional aspects of Israel's formal religion. Just as our Lord represents a clear break with its official priesthood, so the Church breaks with physical descent from Abraham as an ethnic guarantee of true faith. Abraham was the man of faith, and for the Jew the community of faith was established and maintained in Abraham's physical descendants: it was based on the common sense assumption of ancient society, "like father, like son." On the other hand, although heredity may pass on many things, it does not necessarily transmit spiritual and ethical qualities, as several of the prophets and much of Israel's history made very clear.

Faith in the one true God and in his deeds of merciful redemption is not something which can be passed along in the genes. Faith is a spiritual quality, "the assurance of things hoped for and the conviction of things not seen." The Church represents a radical break with the idea that the spiritual succession of faith could be restricted to a nation or guaranteed by the physical and tactual means of human generation. The matter was put very pointedly in our Lord's parable of the husbandmen in the vineyard — the owner of the vineyard (God) sent to his vineyard (Israel) and asked to have some evidence of the fruits (ethical righteousness). But the tenants (priests and scribes), whom he had appointed to tend the vineyard, mistreated and killed his messengers (the prophets), and eventually killed the owner's only son (the Messiah). Jesus ended his parable, "What will the owner of the vineyard do? He will come and destroy the tenants, *and give the vineyard to others"* (Mark 12:1-9). The clue to our understanding of the parable is that the vineyard is Israel, that the fruit of that vine is spiritual, and that because this is lacking "Israel" will be put in the charge of new tenants.[12]

As St. Paul had declared to the church at Philippi, "We are the true circumcision, who worship God in spirit, and glory in Christ Jesus, and put no confidence in the flesh. Though," he observed, "I myself have reason for confidence in the flesh." He then proceeds to give us the evidence of his impeccable Jewish lineage and upbringing. But he went on to declare that he counted all this as loss for Christ, so that he might rather have a righteousness that was not his own works "but that which is through faith in Christ, the righteousness from God that depends on faith; that I may know him and the power of his resurrection, and may share his sufferings, becoming like him in his death, that if possible I may attain the resurrection from the dead" (cf. Phil. 3:3-11).

One could hardly have the contrast put more sharply, and when the writer of the Epistle to the Hebrews takes up this theme in the eleventh chapter of his book, he shows himself to be soundly Pauline in his thought. Here the Epistle to the Hebrews demonstrates that from the beginning the true succession, however it may have been carried on in a particular family's genealogy, was actually a succession of living faith — Moses, the Judges, David and the prophets were men of faith of pure Hebrew descent, but this faith in God's mercy could also justify a person like Rahab, who was a woman, a gentile, and a prostitute! This spiritual generation of faith is the pedigree of the true Israel, says the writer, and for that reason we look

---

[12] The image of Israel as God's vineyard is frequently used in the Old Testament, e.g. Ps. 80:15, Isa. 1:8, 5:1-7, Jer. 12:10, and in an allegorical sense in the Canticles 8:11f. The passages, particularly that in Isa. 5, might be compared with the same imagery used by our Lord in the parable of the wicked husbandmen, and also with John 15.

to Jesus, who is "the pioneer and perfecter of our faith" (Heb. 12:2). The succession is essentially "of the Spirit."

(e.) This is of some importance to our understanding of the Ministry, for we would maintain that in the biblical view of the Church the succession of true Ministry cannot be essentially different from the succession of faith in the Church. This remains a crucial issue between Protestants and those who hold that a form of apostolic succession through the tactual, lineal descent of episcopal consecration is an *essential* mark of the Church. It is difficult to see how Protestant Christians could change their position at this point without being untrue to the gospel, and this must be said not to close the door on ecumenical discussion, but to state the issue clearly. If Protestants are wrong in this matter, then the onus is upon those who think them wrong to produce proofs from the gospel.

Episcopal critics sometimes argue justifiably that Protestants do not give sufficient weight to the implications of the incarnation, for in that act God affirmed the essential goodness of the creation, and the Holy Spirit always seeks to express himself through human channels. They affirm that just as Jesus Christ blessed human flesh and revealed God's willingness to become reconciled to men by becoming incarnate in the womb of Mary, so the Holy Spirit testifies to the goodness of this material world by becoming incarnate in the institutions of the Church and uses them to mediate God's grace to us.

Let us admit with some contrition that there is truth in the criticism. Protestants have sometimes spiritualized their concept of the Church and its Ministry to the point where the institutional forms of the Church are regarded as areas in which the Holy Spirit *cannot* operate. It is a self-defeating process, as we can see, for Christianity is thereby reduced to "spiritual" principles that are considerably less substantial than H. G. Wells' "Invisible Man," and the doctrine of the Holy Spirit becomes little more than the influence of a dead Christ. To spiritualize the incarnation is to end in materialism.

This is not the Bible's teaching. The Old Testament certainly thought of something very alive and dynamically related to human flesh in Israel's understanding of the divine *ruach,* as the almost overpoweringly virile stories of the ancient judges and prophets testify. The same vibrant dynamism is there in the New Testament in the figure of Jesus, in the account of

Pentecost, and in the incredible vitality of the early Church after the gift of the Spirit. While I was at college there was a somewhat pale and anemic student of receding chin and gloomy habits who frequented the innocent haunts of the holy without giving much reason for being alive, and some of our more profane undergraduates referred to him openly as "the holy ghost." The blasphemy illustrates a popular misconception, for no one as colorless as this could be at all like the invincible power of the Holy Spirit that we encounter through the pages of the Bible. This power was never disembodied or expressed in the abstract, for we always witness its creative and energizing work in material stuff, and supremely through human personality. We would maintain that a proper stress on the primacy of the Holy Spirit in the Church, far from leading to a denial of the incarnation, leads inevitably *to* the incarnation.

We must also maintain, however, that in the Church it is the Holy Spirit who holds the initiative, and not the material human forms which he uses: essentially it is the Spirit who produces, guarantees and *characterizes* the apostolic succession, and not the human channels that he may employ.

Let us put it into an illustration. Imagine a young American student of mixed racial parentage in some college of the Midwest, who becomes interested in William Shakespeare through having to write a term paper. He soaks up all the plays and poetry of Shakespeare, he studies life in England during the time that Shakespeare lived, he delves into libraries to learn all he can about the background of the great dramatist's family, and he reaches out to explore the circle of Shakespeare's intimate friends. At the end he is so inspired by his studies that this lad who has not been further east than Chicago feels that an Englishman who lived four hundred years ago is almost as real to him as his own friends, and considerably more real to him than his professors. He is on his way to becoming a writer himself.

On the other hand, let us consider someone living at the same time in Stratford-on-Avon, England, whose name is William Shakespeare, and who is the lineal descendant of the playwright. There have been passed down to him through the family several heirlooms, including a first folio edition of Shakespeare's plays. Our modern Mr. Shakespeare, however, has no taste for literature, and boasts that he has never read a poem in his life; so the volume simply gathers dust in the vault of a nearby bank waiting for the time when its present owner will pass it on to his son. Which one of these two imaginary figures received the real inheritance from Shakespeare?

The illustration has its limitations, for it is the presence of the living Christ and not the inspiration of a dead genius that the Church claims to "inherit"; but the illustration is not all that far from a true analogy, for Jesus himself provided us with a spiritually pragmatic test for the false prophets and others who would profess to speak in his name, "you will know them by their fruits" (Matt. 7:16, 20). And the fruits we look for are the fruits of the Spirit, the signs of Christ's reconciling ministry in our midst. This is the place at which service becomes witness.

In describing the way in which the Church's evangelism spread during the early centuries, T. W. Manson remarked that there were not many great preachers and only a few outstanding apologists. "When we try to picture how it was done," he wrote, "we seem to see domestic servants teaching Christ in and through their domestic service, workers doing it through their work, small shopkeepers through their trade, and so on, rather than eloquent propagandists swaying mass meetings of interested enquirers." And he went on to observe, "It is still true that the best propaganda for genuine Christianity is genuine Christians."[13] If this is true for ordinary members within the Church's ministry, then *a fortiori* how true it ought to be of the pioneering Ministry of the Church!

Of course, the true succession of the Holy Spirit *must* become incarnate in human flesh, through human personality, and in the material forms that the Church perforce adopts within human society. This much not only has to be fully conceded, but also fully asserted: the incarnation is a reality and a doctrine of the Holy Spirit becomes nonsense without it. But we declare with equal emphasis that the Holy Spirit must have his proper priority in the Church, and any attempt to make the essential apostolic succession in the Holy Spirit subject to any material pattern of lineal legitimacy not only fails to take the doctrine of the Holy Spirit seriously, but is also in danger of misunderstanding the true nature of the incarnation.

13 Manson, *Ministry and Priesthood,* p. 21.

III

THE MINISTRY OF RECONCILIATION

The New Testament writers are unanimous in understanding redemption as the purpose of our Lord's ministry among men, and they also show us that from the manward side this redemption centers upon faith in God's redemptive character as it was revealed in Jesus Christ: "God so loved the world that he gave his only Son, that whoever believes in him should not perish but have eternal life. For God sent the Son into the world, not to condemn the world, but that the world might be saved through him" (John 3:16f.). And at the heart of this redemptive purpose there is the intention of bringing about reconciliation — a reconciliation that would reach out to embrace man in all his relationships, to resolve the estrangements between brother and brother (Matt. 5:24), between husband and wife (I Cor. 7:11), between nations and races (Eph. 2:13-16), and indeed, between man and the whole cosmic order (Col. 1:20).

(a.) Yet this reconciliation is by no means obvious from what Jesus himself foretold about the immediate effects of his ministry. In one of the best attested sayings related to his passion he declared, "Do you think that I have come to give peace on earth? No, I tell you, but rather division; for henceforth in one house there will be five divided, three against two and two against three; they will be divided, father against son and son against father, mother against daughter and daughter against her mother, mother-in-law against her daughter-in-law and daughter-in-law against her mother-in-law" (Luke 12:51-3, cf. Matt. 10:34-36). Either on the same or on a very similar occasion Jesus expounded the meaning of discipleship in one of his hardest sayings, when he declared that "If any one comes to me and does not hate his own father and mother and wife and children and brothers and sisters, yes, and even his own life, he cannot be my disciple. Whoever does not bear his own cross and come after me, cannot be my disciple" (Luke 14:26f.). It was a challenge which was considerably softened by Matthew (10:37f.), but its intent can be illustrated in other parts of the Gospels (Matt. 8:21f., Luke 9:59f.), and nowhere more explicitly than in Jesus' own attitude to his mother and brothers when he set out on his public ministry (Mark 3:31-5).

These sayings and incidents suggest that Christ's message would produce the very opposite of reconciliation in immediate personal relationships. It is only when they are put into the total context of his life and teaching that we begin to see how they are related to the great motif of reconciliation in his ministry. Jesus subordinated all human relationships to our primary relationship with God. Reconciliation at this point is the fundamental need, and all other human relationships are dependent upon that. Jesus saw that in bringing about reconciliation between man and man's divinely-given destiny, the sin which maintains its tenacious and insidious grip on all personal and social relationships would have to be rooted out, and that in this process many of our cherished relationships would be turned upside down. Old friends would become new enemies and erstwhile enemies would become our friends, and sometimes in order to be reconciled to God we would find ourselves at greatest distance from those who had been nearest to us. Yet this revolution in human relationships and the new tensions that would appear were but the immediate, temporary results of this most fundamental revision in our relationship to God the Father, who created us and who has given us an eternal hope. They pointed towards the eschatological hope of the Kingdom in which man would be fully reconciled to God, and in which, through the right relation with God, he would discover his true relation to his fellow man and to the whole creation. The redemption of creation is God's purpose, and the revolution in personal relationships would occur inevitably only because the Kingdom must be established on the fundamental basis of reconciliation with God. Nothing could be allowed to rival that. But with the establishment of that Kingdom in the hearts of men the "at-one-ment" with God would reach out to bring reconciliation and peace into all the human relations in which God was recognized as sovereign. The purpose of our Lord's ministry is this fundamental atonement, this reconciliation between man and God.

Reconciliation between man and God. The order is important — it is reconciliation between *man* and God. Theories of the atonement have often thought of our Lord's sacrifice as essentially engaged in winning *God's* forgiveness on man's behalf, and in all the popular theories that followed from Anselm, God was regarded as the one who had become estranged, the injured party whose reconciliation had to be bought. God *is* the injured party, but men in the full flush of their pride and sin are not willing to recognize it. This would not be the place to argue it fully, but as we study the ministry of Jesus, it seems clear that the "estranged party," the obstinate and almost irreconcilable one who is being wooed and reconciled, is man himself.[14] It was *man* who had estranged himself from his Creator and who had voluntarily become an enemy in the face of God's constant love. Whatever truth there is in the older theories of the atonement (and I have argued elsewhere that they all contain some truth),[15] our Lord's whole life seems to have been a public declaration of God's constant love and continuing mercy in the face of our hostility and sin: God watches over the smallest things of his creation with tender care, he sends his rain upon saint and sinner with the same provident impartiality, and God so loves the world that he sends his Son — who "bears the very stamp of his nature" — so that the world might be saved. But it is proclaimed not only by what Jesus said about God directly, for he also tells us a great deal about the kind of goodness there is in God by his teaching about the Kingdom of God, the Sermon on the Mount and the Beatitudes: God is a God who comforts the mourner, welcomes the peacemaker and the one who is pure in heart, who goes the extra mile, and who loves his enemies. More than all this, our Lord's own unvarying attitude towards God as his Father, and his confidence in God's readiness to forgive even the enormity of the crucifixion, probably tells us more about the nature of the God whom Jesus worshipped than all his teaching.

This simply underlines the fact that everything recorded of our Lord's life in the Gospels, his words, his deeds, his own relationships, is a commentary on God's love for us, and a revelation of that love. It is in the *wholeness* of our Lord's ministry, which includes everything from the humility of Bethlehem through the years of witness and service to the sacrifice on Calvary and the victorious hope of the empty tomb, that we see the arms of God ever open and ever waiting to receive us. Forgiveness is there, if only we are ready to show forgiveness ourselves: the

---

[14] I made a tentative beginning in the development of this theme in *The Atonement and the Sacraments,* pp. 287-93.

[15] Cf. *The Atonement and the Sacraments.*

debt is "paid" to man, for he is the one who needs to be reconciled.

(b.) The ministry of Jesus not only reveals God's disposition of forgiveness and mercy towards us, but it also represents the response in fidelity, obedience, and trust which we should make to that love. He is the "beloved Son," "for it was fitting," says the writer to the Hebrews, "that he [God], for whom and by whom all things exist, in bringing many sons to glory, should make the pioneer of their salvation perfect through suffering" (2:10). Our Lord's words and teaching reveal not only the nature of the God whom he claimed as his Father, but they also demonstrate the nature and potential of that humanity which God destined for his Kingdom. Christ's deeds reveal not only the invincible mercy and the almighty power of the One who created the galaxies, but they also demonstrate the spiritual power that is available to men in God's Kingdom. During the events of his last days on earth we certainly have the supreme demonstration of God's love for sinful man, but we also have just as clearly the supreme illustration of one man's fidelity to God. The pattern of the new humanity is presented to us in Jesus Christ, and our Lord shows us that when a person is fully reconciled to God, the effects will sweeten all other human relationships.

In the summary of the Law, Jesus emphasized that true religion does not stop with a demonstration of our love towards God, but it flows out into love of our neighbour; and lest there should be any doubt about who was to be considered as "neighbour" he went on to give a concrete example in the parable of the Good Samaritan. The Kingdom was to be essentially practical. Far from intending that the proclamation of the Kingdom of God should permanently disrupt or embitter social relationships, our Lord had some extremely pertinent things to say about the meaning of true love for one's parents (Mark 7:9-13), responsibility to children (Mark 9:42, Matt. 18:5f., Luke 17:2), and on the proper treatment of a wife (Matt. 19:3-9).

(c.) This extension of reconciliation to human relationships was first, however, to be tested within the circle of the disciples — the embryonic Church. The group had a good number of natural reasons for human friction within itself. Zebedee owned his own boat, and his sons, James and John, appear to have regarded themselves as a social class above such proletarians as Peter and

Andrew; Philip had a Greek name and seems to have been of a speculative turn of mind, whereas Nathaniel is described as a guileless Israelite, and although they are often mentioned together in the record, we wonder how much they understood of each other; Matthew had been a publican and hence a collaborator with the Romans, while Simon Zelotes was a member of the violently nationalistic society of Zealots. So one could go on. But these disciples were told to love one another even as Jesus had loved them, and the Christian Church owes its existence to the fact that they learned how to do it. Yet it must have been a struggle in the face of such ambitions as those of James and John (or their mother) which threatened the unity of the little group. Jesus reminded them on that occasion that the disciple who was ambitious for the highest status in his Kingdom must be prepared to become the servant of all, and on the night of his betrayal he gave them an example of what that meant in practical terms by doing the job of the meanest — he washed their feet. Yet when Peter protested against that action, our Lord told him that if he was not prepared to accept this essential characteristic of his ministry, he had not really begun to understand what the Kingdom was about.

Scholars may not be able to say with any certainty that our Lord's great prayer of intercession for the disciples was uttered in precisely those words, but we cannot doubt that in John 17 the Fourth Evangelist has given us a prayer which truly expressed our Lord's deepest feelings about the little band of men which had shared his ministry and which would now be left to follow in his steps. But we are in danger of missing the point of that prayer if we fail to notice that the unity among the disciples for which our Lord prayed was founded in his own relationship with God the Father:

> I do not pray for these only, but also for those who are to believe in me through their word, that they may all be one; *even as thou, Father, art in me, and I in thee,* that they also may be in us, so that the world may believe that thou hast sent me. The glory which thou hast given me I have given to them, *that they may be one even as we are one, I in them and thou in me, that they may become perfectly one,* so that the world may know that thou hast sent me and hast loved them as thou hast loved me (John 17:20-23).

It has often been remarked that this passage shows the intimate relationship between the unity of the Church and its effective witness, and the fact that this relationship is mentioned twice in the course of a few verses indicates how important it appeared to be in the early Church's understanding of the mind of our Lord. But we must also point out the *closeness* of the unity to which the disciples were called — their unity was to be as close, and as obvious to the world, as the unity of trust and mutual love between Jesus and the Father. The quality of the Church's unity was to be inferred by the disciples from what they had seen and witnessed of our Lord's relationship to the Father, and as they came into ever closer relationship with the Spirit of their Lord, they were inevitably brought into deeper relationship with God and unity with each other. This was to be the ultimate and visible effect of the Holy Spirit's ministry in the Church.

(d.) The apostle Paul understood very clearly the central place which the redemptive work of Christ has in the Christian Faith, and how the reconciliation with God which Christ achieved for us must inevitably permeate and color all human relationships. It is at the heart of Paul's Christian ethics, "For if while we were enemies," he declares, "we were reconciled to God by the death of his Son, much more, now that we are reconciled, *shall we be saved by his life.* Not only so, but we also rejoice in God through our Lord Jesus Christ, through whom we have now received our reconciliation" (Rom. 5:10f.). The members of the Church are united through Christ's reconciling work, and are inevitably brought into union with God and unity with each other.

Paul also insists that human relations are dependent upon the fundamental reconciliation with God. Everything begins at that point, and although Paul sometimes leans towards an interpretation of the atonement in which it is the outraged justice of God which has to be reconciled, yet he leaves us in no doubt that what is done in the ministry and passion of our Lord is God's action. In Colossians Christ is spoken of as one in whom "all the fulness of God *was pleased to dwell,* and through him to reconcile to himself all things, whether on earth or in heaven, making peace by the blood of his· cross" (Col. 1:19f.) — a passage that regards the work of Christ in redemption as cosmic in its scope.

In the same way, Ephesians 2:13-16 shows that the cross —

in which the redemptive ministry of Jesus finds its focus — also brings reconciliation in the most intractable cases of human dividedness. The readers are Gentiles, and the writer is very conscious that he is writing as Jew to Gentiles. This fact, in the normal way of things, would have set up between them an impenetrable barrier of distrust and distaste; "But now in Christ Jesus," he says, "you who were once far off have been brought near in the blood of Christ. For he is our peace, who has made us both one, and has broken down the dividing wall of hostility, by abolishing in his flesh the law of commandments and ordinances, that he might create in himself one new man in the place of two, so making peace, and might reconcile us both to God in one body through the cross, thereby bringing the hostility to an end."[16] Again we notice that the central act is our reconciliation with God effected by Jesus Christ. This is at the center, but like movement on the surface of a quiet lake, the repercussions spread out to the furthest limits of human experience: because Christ reconciles us to our Father, God, we cannot remain hostile to others.

In this passage the writer is speaking primarily about the relationship between Jews and Gentiles, but if we put it into the total context of Pauline thought, we know that he extends the principle to all the circumstances that separate men on the plane of human nature. "For as many of you as were baptized into Christ have put on Christ. There is neither Jew nor Greek, there is neither slave nor free, there is neither male nor female; for you are all one in Christ Jesus." And then bringing it right home to those Gentile readers, he gets to the heart of their unity with their Jewish brethren by specifying the spiritual basis of the New Israel, for "if you are Christ's," he declares, "then *you* are Abraham's offspring, heirs according to promise" (Gal. 3:28f., cf. I Cor. 12:13). Paul saw all the barriers that divide humanity tumbling down because of the reconciliation with God which Jesus Christ had achieved for us through his sacrifice.

We might follow the same theme through many passages in the New Testament — particularly through the sacrifice and intercession of our Lord as the High Priest of the New Israel in Hebrews, or through the ethical implications of our Lord's redemptive work in I Peter, or through II Corinthians 5:16-21:

---

[16] I am assuming, of course, that if Ephesians and Colossians are not directly by the hand of Paul, they are substantially Pauline in thought.

From now on, therefore, we regard no one from a human point of view; even though we once regarded Christ from a human point of view, we regard him thus no longer. Therefore, if any one is in Christ, he is a new creation; the old has passed away, behold, the new has come. All this is from God, who through Christ reconciled us to himself and gave us the ministry of reconciliation; that is, God was in Christ reconciling the world to himself, not counting their trespasses against them, and entrusting to us the message of reconciliation. So we are ambassadors for Christ, God making his appeal through us. We beseech you on behalf of Christ, be reconciled to God. For our sake he made him to be sin who knew no sin, so that in him we might become the righteousness of God.

It has been pointed out that in II Corinthians we cannot be certain when Paul is using the epistolary "we" and when not,[17] and this is tantalizing because it would help us a good deal to know, in relation to the church at Corinth, whether the apostle was thinking primarily of himself, or himself and his co-workers. Or do the first person plural pronouns of verses 19 and 20 go further to include the whole Church in a proclamation to the world? Of this we can be sure, however, that whatever the logical extension of Paul's thinking about his own ministry to Corinth in a ministry of the Church to the world, this passage is primarily concerned with a particular ministry which he, and possibly others, exercised on behalf of the people at Corinth. Leaving aside the question whether it was the duty of everyone who received the gospel of reconciliation to proclaim it (vs. 18), Paul announces, "We are ambassadors for Christ, God making his appeal through us." Here we see a form of Christian Ministry which centers in the proclamation of God's redeeming love in Jesus Christ; and this, when Protestants have been most true to their biblical insights, has been the historic Protestant assertion about the apostolic ministry in the Church. It is expressed in and through men, but that which is expressed is the apostolic succession because that will bear the unmistakable accents of the Spirit. As Daniel Jenkins insisted some years ago: "It is their *testimony* which constitutes the Apostles as Apostles. . . . It is not their faith or their zeal or their religious genius or any

---

[17] Hanson, *The Pioneer Ministry,* pp. 49ff.

other special charismata they possessed, like the gift of the Spirit by the laying on of hands, and certainly not any accident of historical association, but their *testimony* which constitutes the Apostles."[18]

True — and yet we cannot quite end there, for the testimony itself was much more than uttered words. As we put Paul's words within the framework of his whole life of witness, we recognize that God was making his appeal to men through the *total* life of the apostle: Paul's whole life — what he did, where he went, how he reacted to situations (see II Cor. 12), no less than what he preached — was a living proclamation of the gospel and a call to commitment.

The implication for the modern forms of Christian Ministry must be obvious. The Minister has the primary charge to proclaim reconciliation with God, to be an "ambassador for Christ," but Ministry is most truly itself when it is not limited to the preached word of the pulpit or the preached action at the altar, but when it becomes a testimony through the whole of a reconciled and therefore reconciling life.

IV

CHRIST AND HIS BODY

The metaphor of the Church as the Body of Christ is used in no less than four of the Pauline epistles. It stresses the organic unity of a body to its head, the organic relationship of the members to each other, and the fact that within their various functions all the parts of a body are necessary to the health of the whole.

With these built-in lessons about the nature of the Church we can understand why the metaphor of the Body of Christ has been a favorite in the ecumenical movement. "Jesus Christ," declares the *Lund Report,* "is the King of the new People of God. He is 'the chief cornerstone in which the whole building, fitly framed together, grows up into a holy temple in the Lord.' He is the head of the Church which is His body. Through His Spirit Jesus Christ is present in His Church. Christ lives in His Church and the Church lives in Christ. Christ is never without

---

[18] D. T. Jenkins, *The Nature of Catholicity* (London: Faber & Faber, 1942), pp. 24f.

His Church; the Church is never without Christ. Both belong inseparably together, the King and His people, the keystone and the temple, the Head and the Body. As members of His Body we are made one with Him in the fellowship of His life, death and resurrection, of His suffering and His glory. For what concerns Christ concerns His Body also."[19]

Those who drafted the report were too aware of the richness of the New Testament images about the Church to ignore others like that of the king and his people, and the keystone to the temple,[20] but when they wish to expand the implications of the unity between Christ and his Church, it is to the metaphor of the body that they return. Nor is this surprising, for this image does express, perhaps better than any other, the organic and living relationship of Christ to the Church. Thus Lesslie Newbigin uses the image of the body to emphasize the "catholic" element in the nature of the Church, the claim that "the Church cannot live except as a visibly defined and organized body with a continuing structure."[21]

We must recognize that there are dangers in the ecumenical popularity of this image — the danger of allowing it to control and govern all other New Testament insights into the nature of the Church. A wise and respected teacher once wrote, "I beg you to beware of the ecclesiastical misuse of Paul's metaphor of the Church as the Body of Christ. It is an entirely appropriate metaphor as he uses it, but if it is taken, as it so often is, not as a metaphor but as a metaphysical statement, its consequences can be disastrous for theological thought. The Church is the Body of Christ and the Bride of Christ. We have no more reason for taking the former than the latter as a proposition in metaphysics."[22] The warning is well taken. On the other hand, we cannot ignore it simply because it may be misused, and it has a particular appropriateness in our study of the Church's ministry at least in the following four points.

First, we notice the emphasis which this metaphor puts upon

---

[19] *The Report of the Third World Conference of Faith and Order at Lund, Sweden, August* 15-28, 1952, (London: S.C.M., 1952), p. 7.

[20] Cf. Paul S. Minear, *Images of the Church in the New Testament,* (Philadelphia: Westminster Press, 1960).

[21] Lesslie Newbigin, *The Household of God* (London: S.C.M., 1953), p. 72; cf. also especially *ibid.,* ch. iii.

[22] Nathaniel Micklem.

the living and organic relationship of the various parts of the Church to Jesus Christ, and through him to each other. We are made to realize the indispensable place that all talents and all members have in the life of the Body for its health, efficiency, and service, and it is clear that in the thought of Paul the differences that tend to divide us in the natural world — race, language, sex, class — are irrelevant to the Church, for as a member belongs to Christ in the Church, so he belongs to all his fellow-members.

But how legitimate is the popular Free Church claim that this metaphor justifies a concept of simply "spiritual unity" between otherwise separated denominations? One might doubt whether "spiritual unity" that refuses to commit itself to a physical manifestation could have very much to do with the Holy Spirit that was incarnate in Jesus Christ. Our main cause for doubt, however, is that Paul does not speak of several "bodies" co-existing and acting as if they and they alone were "the Body" separately joined to the Head. The idea would be entirely foreign to him. Indeed, such a concept would destroy the whole metaphor, and it raises acute problems for us if it is seen in relation to the metaphor of the vine and the branches in John 15. I have difficulty in accepting the "catholic" definition of the historical Church, but the insistence that the Church's unity must be organic and visible seems to me to be entirely justified by the New Testament. If you wish to take these parts of the New Testament seriously, the ecumenical issue cannot be spiritualized away.

Secondly, I would point out that the most profound aspect of the metaphor is that the Church is likened to the Body *of Christ*. Within the biblical passages on the Body there are in fact two metaphors, and beyond the metaphor which compares the relation of Christ and his Church to that of the human head and its body, there is the much more startling claim that the Church is to be likened to Christ's *own body.* i.e., *Christ's* body reveals to us what the Church is entended to be. That which our Lord's human frame was to him in this world — obedient and visible vehicle of his Spirit, the living embodiment of his redemptive service — *this* is what the Church is to be. This in a metaphor, declares the apostle, is the Church's task; and if we cannot ignore the "catholic" demand that we face the implications of the metaphor for the Church's unity, then equally we cannot ignore the "protestant" claim that the Church reveals its true relationship to Christ by the kind of Spirit it manifests and the kind of service it offers: "By their fruits ye shall know them" is still the ultimate test.

Thirdly, as we have hinted already, the metaphor suggests the corporateness of the Church's mission. It would seem to be obvious that all who belong to Christ not only belong to him but are needed for his work. The apostle reminds us that although some parts of a human body seem to enjoy a certain primacy in perceiving, in creating, in movement, in doing, they are by no means independent of each other or of the rest of the body: all parts of the body with their various gifts and skills are *necessary* if the wishes of the mind are to be made effective. So it is with the Church (I Cor. 12). This undoubtedly indicates something of the mutual ministry that Ministers and laymen should exercise toward each other in the total life and ministry of the Church; but it also causes us to reflect upon the defectiveness of our church life and of our varying forms of ordination because of our divisions — for the Church as the Body of Christ does exist on earth, but, as Oliver Chase Quick observed, "It does not exist completely or exclusively in any one of its divided fragments."[23] While schism persists every ordination is defective, for P. T. Forsyth pointed out, "That is ordination, which no single congregation has power to give, but only the greater Church."[24] Therefore, while the Church remains divided, the Ministry which should be a sign and seal of her apostolic unity[25] is the symbol of the Church's great betrayal.

Fourthly, the metaphor sets before us the nature of the Church's mission, which is to witness to the glory of God in Jesus Christ. Here we must be careful to insist that we are speaking of a metaphor, but I would maintain that within the limits of metaphor it is permissible to speak of the Church as a continuation of the redemptive incarnation. The Pauline image of the Body seems to have this thought behind it.

The incarnation was necessary to fulfill God's purpose towards men, and yet "it is by no means obvious that in Jesus Christ we do recognize very man, and not, say, an idea of man; and very

---

[23] O. C. Quick, *The Christian Sacraments* (London: Nisbet, 1948), p. 147. First pub. in 1927.

[24] P. T. Forsyth, *The Church and the Sacraments* (London: Independent Press, 1953), p. 136. First pub. in 1917.

[25] Cf. *ibid.*, pp. 134f.

God, and not, say, a demigod."[26] The Church is to take its pattern from the incarnation of Jesus Christ, it is to be *like* the body of Christ. Just as God the Creator used the flesh and blood of a human body to give us Jesus Christ and not an angel, so he employs the institutional forms of men to proclaim the gospel in terms of community. According to one of the accounts in Genesis the creation is described in the picture of God using the dust of the earth to create man, and then he used this same humanity to give us the Mediator. In like manner he uses the material stuff of redeemed flesh and blood — even if it is still mixed with some of the clay — to bring into being the Church.

God's glory is the obedience of the Son in redeeming the world: "Now is my soul troubled. And what shall I say? 'Father, save me from this hour'? No, for this purpose I have come to this hour. Father, glorify thy name" (John 12:27f.). The Church also exists to glorify God. Taking its pattern from the human form of Jesus, the Church is to be a kind of redemptive incarnation — its work is to forward the work of the world's redemption in and through Christ. But the Church could not be an agent of redemption unless first it had been redeemed *by* him: it does not exist in its own right, by its own worth, or as an end in itself. As our Lord witnessed to the Father, so the Church is intended to witness to its Lord: it is no more than clay in which the impress of our Lord's redemptive work can be seen. While it exists here, this Body of Christ will have to travel through the world bearing something of the mud and dirt even as our Lord's human body did; it has to identify itself with the Son of Man in that penal area where sin permeates all human relationships. Yet if it is truly to be his Body, it will witness in many unconscious ways to the truth, bearing about in its own members the dying of the Lord Jesus that the life of its Lord may be made manifest. Because of sin — our sin — it will be a broken and a lacerated body; only as it makes its witness in obedience to Jesus Christ and in compassion for the world does it have any claim to be the Body of Christ.

The Church continues the ministry of our Lord, but let us have no doubt about the source of its witness and its service.

---

[26] Karl Barth, in *Revelation,* a symposium edited by John Baillie and Hugh Martin, (New York: Macmillan, 1937), p. 58.

"The One great Minister sent of God on this embassy of reconciliation is Jesus Christ, the Son of the Living God. He is his special servant in accomplishing this work."[27]   That sounds remarkably like T. W. Manson, with whom we began this chapter, but it is not, for it comes from the sermon of an American preacher on the frontier about one hundred years ago. But whether you take the thought from T. W. Manson or from James Challen, it points to the source of the Church's own ministry and of all Ministry in the Church, and to the place where the only valid "theology of Ministry" can begin, to the redemptive ministry of Jesus Christ himself.

[27] From a sermon by James Challen of Davenport, Iowa, which appeared in William T. Moore's *The Living Pulpit of the Christian Church* (1867), and cited in *The Reformation of Tradition,* ed. Ronald E. Osborn, St. Louis, Mo., 1963), p. 83.

chapter four

The Ministry of the Church

I

The Pioneer People

We like the story of Cinderella because virtue is rewarded in the end, and I suspect that we sometimes find the Christian gospel comforting for much the same reason. Of course, we are right, the faithful are rewarded in the end; but suppose we have our values the wrong way around. Suppose, for example, instead of Cinderella being chosen to leave the position of servant in the kitchen to be a princess in the castle, her prince joins her in the kitchen as a servant; suppose she found that to be the royal bride meant taking up the role of a servant and making a "heaven" of that, would not that make a difference to the story? It would put quite a different twist on the theme of virtue rewarded, and it might cause many young ladies to review their ambition to marry the prince for "love alone." Yet this is probably nearer the truth of the love match between the Church and her Lord than is the conventional picture of a Cinderella heaven.

God's purpose, as the Bible speaks of it, is the redemption of his creation, in which the salvation of mankind is supreme. The task of the people of God has always been directed towards this end. Israel *is* to exemplify the reconciliation between God and man through her own life of worship and of faith — she *is* the

101

redeemed of the Lord — but this redemption is never an end in itself, it is always directed to the salvation of all mankind. It was always Israel's temptation that, in claiming the privileges of her own deliverance, she forgot the responsibility to which that redemption called her. The people of the Old Testament were superseded as God's instrument, and perpetrated the blasphemy of the crucifixion simply because they could not recognize that within the promise of their own redemption they held responsibility for the redemption of the world. Indeed, the people of God cannot exemplify the meaning of reconciliation between God and man unless they exemplify God's righteous love and compassionate involvement in mankind's redemption. Israel is in that sense simply a pioneering people, a people that pioneers the Kingdom of God, the first community to tread the way by which we all come to our King. We may certainly agree that this implies a kind of primacy and leadership, but it is leadership of a particular quality which is at the very opposite pole of what 'primacy' and 'leadership' connote within the kingdoms of men. We do not know who wrote the Servant Songs of Isaiah, nor are we very sure who was meant to be the "Servant," whether the prophet intended it to be the figure of Israel, or the Remnant, or a particular witness like the prophet Jeremiah, but we recognize that the Songs represent the very apex of Israel's religious insight because they enthrone the idea of obedient service. The Servant gets his reward and shares his portion with the great in bringing many to righteousness, in pouring out his soul to death and in making intercession for those who transgressed. Ministry bears its own reward.

The task of the people of God is to interpret this in community. However unique the mission of the pioneering Servant may be, the meaning of the reconciliation between God and man must eventually prove its relevance in terms of reconciliation between man and man, and perhaps this is why "the supremely important sermon only the Christian fellowship can preach." In the final issue the value of the reconciliation with God that the Church proclaims is judged by the world in terms of its practical effect upon human relationships. That is the way in which our Lord wanted it to be: if the writer of the Fourth Gospel interpreted Jesus correctly, there is no way of evading the relationship between the unity of the disciples and the evangelism of the world that occurs twice in the High Priestly prayer of John 17 (vss. 21-

23). We see the ecumenical dimension in these days not as an optional extra which the Church may wish to take up for its own increased efficiency, but as an imperative command to those who profess Christ's work of reconciliation. The affirmation of atonement becomes a betrayal of Christ where the Church's unity is denied or ignored.

Moreover, the task of witness is that of the *whole* community of God's people, and we have seen that this must engage every member in and through his (or her) involvement within the secular world. It is hardly necessary to point out that before this can begin to be effective, the task of lay training and of interpreting the gospel through our many secular vocations is enormous. The need for adult education among the whole people of God stands clear as one of the most pressing demands on the Church's money and time, for without it the Church is in danger of being simply an association for mildly charitable purposes. What her membership needs to know is how the Church can really be the *Church,* the people of God, the apostolic community that witnesses to the victory of Christ. In the Church there will be many differing gifts, many different stages of maturity, but the work to which the Church is called requires the witness of every member, in the place where he (or she) lives and works.

We have drifted far from the time when those who were scattered abroad through persecution thought it their privilege and their duty to be "preaching the word" (Acts 8:4), yet the New Testament writer was speaking about ordinary Christians, not the apostles. The danger into which we have fallen is due to the fact that evangelism is no longer the burning concern of every church member — it has been handed over to professionals.

Let me take my illustrations from Britain rather than America, for I know it better and the process has been at work a little longer. Every year since the end of World War I names have disappeared from the church rolls of British denominations — the names of people who had once been members of the Christian Church. Presumably each one of them at some time or other had stood up before his fellow Christians and solemnly confessed faith in Jesus Christ and vowed to follow him through life. They are no longer in the Church. Yet very few of them have been converted to Communism or atheism or anything else, and probably few of them realized that they were leaving the Church at all. It just happened. I will tell you how it happened.

Two of them were married from the young people's society of a local congregation, and moved to a new district because they found just the house they wanted. Of course, at first there was a lot to do in the house and garden, so they did not find much time to go to church on Sunday, and when the baby arrived it always kept one of them at home and the other one did not want to go alone. In the 1930's they bought a little car and they started to take trips together out into the country. By the time of World War II they were lost to the Church before ever Hitler's bombs destroyed their faith.

Or let us take a different case — a couple who since 1945 have retired to the warm southwest coast to their dream cottage. They were extremely careful to ask the estate agent (realtor) about the soundness of the house's construction, whether it had good drains, and adequate water and electricity supply, and whether it was reasonably near the shopping center. No, they did not enquire about a church, and it is not a very easy journey into the village on a Sunday, so they just gave up going. "After all," Mr. X remarks laughingly, "we attended church for a good number of years when we lived in town, so I suppose we have learned all the parsons can tell us!" They are lost to the Church. They did not intend to leave — it just happened.

You will probably remark that this has little to do with evangelism, but I insist that it does. Surely the fault in the cases I have described is in the fact that the Church is regarded simply as an association for our own spiritual nurture or titillation, instead of the community in which we learn to be witnesses for Jesus Christ. For example, that young couple in its new housing area, surrounded more likely than not with hundreds of children from homes where the name of Jesus Christ is little more than an easy blasphemy, had a primary duty before house, garden, or even family, to gather a Sunday School for the children or a social club for young people. And that older couple, finding themselves in a district where there is no church and possibly with neighbours in a similar position, does it never occur to such people that they could start the church in their own homes and among their own friends? Surely we have to learn that whether we are scattered by reason of persecution as was the earliest church at Jerusalem, or because of the complexity of modern society with its multitudinous opportunities, we are first and foremost Christian witnesses in the home, in the business, in the profession. The opportunity has been given to us to found the Church of Jesus Christ in the place where we are set.

In former times evangelism sometimes appears to have been a matter of a strong voice and an invincible prejudice. Let us gladly admit that the Church today needs evangelism of a very different quality. Let us also gladly admit that the need is for those who will witness *within* their daily work rather than *despite* their daily work, that the Christian needs to be as open to the truth that comes from the colleague of different faith, or of no faith, as he is ready to give an account of the faith that is in him. Let us welcome the pioneering work of the lay academies, retreat centers, and "third orders" where the church member can learn to understand the witness of his profession, where he can forget the temptation to pious monologue and will share exposure to serious dialogue, where above all he can replenish the spiritual reserves that alone can keep him effectively in the Church's front line. But let us not forget that the main task *is* evangelism. It is to bring men and women into confrontation with Jesus Christ, and to bring such people into the living community of the Church where God's grace in reconciliation is proclaimed in Word and Sacrament.

Those of us who have worked in a parish must humbly concede that the Church is often a denial of what it should be, and perhaps God in his mercy is raising up his Church in new forms that will supersede the traditional parochial structure as we have known it. We hope that Ministers will have the grace to welcome the changes as evidence of the Holy Spirit's power in our day. Until God's will is revealed in the power of his Spirit, however, let us not fall into the opposite error of worshipping novelty. The Church has to find new forms in which to supplement the conventional parish for those who are completely disenchanted by the social odor of our parishes. Possibly we have to think in terms of "orders" that will be roughly equivalent to the religious orders of the Middle Ages. They grew up side by side with the life of the parishes, but they were nourished by the same Word and Sacrament and held together in Christian fellowship. Until the reader of *Saturday Review* is prepared to accept the avid viewer of the Ed Sullivan Hour within a single parish life, the Church will probably have to find forms in which both can receive the ministry they demand apart from each other.

Let us not fool ourselves, however, that this is the Church as it should be. A group of "classless" intellectuals who all share the same radicalism can be just as much a cozy club denying the radicalism of which the gospel speaks as any bourgeois congregation in suburbia; a group of factory workers which insists on maintaining the group as a closed shop on factory premises would be just as perniciously sectarian as a white ghetto church in Mississippi, or the white-collar congregation in Greenwich, Connecticut. Some few years ago the leaders of the Evangelical Academies in Europe met at the Ecumenical Institute, Château de Bossey, seriously to examine how far they were fulfilling the evangelical task which they had seen at the beginning. One of the directors of a Swiss academy admitted that he was extremely puzzled about what course he should take in the future. As the result of his industrial conferences some factory workers had become soundly converted to the Christian Faith; but they would have nothing to do with the traditional parish churches in the places where they lived because the congregations were snobbishly middle class, pompously stuffy, and falsely pious. The new converts were content to get their spiritual nourishment through the regular meetings and Bible study at the Evangelical Academy. "And now," he added, "they want me to administer the Lord's Supper to them. What must I do? Do I send them back to their proper parish church, where they will be stifled in two weeks? or do I give them what they want, and become, in fact, a sect?"

It is a genuine dilemma; it may indicate that we are only prepared to be reconciled to our brother in a very limited sense, and until we learn the gospel better, there may be a place in the organization of the Church for orders that can exist alongside parish life. But let us see that our Lord is just as grieved at the factory worker who refuses to accept his middle-class neighbour as a brother in Christ as he is with that middle-class neighbour when he settles himself comfortably into the ecclesiastical club on Sunday at 11:00 A.M. Are we willing to be reconciled to each other? That is the question that runs all through our society, and if the well-to-do in suburbia bear a heavier responsibility today, it is because they have set their stamp on the Church, and therefore they should be the first ones to face the claims of the Lord they profess.

The last few paragraphs indicate that the problem of the Church's unity (another way of speaking about the reconciliation into which our Lord brings us) arises every time the Church seriously undertakes her evangelical task. It was raised in the nineteenth century on the foreign mission field, it was raised by the denominations on the American frontier, and it is raised today acutely in the work of an evangelical academy or the witness of an inner-city mission. As soon as we treat the Church's evangelical mission seriously, we have to face the ecumenical reality. We meet it in a relationship to new and possibly smelly and grubby converts, or snobbish and highbrow converts; or in our relationship to other (and apparently erroneous and rival) Christians; or in the issue of our divided witness in the face of a hostile or (worse) mildly amused majority that professes some other form of faith or non-faith. Only churches that have forgotten how to evangelize and which are content to maintain themselves through the unearned increments of an expanding population or by a gentleman's agreement about the exchange of members, can be content to accept our plurality of denominationalism. To bring people face to face with Jesus Christ is the Church's main task in this world, and it is the vocation of those who bear her witness in the office, factory, market, or home.

But what about the claim that we need to send the Church's members to work in political parties, trade unions, and other areas of secular concern? Of course the Church needs her representatives in these places — in the rapidly expanding complexity of our world responsible Christians will have to be ready to take more responsibility. Do we then need to provide lay people a doctrine of work and vocation? Yes. Do they need to be brought into dialogue with those of other faiths? Yes. Do they need new forms of simple spiritual discipline — a "worldly spirituality" such as that to which Bonhoeffer looked?[1] Yes. Do they need lay academies, and retreat centers, and training institutes? Yes, yes, yes. But most of all we should know that the need of the world is to be confronted with the gospel of Jesus Christ, and the task of the Church is to do that. By all means let us evan-

[1] Dietrich Bonhoeffer, *Letters from Prison* (London: S.C.M., 1954), pp. 121ff. See also "Towards a New Christian Style of Life?" *Laity* (Geneva: W.C.C., June, 1958, No. 5), ed. Hans-Ruedi Weber.

gelize, if evangelize we can, by the quality of our professional work and the exercise of our vocational skills, but let us also understand that the Church's task is witness, and that call is to each member. When Christ canvasses for evangelists, the pledge can be redeemed only in the currency of service and commitment. No other check will pay it.

Christ calls the Christian individual, but "the supremely important sermon only the Christian fellowship can preach." Ultimately reconciliation can only be demonstrated in community; "even as thou, Father, art in me, and I in thee, that they also may be in us, so that the world may believe that thou hast sent me" (John 17:21). The unity of the disciples is to be as close and as manifest as the unity between Jesus and his Father, and unity is the identity of heart and will that reconciliation makes possible. To be reconciled is to be made "at one" — with God first but also inevitably with those who share the same atonement; whether they are black or white, whether they are rich or poor, whether they are American or Chinese, whether they speak English or Afrikaans, whether they live here or there, whether they are politically to the right or to the left, whether they are dirty or clean, man or woman, diseased or healthy, intelligent or stupid, Catholic, Orthodox, or Protestant, and — perhaps the most difficult — whether they are morally upright or morally outcast. This is what the Church should be like. How do you feel about joining it?

This puts into question at once the kind of fellowship the Church is supposed to be. It is a worshipping community, but is it simply a community of individuals who come to a common place for worship and then have no relationship to each other for the rest of their time, like comets whose orbits intersect briefly but only to swing away in totally unrelated arcs? D. T. Jenkins has pointed out this difference between the "Catholic" and the "Free Church" concept of the Church. It puts pressure of a unique kind on the latter in its attempt to be the Church of Jesus Christ. "It is not hard," he says, "for the Guards officer and the distinguished novelist and the artistic peeress to hear Mass in the same church as the Irish labourer and the elementary schoolteacher's wife and the secretary of the funeral club, if that is their sole association. It becomes more complicated if they are also expected to attend church meetings [i.e., in the Congregational sense of 'church meeting'] and serve teas at church social gatherings and send their children to the same Sunday schools."[2] We can justly condemn the "Free Church" for its tendency to become a "one class church" and in its suburban setting to have many of the less agreeable features of the exclusive country club. There are plenty of people who will join in the chorus with us, but we also need to reflect that while we properly condemn the result, the reasons for this tendency in 'Free Church' congregations are not all bad. I believe Jenkins rightly asserts that such a Church "can claim, as against those denominations who are perhaps too ready to glamorize their alleged universality, that it has made a determined attempt to create a genuine Christian fellowship in the place where it matters most and where it is most difficult and costly, in the particular local congregation."[3] It is not only the fact that the Church should welcome all kinds and conditions of mankind into its fold, but it is equally important that when they enter they should find themselves in the midst of a living, caring *fellowship,* in which each bears a mutual ministry for the other. That is one reason which makes it so hard to realize the universality of the Church in a typical Free Church congregation in America or Britain: the demands of Christian charity are more insistent. They are no less a part of the Church's essential nature.

Of course, our dislike of certain classes of people is the measure of our failure to be reconciled to the God who is Father of us all. Through that which Christ has done upon the cross the one great barrier between us and God came tumbling down, so that the little things that seem to be between us are but ripples in the sand in comparison. "But now," declares the apostle, "in Jesus Christ you who once were far off have been brought near in the blood of Christ. For he is our peace, who has made us both one, and has broken down the dividing wall of hostility . . . that he might create in himself one new man in place of the two, so making peace, and might reconcile us both [Jew and Gentile] in one body through the cross, thereby bringing the hostility to an end" (Eph. 2:13-16). The early Church tried to live in that spirit, and the pagan world looked on and remarked how these Christians loved one another. It was not a sarcasm,

[2] Daniel T. Jenkins. *Congregationalism: A Restatement* (London: Faber & Faber, 1955), p. 45.

[3] *Ibid.*

but sober reflection on observed fact: the Christian fellowship had become the supremely important sermon. We can make no further comment. That is what the Church should be, in the local parish, in the relation of national denominations and international confessions, in every aspect of its life. Our failure to make it actual is the measure of our need for the healing of the cross.

II

The Church and its Ministers

What we have said in the preceding paragraph is no more than to admit that the Church falls short of its own messianic vocation. The call of the people of God was from the first to be the messianic, pioneer community to lead mankind into God's Kingdom, but as the writer of the Servant Songs understood, it was to be of a quality very different from that which the kingdoms of men recognized as leadership. It has been the temptation of the people of God to claim the rewards of being the Chosen people without recognizing the nature of the role for which God's people are chosen.

As with Israel in the Old Testament, so with the Church. We have seen the way to the Kingdom. We have seen the quality of messiahship in Jesus Christ. The mission of the Church is to interpret the meaning of one man's obedience into terms of a living community, and to proclaim this through word, deed, and the nature of its fellowship. But it constantly falls short of its vocation, and if there is anything characteristic of the Church, it should not be arrogant claims about its election, but penitence, a sense of need, a humility before God and the world, a dependence upon God's grace. Christ has given to his Church a high calling, but it is the high calling of service, of obedience and self-denial for the sake of the world which he came to save.

Once the essential character of the Church's own ministry is seen, then the particular function and nature of those whom he calls to be Ministers within his Church becomes more clear. They are to lead the Church into the recognition of its own total, corporate ministry. Their ministry is no different from the Church's ministry, but they are given by Christ to his Church to lead it towards that ministry which only a corporate fellowship can fulfill. The Church's ministry and the particular ministry of

Ministers within the Church are not different in kind, for they both find their source and inspiration in the only essential Minister, Jesus Christ. Nor do Ministers stand over the Church as a caste apart, for it becomes the "glory" of a true Minister when he can lead the Church to undertake corporately the ministry that he is sent to exemplify. If he proclaims the Word of God to a congregation, it is in order that this congregation may proclaim that same Word of God to the world by its character, to live the reconciliation that Christ came to reveal. If he administers the sacraments in the midst of the Church, it is in order that the Church herself may portray the great representative Sacrament, immersed, broken, poured out in the service of men. If the Minister stands as representative of the people before God and intercedes on its behalf, it is so that this same people may be itself a living prayer for the world. Everything the Minister does as Minister for this people is of the same character as the ministry of God's people to the world, and with the intent of expounding that ministry and preparing them for it. It is within this total ministry of the Church that his ministry has its place and finds its meaning. P. T. Forsyth had gone a long way ahead of us when he wrote, "The ministry is sacramental to the Church as the Church itself is sacramental to the world. For the Church is sacramental as a living element and vehicle of Christ's redeeming grace."[4]

The only human ministry which is of the *esse* of the Church is the Church's own ministry to the world, and it is of the essence of the Church because it takes its character directly from the ministry that Christ fulfilled. Without this ministry the "Church" ceases to be the Church. The particular ministry of those whom Christ calls out and gives to the Church also belongs to this *esse* but it does not constitute it. And it shares in it not because Ministers are specially gifted, not because of careful training, nor even because they have the Church's recognition, but as their ministry takes its character from the ministry of Jesus Christ and leads the Church towards the fulfillment of its own corporate ministry. Where these features are missing, no rite or act of formal consecration, however impressive, can make a ministry valid, for "only that gospel validates the ministry which created it."[5]

---

[4] Forsyth, *The Church and the Sacraments,* p. 133.
[5] *Ibid.,* p. 140.

It should be clear from this that there can be no false opposition between the Church and its Ministers, for both find their
source and inspiration in the ministry of our Lord. In times past
"Catholic" and "Protestant" have argued *ad nauseam* whether
the Church or the written gospel should come first in the allegiance of the Christian, rather in the spirit of the old riddle about
the chicken and the egg. We have begun to see how irrelevant
those discussions were, for Christ is the source of both — he is
the source of the gospel written and lived, the representative of
the redemption about which Scripture and the people of God
both testify. In the same way, I suggest, it is equally beside the
point to argue for any priority as between the Church and the
Ministry. Our Lord was representative of the people of God,
the Church; but as he led this people into an understanding of
what God calls it to do, he personifies Ministry, all ministry,
the very purpose for which Ministers are given to the Church
and the Church is given to the world.

Any question of priority of a minister over the Church becomes a denial of this essential ministry of our Lord. If it is
possible in any sense to speak of "priesthood" in the Christian
Church at the human level, it is only possible as it reflects the
character of our Lord's High Priesthood, and in this the fundamental theme is that of humility and sacrificial service. If the
question of priority arises at all, it is only in terms of a minister's
self-oblation on behalf of Christ's people — an example and an
offering which is given to the Church by Christ through his servant, so that the Church itself may respond in ministry to the
world. Priority in humility, in obedience, and in service are the
forms of status recognized in the Kingdom of God: in a profound sense the Minister represents Christ before the people of
his parish.

Yet to say this is to reveal at once the temptation and the dilemma within which a clergyman is set. He is to represent Christ, and
yet he knows he cannot represent Christ. As soon as he magni-
fies his own call above that of the Church which he is called to
serve, he is launched into the sacrilege of professional sacerdotalism with its hell-bent claim to recognition, its worldly
prerogatives and pious dignities. "You know," said Jesus, "that
in the world the recognized rulers lord it over their subjects, and
their great men make them feel the weight of authority. That is
not the way with you." In contrast to the secular ideas of lord-

ship Jesus Christ's definition of leadership in his Church was extremely clear and specific — "whoever wants to be great must be your servant, and whoever wants to be first must be the willing slave of all. For even the Son of Man did not come to be served but to serve, and to surrender his life as a ransom for many" (Mark 10:42ff., NEB).

These words were spoken to disciples who represented the Church in embryo, and who were to be the first apostles; and yet if the later history of the Church has been a denial of its Lord, it has been in large measure due to the fact that concepts of the Ministry were taken from the very examples of secular lordship against which Jesus witnessed. Our Lord explicitly pointed to the contrast and showed us where we were to look for our example of the Church's Ministry — "here I am among you like a servant."[6] Most of our present uncertainties about the Ministry stem from the fact that we have mixed the idea of ministerial leadership in the gospel with dreams of status and authority from other sources. So we base the authority of the clergy on the manner of its consecration or recognition, upon the offices it performs, or even upon the way in which the churches select their Ministers, rather than upon the essential character of service.

We might well ask, "Who can fulfill such a Ministry?" To describe its nature makes us realize that we all fail and have sinned. Yet I believe a Minister should derive some encouragement from the fact that the very failure which, from the human point of view, is inherent in his vocation can be used by God to remind the Church of its own ministry. The Minister's mission within the Church is no more impossible than is the Church's mission to the world. He should stand first in his sense of penitence, first in his need of forgiveness and of God's sustaining grace.

He does not stand alone in his ministry. If his task is to build up the Church, the whole community of Christ's people exercises its own pastoral concern for him as a member who stands in its midst, no less in need of Word and Sacraments and pastoral care than any other member of the fellowship. Church and Minister perform a mutual ministry to each other, and only those who have tried to *minister* to a congregation, rather than to gov-

[6] Cf. the Lucan version of the incident, Luke 22:25-27.

ern or *administer* it, know how deep this ministry of the fellowship towards its Minister can go. No true pastor will feel adequate to fulfill his ministry to a congregation of God's people. He is conscious that he receives far more than he can ever give to them, and, as he reflects upon the faith and the courage and the sacrifice of those to whom he is called, he will be humbled. This humility *is* his ministry, and for a Minister to reach this point is to make him what he should be, for it is humility before the face of Christ's redeeming work.

III

MINISTRY AS FUNCTION

The President of a corporation, the Dean of a faculty, the Governor of a state, and the Commander of an army corps all hold offices in which they perform certain functions of administration. In fact, the functions define the nature of their office, and if they did not carry out these functional responsibilities there would be little justification for the office.

The Minister of a local congregation also performs functions which are descriptive of the office that he holds, and from the point of view of a sociologist a Minister will be seen in terms of the functions he performs just as a bank president or an attorney has to be seen in terms of his. On the other hand, to a theologian who sees the Ministry as an outcome of the Church's divinely-given nature, the functions of Ministry become very secondary. There is always a sharp cleavage between the "theological" view of the Ministry put forward by a "high church" theologically-minded Anglican, for example, and many liberal American Freechurchmen whose view of the Ministry is essentially functional and pragmatic.

This is a false opposition. The New Testament itself is pragmatic in that it *is* concerned with results — the ethical and spiritual results of the gospel, but nonetheless results: the gospel is intended to "make a difference," and that difference is seen in the kind of people, the kind of community it produces. According to the New Testament, Christians are expected to act in certain ways, and what a Christian believes about God and Christ should have an effect upon the way Christian masters treat their servants, Christian husbands treat their wives, Christian parents treat their children, and upon how members of the Church treat each other and those outside its fellowship. The Pauline epistles are full of exhortation about the practical implications of the Christian Faith. There is a very clear pragmatism that runs throughout the New Testament, and the highest test of a person, or a doctrine, or an attitude is the pragmatic test given by our Lord himself, "By their fruits ye shall know them."

Presumably if Ministers are given to the Church to help it achieve certain results, the functional aspects of their calling are not irrelevant. A Minister is appointed to serve the Church by the exercise of gifts that have certain realistic goals within the fellowship, and related to the Church's mission in the world. It is in that sense functional, and properly so, for it is the Protestant contention that the existence of the Church has little significance if it does not forward the mission for which it came into being. In a time of social injustice the pragmatic American churchman is rightly suspicious of supernatural claims about any Ministry that preaches loudly but refuses to risk getting its hands dirty in the struggle of the downtrodden: the social gospel may not be all there is in the gospel of Jesus Christ, but the objectives for which it strove are certainly there. The Minister has a job to do, and doing it is a very important part of his ministry.

This functional aspect of the Ministry — the fact that a Minister has a task to perform for the Church — is illustrated by those times in church history when God took special measures to raise up "Ministers" to do the things which needed to be done. When Cardinal Sadolet admonished John Calvin for daring, as an unordained layman, to exercise his ministry among the churches, Calvin likened himself to a private soldier who sees his company routed and who snatches up the colors and rallies the troops to withstand the enemy's attack. He claimed that he was no traitor to the Church, "unless indeed he is to be considered a deserter who, seeing the soldiers routed and scattered and abandoning the ranks, raises the leader's standard, and recalls them to their posts."[7] That is the action of a true Minister, whether recognized by the Church or not.

I am reminded of a further example from church history. Some few years ago Dean Ronald Osborn was lecturing at

[7] Calvin, *Reply to Sadolet;* cf. *Calvin: Theological Treatises,* ed. and trans. by J. K. S. Reid, [*Library of Christian Classics,* Vol. XXII], p. 248.

Bossey on the development of Christianity in America. He was
lecturing to a group of students in the Graduate School of Ecumenical Studies, and to many from Europe and Britain the story
of Christianity on the American Western frontier was fascinat-
ingly new. Dr. Osborn described the remarkable evangelism
carried out by the frontier riders of Methodism, the deacons
and lay elders of the Disciples and the Baptists, and of the simple forms of communion service that were held in farm houses.
At last one English Anglican student could not restrain himself.
"Do you mean to say," he asked incredulously, "that the service
of Holy Communion was conducted by men who had not been
properly ordained?" I remember that Dr. Osborn paused for what
seemed to be a long minute, and then he smiled and said slowly,
"Do you know, it has just occurred to me, that if some parts of
America had waited for the Lord's Supper to be celebrated by an
episcopally ordained clergyman, they would be waiting still."

I am not concerned at this point with the fact that these illustrations concern those who were technically "laymen." They
were raised up to exercise a true Ministry, and they show us that
in Protestant understanding Ministry *is* concerned with function.
We must resist the kind of theological snobbery that refuses to
see any relationship between Ministerial orders and the practical
tasks of building up the Church for worship and witness. There
is nothing wrong with American pragmatism being applied to
the Church and its Ministry as long as it maintains clearly the
objectives of the New Testament. On the contrary, it can be a
most useful test for judging the Church's organizational effectiveness, and for stripping from her work the unnecessary gargoyles
and dim religious windows that obscure true beauty.

But the objectives of the Church's life and work *must* be those
of the gospel. That is where pragmatism so often breaks down in
relation to the Church. The New Testament talks about practical
goals, a firmer faith, a stronger hope, a deeper love, but they
are not goals that the "practical man" recognizes as practical.
The pragmatism of the gospel is not directed towards the production of bigger and more elaborate church structures, longer
church rolls from a higher income bracket, or more efficiently
organized religious communities; rather, it is directed to building
up the household of faith so that the Church can witness to
the power of the living Christ. There is a great deal of difference
between a functional view of the Church that has practical effi-

ciency as its ultimate goal, and one which tries to fulfill the pragmatism of the gospel. Fundamentally, if we insist on the relation between Ministers and the functions they perform, it is not because this kind of Ministry gets things done and makes a better showing in the reports to Annual General Meeting, but because our God is a God who *acts* in history and uses the actions of men to forward his redemptive purpose.

Perhaps we can make the point best by referring to Philippians 2:5-11, a passage that admittedly bristles with difficulties, as a comparison of the English versions shows clearly. It was evidently introduced by the apostle "for a practical purpose,"[8] an ethical purpose related directly to the readers whom he is addressing. They are exhorted to treat one another in the same spirit that they have seen in Jesus Christ, who, the apostle reminds them, did not regard equality with God as something to be snatched, "but made himself nothing, assuming the nature of a slave. Bearing the human likeness, revealed in human shape, he humbled himself, and in obedience accepted even death — death on a cross. *"Therefore,"* he goes on to declare, "God raised him to the heights and bestowed on him the name above all names, that at the name of Jesus every knee should bow — in heaven, on earth, and in the depths — and every tongue confess, 'Jesus Christ is Lord,' to the glory of God the Father" (NEB). It seems from the passage that this outpouring of himself by our Lord is the reason for his exaltation, the reason why the confession "Jesus is Lord" redounds to the glory of God the Father. If we recognize what it meant in the life of our Lord to glorify the Father (cf. John 12:27f.), we gain some insight into Forsyth's comment on the opening words of the Westminster Shorter Catechism: "First we glorify God, then we enjoy him forever."[9] The order is important, and the meaning we give to 'glorify' in this setting is even more important. In the mind of the apostle in Philippians our Lord's voluntary humility and willingness to serve partakes of the very character of God himself. If this is so, then the New Testament concept of Ministry begins in the nature of God himself. The New Testament schol-

[8] J. Hugh Michael, *The Epistle of Paul to the Philippians* (London: Hodder & Stoughton, 1928), p. 83.

[9] P. T. Forsyth, *The Principle of Authority* (2nd ed.; London: Independent Press, 1952), p. 13.

ars must tell us how far this inference is justified, but I cite the passage because it appears to show that we shall get our goals in the Ministry straight only as we keep New Testament *theology* in the foreground.

IV

The Ministry as Christ's Gift

The Ministry is functional, but it is not merely functional. The Letter to the Ephesians speaks of it as a gift of the ascended Christ to his Church. Or rather, the writer speaks of several different forms of Ministry which are given to the Church: "And these were his gifts: some to be apostles, some prophets, some evangelists, some pastors and teachers, to equip God's people for work in his service, to the building up of the body of Christ" (Eph. 4:11f., NEB). We have already commented to some extent on this passage, [10] but it is clear that the apostle relates the Ministry to various functions in the Church, and that these functions have a direct bearing upon the Church's own service and witness. The functions of Ministry are given to prepare the Church to serve the risen Christ, and in that sense it has a practical meaning. As Forsyth said almost fifty years ago, "The first test of an effective ministry is its effectiveness on the Church."[11] There is a down-to-earth practicality in the New Testament which recognizes that there is a job to be done. Results are not irrelevant.

But the Ministry is more than a practical expedient, for it is Christ's gift to his Church. To continue with Forsyth for the moment, "The Minister," he declared, "is much more than a leading brother as the Church itself is more than a fraternity. He is neither the mouthpiece of the Church, nor its chairman, nor its secretary. He is not the servant, nor the employee, of the Church. He is an apostle to it, the mouthpiece of Christ's gospel to it, the servant of the Word and not of the Church; he serves the Church only for that sake. The Ministry is a prophetic and sacramental office; it is not secretarial, it is not merely presidential. It is sacramental and not merely functional. It is the outward and visible agent of the inward Gospel Grace."[12]

---

[10] *Supra*, p. 29ff.
[11] *The Church and the Sacraments*, p. 131.
[12] *Ibid.*, p. 132f.

Is Forsyth claiming too much for Ministers? For there *is* a sense in which the very essence of Ministry is in the *service* which it renders to the Church. On the other hand, perhaps what we see in this passage is Forsyth wrestling with this "giveness" of the Ministry. He is asserting that the Minister is not a servant of the Church in the sense that one might employ someone to perform tasks that we are too busy or too uninterested to perform ourselves; but he is a servant in the sense that he has been sent by the One whom we all recognize as Master. A parallel may be seen in the case of a doctor or a farmer who has been sent to a primitive country as part of an international aid program. He may give years of devoted service at considerable self-sacrifice to the people who need his help, but in the final issue he does so because his primary allegiance is to the United Nations or to the agency that has sent him. So it is with the Minister: he serves the Church because he is first and foremost the servant of the risen Christ and is given to the Church by Christ.

The theological root of our concern about the place of Ministers in the Church is in this "giveness," for what Christ has given to his Church let no man call irrelevant. As it makes manifest the essential ministry of our Lord himself, it is a pledge of his presence in our midst. Human nature being what it is, a Minister may have entered the Ministry with mixed motives; he may have rather fancied himself in pastoral office, or liked the idea of declaiming to a captive audience from a position four feet above contradiction. No one denies that in making our decisions unworthy motives enter into Christians as they enter into others; but no Minister is truly a Minister unless there is a sense in which he has heard Christ say to him, "You did not choose me: I chose you. I appointed you to go on and bear fruit, fruit that shall last" (John 15:16, NEB). The Church has the responsibility beyond all the conflicting and distracting motivations that may be present to discern and recognize this authentic note in a Minister's call, and to say that this man is Christ's gift to his Church is to say no more (and no less) than that he has come to this congregation through the call of Christ. His service to the Church is given because of that, and it is offered in the spirit of the essential ministry which is our Lord's own.

But how difficult it is for modern twentieth-century Americans (or British or French or Germans) to think of a Minister as a gift. Here we see him day by day moving about our society, neatly dressed like any other moderately well-heeled executive, and doing with varying degrees of competence what we expect any professional man to do. He joins the same service clubs, and although he may avoid the nineteenth hole of the golf course,* we understand that this is an occupational liability, such as being called out in the middle of the night if you are a doctor or marking papers if you are a teacher. The idea of thinking about anyone as a gift from God is foreign to Anglo-Saxon pragmatism.

Is it? If you are happily married, let me ask you a personal question. How do you think of your wife? Do you regard her primarily as a paid housekeeper, or as a professional playmate and companion, or as nursemaid for the children and a cook for the family? If any man thinks of his wife principally in those terms, he will be lucky if his marriage lasts, and he will not deserve much happiness from it. Yet in the cold eye of the physiologist marriage is primarily a matter of organs and glands; to a sociologist it may be mainly a question of economics; and to a psychologist it resolves itself into a number of emotional urges. But how do *you* think of her?

Surely we come nearest to the truth we know when we think of the woman we love as a gift from God to us. We do so because any description of marriage in terms that might satisfy the physiologist, the sociologist, or the psychologist, that does not also speak about love, would fail utterly to describe *our* marriage, for love comes as near to divinity as anything we know in human experience. This is not something that we could command or create. There is no fallacy as ephemeral as the petulant insistence of Western eroticism that it can *make* love. It can't be done. True love is a gift, a gift that we know we do not deserve, which comes from we know not where — as if someone had bestowed an act of pure grace upon us.

It is like that with all true Ministry. In various ways the Minister proclaims the love of God in Christ, but in the deepest sense the relationship of a Minister to the congregation he serves, and of the people's relationship to him, must exemplify the love which they proclaim. Without it there can be no true Ministry, but where it exists there will be effective Christian witness even though the people have many shortcomings and the parson is a man of very moderate talents. Let us emphasize that this pas-

---

* A British — and American — euphemism for the bar!

toral relationship which binds Minister and people together is not a sloppy, sentimental emotion. It is unlike civil marriage, for it finds its center not in the two parties of the covenant, but in Jesus Christ through whom they have been brought together, and in whose Spirit they are held together. It is a mutual ministry that the Minister and people exercise towards each other, "each preferring one another," in which the goal is not present happiness or even a contented fellowship, but God's will for each member. So the Minister is given by Christ to the Church until that time when the unity inherent in our faith is achieved, to the time when we all have achieved the kind of maturity which can be "measured by nothing less than the stature of Christ."

Is this too "high" a doctrine of the Ministry? It is difficult to say this if it is the view of the Minister's calling put forward in the New Testament; and perhaps we have less to fear from it as we realize that no man can undertake this call who feels himself worthy of it. The only justification for a Minister's acceptance of the call is that he stands as first among penitents. J. A. T. Robinson bids us have as high a doctrine of the Ministry as we like, as long as our doctrines of the Church and of the Kingdom of God are higher.[13] Perhaps we could push it further by saying that we can have a high doctrine of the Ministry only as our doctrine of Christ is highest of all.

Let me end this section with a parenthesis, which I include not because it has immediate bearing on the *meaning* of 'ministry', but because it is an issue that arises directly *from* the view of Ministry that we are setting forth. It is the vexed question of women in the Ministry — a question that seems so often to have been debated on the basis of scriptural literalism rather than from the standpoint of what biblical theology says about the doctrine of man and the nature of God's call to men. We must remember that the cultures of biblical times were predominantly, almost exclusively, masculine. We can do no more here than touch upon this subject, which rightly exercises the Church at a time when it is seeking to realize the fulness of its own call. But I would ask the reader to reflect upon the issue in these terms: if an adequate doctrine of the Church demands that we should recognize the calling and talents of all the Church's members, can we so circumscribe the work of the Holy Spirit that

---

[13] *The Historic Episcopate,* p. 15.

women are excluded from the call to the Ministry? Is there anything intrinsic to the fact of being a woman that prevents a Christian from being called to the kind of spiritual leadership that Ministry implies? If the Christian doctrine of man maintains the real equality of all "men" in the sight of God, then God may be asking the Church in these days to recognize those whom he calls into his service without respect of race, color, social position, *or sex*. I suggest that this is not fundamentally a question of feminist aspirations, equality of status, or even of strict justice, but of our willingness to recognize and receive all God's gifts in Ministry to his Church.

V

The Church, the Ministry, and the Atonement

Does Christmas or Easter have priority in our understanding of Jesus Christ? Obviously both events are indispensable to that which the Church believes about our Lord, for without Christmas the events of Easter are meaningless and without the death and resurrection the nativity and incarnation are equally irrelevant. There is a sense, however, in which the incarnation has to be seen in terms of the atonement. Protestants approach the Christmas story through the events of the Easter weekend: it is because of what we see on the cross and in the empty tomb that the truth behind the Christmas stories becomes credible, indeed, necessary. This I have argued at length elsewhere, because essentially it is the way in which the New Testament writers themselves seem to have approached the mystery of the person they confronted in Jesus of Nazareth.[14] The point of that confrontation, certainly for man, was in the cross and the resurrection. Golgotha and the Garden put all the previous events of that life into a new focus, and revealed a purpose behind the nativity of this Man by which alone Easter itself could be explained. Given the experienced facts of the crucifixion and resurrection, then the annunciation to Mary, the choirs of angels, the star, the prophecies of Simeon and Anna, the shepherds and the wise men are no longer pious legend, but they are the poetry behind a miracle too vast to be continued within the prose record of Caesar's census. As St. Paul hints on more than one occasion when he bursts

---

[14] *The Atonement and the Sacraments*, pp. 282-8, 297-301, 371-4.

into something akin to poetry, only a doctrine like that of the incarnation could possibly do justice to the facts about Jesus Christ which the early Church had experienced and in which it rejoiced. They saw the man, the way he lived, the manner of his death, the things that happened after his death, and they were forced to ask themselves, "Who is this?" Christ was judged by his "fruits." This should be the background against which we should set all our claims about the Church and its Ministry. It is in this sense and at this point that Christology becomes the only proper beginning for ecclesiology.

The Church exists to witness to the reconciliation that was first revealed in the work and person of Jesus Christ. The act of witness begins in our being reconciled with God, with the forgiveness that is offered to us in Christ, with the willingness to forgive and to be forgiven. The Church's primary duty is to proclaim this reconciliation, and it does so first of all as we accept the redemption that is offered. It must be accepted as a free gift of God's grace: we cannot make ourselves worthy of it, we cannot buy it, we cannot qualify for it by reaching a decent standard of morality or by secret illusions of being "holier than thou." We accept it as a free gift from God, or we fail to accept it at all. This is the heart of the message that the Church proclaims in the name of Christ.

There is, however, a second part to the proclamation, which is more difficult to speak about because it is to be doubted whether it should ever be or can be the result of conscious effort. As God's people appropriate the assurance of atonement for themselves, they *ought* to begin to demonstrate what this reconciliation means by the kind of people they become. Put bluntly, to confess the name of Christ should have an effect upon the kind of people we are. The evidence of the Spirit's presence *should* have its own living witness in the "fruits of the Spirit," both in the individual Christian and in the Christian community: it should make a difference. The Puritans were right to insist that the Church should consist of "visible saints."

The Puritans also illustrate the danger we are in when we make that claim. There is not only the danger of identifying the "fruits of the Spirit" with our own preferred standards of ethical achievement, but there is also the worse danger of thinking that if we can generate a sufficiently high standard of morality, we thereby guarantee the Holy Spirit's presence in our midst. Beyond this is the danger of spiritual pride. And yet to be a Christian *should* make a difference both to the individual and to the community of faith of which he is a part.

Perhaps we keep the issue in a more healthy perspective when we recognize that the Christian is not given salvation so that he can wallow in the cozy feeling of being "at one" with God, but so that the world may be saved. Jesus certainly had the sense of being at one with his Father, but he revealed that unity with the Father by giving himself completely to the salvation of the world. If Jesus had settled back in the knowledge of his own ethical uprightness and rested in the assurance that he was God's Son, he would have denied his Sonship. His unity with the Father was revealed as he accepted his part in God's purpose for the world. So the Church's acceptance of reconciliation with God can never remain enclosed within the assurance that it is "saved," for salvation demands witness. The reconciliation of which the Bible speaks begins with the renewal of the broken relationship between man and God, but it will flow out to baptize all our relationships. It will inevitably proclaim also the reconciliation between man and man, between man and woman, between man and the whole created order, between man and his alienated self. If the Church rests in a comfortable doctrine of its own salvation, it denies the very salvation that it claims.

This puts the claims of the Church about its divine origin into a different light, for if the Church herself came to an understanding of Jesus as the Christ through what he accomplished for our salvation, she must expect the world to judge her by the same standard. If Christ himself was judged by the quality of his deeds, if he humbly refused to allow others to call him "good" in comparison with the Father, then there is no place for the Church to make large claims of divine origin or infallible authority. The Church cannot make any claims about her own sanctity or supernatural authority over the world, for as soon as she does so, she parts company with her Lord. Only the works of the Spirit can reveal the presence of the Spirit, and the New Testament seems to tell us that where the Spirit is most present he points men away from himself to Jesus Christ (John 16:13-14). The origin of the Church and the character of her great Original are to be made manifest not in the largeness of her theological claims or in the imperiousness of her demands, but in the quality of her service.

How much more, then, is this true of the Church's Ministers! If a man's ministry is given to the Church so that the members may be helped to realize their own corporate mission, then all that we have said about the Church in relation to the world is true in a Minister's relationship to his congregation. A minister proclaims the redemptive, reconciling work of Christ. He may share many of the same doubts and problems with the members of his congregation, for he is certainly no less subject to human frailty than they are, but the Church has the right to expect of its Ministers that they have themselves stood humbly beneath the cross and have received the assurance of that forgiveness which Christ made manifest. A Minister may be just as imperfect as his congregation, with similar faults and prejudices, and yet he will reveal his ministry as he moves among his people by showing something of the breadth of the reconciliation that was revealed in Jesus Christ. He will be one who knows he can make no claims about his own sanctity, but who makes infinite claims for his Lord. And in the final analysis no claim of valid orders or historical succession, or even the claim to faithful preaching can justify his ministry as a true ministry, but only the spirit that is content to be a servant of Jesus Christ.

The Minister lives within the paradox of representing to the Church more than he can ever be, just as the Church witnesses to the world in the same capacity. The vocation to which both Church and Ministry are called is essentially that of witnessing to God's saving grace in Jesus Christ, and it is a ministry that can make no claims to special ability or extraordinary holiness. We fulfill this ministry only as we proclaim in word and deed that we stand first in need of the same grace. Only as we recognize our constant need for penitence shall we avoid the danger of denying by our deeds what we proclaim with our lips; and only thus shall we point away from ourselves to that essential ministry of Christ in which all Christian vocation is centered.

chapter five

Ordination

I

GENERAL ORDINATION AND THE ORDINATION OF MINISTERS

Whenever a group of concerned Christians begins to discuss the nature of the Ministry seriously, sooner or later someone will ask a question that goes something like this, "Well, what *difference* does ordination make? The Church speaks about the responsibility of every Christian to witness in his profession or job. How can we say that a Minister is any different from any other member of the Church? — except, perhaps, in the fact that he does not have to put his faith or his Sunday ethics to the test quite as constantly. If we 'ordain' one man to do a job in the Church, then we should ordain every man to do a job in the world."

Although I have sat in many audiences in which this issue has been raised in one form or another, I have not yet heard a reply from the platform which did not either evade giving a straight answer or sound pompous; frequently both.

The short answer is that the Church does ordain every man to his work in the world in the sacrament of baptism. The ecumenical demand for a "theology of the laity" has led to this insight. The point at which Jesus understood his own special commission, the place where the special blessing of God's Holy

127

Spirit was made manifest, was at his baptism by John, and if there is any analogy between the life of Jesus and the life of the Church, we can agree that "similarly through our baptism Christ incorporates us for participation in his ministry."[1] The sacrament certainly means that the assurance of salvation is given to *this* individual, but biblical theology is forcing us to recognize that the assurance carries with it direct responsibility to the world which our Lord came to save. Baptism can never mean, as some Christians have interpreted it, that the baptized person can contentedly rest in the security of his own salvation and let other poor sinners "go hang." Our Lord's commission to the apostles, that they should go into the world to preach and baptize in his name, is given to a Church which is baptized for the purpose of proclaiming Christ's gospel. "This is his charge to the Church and his charge to every baptized person. The place of the baptized is wherever in the world there is room for service, for the baptized, like his Lord, is a servant. Baptism proclaims that, as the Christian has been called out of the world, so he returns to the world as its servant; for only in his union with the world's Redeemer is he free to participate creatively and fully in its common life. . . . Baptism is the ordination into the apostolic, charismatic and sacrificial ministry of the Church."[2]

So speaks a document prepared by the World Council of Churches' Department of the Laity for the Fourth World Conference of Faith and Order at Montreal in 1963. There is plenty of basis for this view of baptism in Reformation theology. The groundwork was adequately laid by Martin Luther in his treatise *On the Babylonish Captivity of the Church,* when he declared

[1]"Christ's Ministry and the Ministry of the Church," *Laity,* No. 15, May, 1963, p. 16.

[2] *Ibid.,* pp. 17, 18. The particular document was written as a contribution of the Department on the Laity to the Faith and Order Conference at Montreal, and submitted to the third section of that conference on "The Redemptive Work of Christ and the Ministry of His Church." The concept of baptism as the general "ordination" of Christians is clearly basic to the thinking of this department, and it may be traced to other writings from the same or similar sources. Cf. *Laity,* No. 9, July, 1960, "Ministers of the Priestly People" [especially the article by Hans-Ruedi Weber, and p. 11], George Hunston Williams, "The Role of the Layman in the Ancient Church," *The Ecumenical Review,* X (April, 1958), 231; it is also implicit in Hans-Reudi Weber's articles "The Laity in the Apostolic Church," *ibid.,* XIII (Jan., 1961), 203ff.

that "baptism is the first of the sacraments and the foundation of them all,"[3] but the Reformer made the issue even more pointed by his insistence that monastic vows should be discouraged and his denial that Orders could be regarded as a sacrament.[4] The foundation of his argument in both cases is the entire adequacy of God's promise in baptism. "We make an ample vow at baptism, a greater one than we can fulfil," he declared, "and we shall have enough to do if we give all our efforts to this alone."[5] The doctrine of the priesthood of all believers has its origin in this insight.[6] Therefore, the accent upon baptism as the general "ordination" of every Christian represents a natural focus for an ecumenical theology that is trying to give the layman his proper place in the total doctrine of the Church. Its significance for the subject of this chapter is seen in the fact that it brings into even sharper focus the question with which we began, for "if baptism is the basic ordination of each Christian," the modern writers ask, "what does special ordination add? What does it do that baptism does not? Thus: what is a minister that a layman is not?"[7]

We must try to respond in part to that question.

In the first place, it is absurd to represent baptism as the general "ordination" of Christians when what we mean is infant baptism. In the act of ordination there is at the centre both God's call and man's response, and neither has much relevance for us without the other. In the sacrament of baptism, as it is most generally practiced, there is the declaration of what God in Christ has done for this individual, but if we go on to spell out too specifically what this is to mean in terms of this infant's personal engagement in life, the rite becomes forced and meaningless: it demands the voluntary response of the individual. This sense of voluntary obedience is quite clearly central to the accounts of our Lord's baptism by John, and it shows the need for an act of con-

---

[3] *Luther's Primary Works,* ed. Henry Wace and C. A. Buchheim (London: Hodder and Stoughton, 1896), p. 342.

[4] *Ibid.,* pp. 358-65, 390-401. The first of these passages on religious vows is of particular interest because it is inserted in the section dealing with baptism, and emphasizes the fact that Luther regarded baptism as the charter of a Christian's liberty.

[5] *Ibid.,* p. 359.

[6] *Ibid.,* pp. 353-7, 365, 399.

[7] *Laity,* No. 15, p. 22.

firmation in which the responsibilities of baptism are taken up with the glad acceptance of its promises. As Karl Barth exclaimed, "Infant-baptism calls aloud for such a completion and supplementing."[8]

There is no need to reopen at this point the whole debate about the rightness or wrongness of infant baptism as an adequate mode, about which I have probably said enough elsewhere.[9] My concern at this point is to introduce some realism into the discussion, so that we do not assume too readily that because baptism as it is in the New Testament may represent adequately the "ordination" of the people of God under the New Covenant, the same can be said for baptism as it is presently practiced by most churches.

The real equivalent to ordination in the experience of the serious church member is not "baptism," but the whole process of baptism-confirmation. It is in confirmation that the vows which have been made vicariously on behalf of the infant are taken up by that individual with some understanding of what they involve in terms of service. It is at confirmation that this same individual Christian is conscious that he or she stands on the brink of a new world of experience, when the responsibilities of working for a living in the secular world are beginning to be realized. This is the time when the meaning of baptism becomes clearer, and one begins to realize that salvation also involves our willingness to "stand up and be counted" for and with Jesus Christ. To say that baptism represents the ordination of every Christian is therefore valid only if we include the whole sacramental act — not only the actual rite of baptism but also its response in confirmation.

Secondly, baptism-confirmation and ordination say similar things about the Christian's vocation, but they do not have identical emphases.

The sacrament of baptism certainly sets the individual within the context of the Church, but the emphasis is centered in God's promise and God's promises to *this* individual. True, in the words of one service of baptism we ask God to "Sanctify to us all the ministration of this Sacrament, that, acknowledging both our need of cleansing and thy purifying grace in Christ, and being

---

8 *The Teaching of the Church regarding Baptism,* trans. Ernest A. Payne, (London: S.C.M., 1948), p. 47.

9 *The Atonement and the Sacraments,* ch. x, pp. 319ff.

recalled to the promises and vows of our own baptism, we may abide in him unto our life's end."[10] But even in this we are recalled to the obligations of our own baptism. The emphasis is necessarily upon the individual, and in confirmation this is brought home to us as we take up the responsibilities of being a Christian within our own circumstances. Certainly, the members of a local congregation share in a mutual ministry to each other, and because we are all called to similar service and witness, we should all be involved in the problems and choices of each individual member. But finally it is *this* individual who must take responsibility for working out the implications of his own call before God. A banker or a farmer shares with his Christian brother who is a factory machinist the responsibility for service and witness in the world, and can to that extent help him in his understanding of his own vocation; but only to that extent. In the end only this particular machinist can discover what is involved in being a Christian and a machinist at this particular time and in this particular factory. We share the same call and the same promises, but it is the hope and the glory of the Church that the circumstances shall be as wide and as diverse as human experience. The sacrament of baptism-confirmation therefore applies to every member and is in that sense a general ordination, but its point of reference under God is to the particular Christian.

It is the thesis of this chapter that ordination to the Ministry approaches Christian vocation from a precisely opposite angle, and that this is its value to the Church. It is a churchly act, not because this man and his vocation are chosen for special ecclesiastical dignity, or because his work is mainly within the Church, whereas other vocations are engaged within the world, but because this *vocation* brings before the whole company of Christ's people what its own corporate vocation is within the world. The act of ordination applies to only one member, but its point of reference is to the whole Church.

Thirdly, in the sacrament of baptism-confirmation the gospel emphasizes the equality of all the faithful in their work before God. But the gospel does not resolve the question of "status"

[10] "Order for the Administration of the Sacrament of Baptism," in *A Book of Public Worship Compiled for the Use of Congregationalists,* by Huxtable, Marsh, Micklem and Todd (London: Oxford Univ. Press, 1949), p. 162.

by imposing a flat uniformity that recognizes no differences; it rather adopts a revolutionary concept of status which turns the world's standards upside down and in which "the last shall be first." If the act of ordination simply invests the Minister with a title and the accoutrements of a worldly status, then it has become a denial of the very ministry to which he is called. It is a very different matter if it commits him to the "status" of the gospel, in which the idea of servanthood is paramount, in which the brethren are enjoined to give pride of place to each other in showing their esteem (Rom. 12:10).

It is only within a context in which the Church seeks to honor its own servant and in which the servant recognizes the character of his service that ordination is to be regarded as a Christian rite. Furthermore, it is set within a community which not only recognizes differences of ability and function but rejoices in them, and which now accepts as a gift from its Lord this particular talent through which the Church will be helped to be loyal to its faith and fervent in its mission. If ordination today means something very different from that, the Church itself is to blame; it means that in the government of their own affairs denominations have looked for a different kind of Minister than that which is shown to us in the ministry of Jesus Christ.

We grant that there is always the temptation for the Minister to think of himself more highly than he ought to think, and congregations often do a good deal to inflate that ego. At my own ordination I remember John Marsh of Oxford reminding me that although a young Minister was called to be a shepherd to Christ's flock, he could very easily degenerate into becoming its pet lamb. Where the Minister is lauded for the wrong gifts and graces, where the Ministry is never free from the striving for professional recognition, where too much adulation is given to a man for his personal brilliance or persuasiveness, who is primarily at fault for receiving that kind of Ministry and for honoring that kind of Minister? Ordination has little significance except as *an act of the Church which brings to a focus the nature of the Church's own ministry;* but if it is an act of the Church, then it must be the Church that takes the principal responsibility for the gifts it calls forth into its Ministry and for the kind of status it accords to those in its service.

II

THE MEANING OF ORDINATION

Those who wrote the paper submitted by the Department on the Laity posed the extremely pertinent question, "If baptism is the basic ordination of each Christian, what does special ordination add?" But I question whether this is the way in which the issue should be put, because the use of that word 'add' suggests a quantitative difference in the Minister from that of the whole Church. It suggests the very attitudes which they criticize when they accuse ordination of meaning "too often not setting apart *within* and for the ordained people of the baptized, but setting *over above* and apart *from* the laity."[11] It implies, perhaps unwittingly, that we can think of ordination only in terms of something added — presumably added to the ordained Minister.

Insofar as ordination has been allowed to represent, explicitly or implicitly, a view of the Ministry that regards the Ministry almost as a separate caste within the Christian community, they are right to question it; but if we concede that baptism represents the basic ordination of each Christian, the basic question then is whether "special ordination" adds anything to our understanding of *all* ordination. Or, as I would prefer to put it, what different facet of meaning to "ordination" does the special ordination of Ministers convey that cannot be gained from baptism?

(a) I hope it will be seen from the previous section that there is one significant difference of emphasis. Ordination of a pastor to ministry within the Church objectifies to the Church its own ministry within the world.

To a casual observer the act of ordination may very well appear to be the most personal and individualistic rite in the Church's book. It selects one member and seems to concentrate upon his confession of faith, his religious experience, his capacities and his vocation. I suggest that this is a superficial understanding of what is being performed in the service of ordination. The misunderstanding is only possible when the rite has been divorced from the *Church's* ministry within which a pastor's vocation is set, and when it is performed without specific reference to the essential ministry of our Lord himself. Our Lord

---

[11] *Laity,* No. 15, p. 20.

personifies all ministry. He incorporates within himself the ministry of God's people, the true Israel; but he does so as the great Pioneer, the great Minister who leads God's people into a truer understanding of what it means to be the servants of God. In his person God's people and its Ministry are not two separate entities: that to which he points in his leadership is that which he is.

The Epistle to the Ephesians shows us the relationship between the ministry of our Lord and the different forms of Ministry in the Church when it speaks of these existing for the upbuilding of the body of Christ (i.e., the Church), and goes on to declare, "So shall we all at last attain to the unity inherent in our faith and our knowledge of the Son of God — to mature manhood, measured by nothing less than the full stature of Christ" (Eph. 4:12f., NEB). The words are so familiar that they may lose their impact, but the plain meaning seems to be that apostles, prophets, evangelists, pastors and teachers are given to the Church so that the whole Church may become what Christ is, so that its ministry may become what Christ is, so that his ministry may become the Church's ministry. If we interpret these words in this way, we cannot drive a wedge between the task of these "special" ministries and that which the Church is called to be, and presumably when the writer speaks about such ministerial functions, he is not suggesting a special caste that is separate from the body of Christ. No group of Christians, ministerial or lay, can claim to "add" anything to the "full stature of Christ," which it is the Church's vocation to become, and which may be summarized in the one word, *ministry*. Individuals are given to the Church to lead it into a fuller understanding of what this means and how it is to be implemented, but they stand within the same need themselves, as those whose proudest claim will be that they are members and servants of the same body.

This Ministry is necessary. It is leadership into servanthood, and it continues for as long as it takes the Church to reach its goal. It is not irrelevant, something that can be pushed aside, for insofar as it bears this character, it is Christ's gift to the Church, given that the Church may attain its own essential ministry in Christ.

Of course this kind of leadership may go unrecognized and even spurned by the Church: the 'Ministers' whom our Lord gives may not always be given formal recognition by the churches as institutional bodies. Ordination, however, is the rite by which the Church seeks to recognize those who have been sent by Christ for this leadership, and to the degree that it does this, it expresses the fundamental truth that the Church exists for ministry.

Ordination is undoubtedly a high point in the life of one individual Christian, but far more fundamentally it is a high point in the life of the Church. The ordained is presented to the Church not so much as an individual called to exercise particular ecclesiastical functions, but as one who within his person represents to the Church the nature of its own corporate vocation. He stands within the congregation as a servant, as the Church stands before men. In the service of ordination each member of the Church certainly should have brought home to him (as in the sacrament of baptism) the meaning of his own individual vocation, but he should also be brought face to face with the corporate vocation of the community in which he shares. In the service of ordination the Church is seen primarily not as an aggregate of individuals engaged in their own callings, but as *the* Minister within God's world. Therefore, far from being one of the most individualistic actions in church life, it ought to be one in which the sense of unity and corporateness is most pronounced. As we see within the record of one selected Christian's life how the Holy Spirit has led him to this point, as we see the implications of total commitment *for this man*, of fidelity to the historic faith, of life centered in worship and prayer, of what it must mean to be an intercessor for and a servant of the people, so this one man's life becomes an object lesson of the role which the Church bears. We are identified with our pastor in this, for this is a role in which we all share. The ordination of a pastor, far from making him something different from the rest of the church's members, should emphasize his essential unity with the ministry of the whole Church; for in his single person Christ's call to his whole Church is personified and made visible before us.

We are deliberately approaching the question of the ordained Ministry through the doctrine of the Church because I would maintain that a "total ecclesiology" is just as necessary as the setting in which to see the Ministry as it is for a proper consideration of the laity. Indeed, I would affirm that the doctrine of the Church and the nature of the Ministry are so intimately related that we cannot understand the one without the other.

(b) Let us return to the Church's role in this world. It takes its character from Jesus Christ, and it is servanthood. As we have already emphasized, the Church is to be the living, witnessing community testifying to the reconciliation that Jesus Christ achieved between God and man, and further to the meaning of this reconciliation within all human relationships. Wherever Christians are unwilling to be reconciled in the spirit of Christ, they deny their Lord.

This is the reason why churches segregated on the basis of color, whether perpetuated from the side of white or black, should be the concern of us all; they deny by their deeds what the Church professes with its lips, that in Christ the dividing wall of hostility has been broken down between men, and that we have become all "one man" in Him. It is also the reason why the ecumenical concern of these days cannot be brushed aside by anyone who takes the meaning of Christ's atonement seriously; in promoting rivalry among denominations we deny with our deeds what we profess with our lips. We have all sinned here, for if Protestants have often taken the divisions of the Church too lightly, Catholics have often interpreted its unity too exclusively.

The high point in the Faith and Order Conference at Montreal in 1963 was to hear a Roman Catholic Cardinal, Paul-Emile Léger, lead the representatives of Catholic, Orthodox, Anglican, and Protestant churches in the following prayer of confession: "Blessed art thou, God, the Father of our Lord Jesus Christ. We have sinned against thee, we have introduced divisions into thy work of unity. Even in our proclamation of thy truth, we have often been narrow, exclusive, and lacking in love. We have forgotten the beam in our own eye in order to judge the speck in our brother's eye. We have lived, ignoring them, and scorning them; we have often wanted to conquer and subjugate them. But thou, Lord, Father of mercy, thou wilt break our heart of stone and give us a heart able to repent. Glory be to thee throughout the ages."[12] I speak personally, but never have I as a Protestant felt more reconciled, more essentially "at one" with the Roman Catholic Church than at that moment, when in the person of Cardinal Léger it laid aside all pretensions and made confession with the rest of us before Almighty God.

[12] Order of Worship for the Ecumenical Gathering held at the University of Montreal, 21st July, 1963.

The Church has its own glory, but it is glory which can only be derived from the ministry of its Lord, born in a stable, lived out in service, and finally given in sacrifice for the world. It is a glory which it can never claim as a right, never self-endowed, but which will be made manifest before men by the Father only as the Church is prepared to bear the marks of his Son. We have all been far more concerned to assert the glorification of the Church, whereas we are called by God to reveal it. We have interpreted that glory more in terms of the splendor associated with thrones and empires than in terms of the Suffering Servant and the Prince of Peace. In every echelon of the Church's life we have acted and spoken as if the gospel gave us the right to enforce recognition from men, whereas the gospel grants the Church's right only to be obedient to the Lord in service.

Precisely the same may be said of the Ministry, for all Ministry is centered in the Church's own ministry. Only a truer understanding of the nature of the Church can lead us to a truer understanding of the Ministry. Like the Church itself, pastors and priests have their own "glory," but it becomes false when it becomes a claim to worldly domination rather than the acceptance of discipleship and apostleship. Indeed, as soon as Ministers begin to expect the kind of recognition that leadership brings in secular life, they deny the very thing that they are supposed to exemplify. Perhaps the theology in which clergy sometimes try to justify their office would be more convincing if it were directed toward clothing our ideas of *episcopē* with the simple robe of Christ rather than with the royal purple. As Luther tartly observed in *The Ninety-Five Theses,* "The true treasure of the Church is the Holy Gospel of the glory and grace of God. This treasure, however, is deservedly most hateful, because it makes the last to be first."[13] If all ministry is derived from the ministry of our Lord, then it can claim nothing but the right to serve, and to reconcile through service. "In the Kingdom of God," T. W. Manson remarked, "service is not a stepping-stone to nobility: it *is* nobility, the only kind of nobility that is recognized."[14]

Ordination should also personify before the Church what it means to be redeemed and reconciled by Christ, for in the ordination service we have re-presented to us the two sides of faith

[13] Theses 62, 63, *Luther's Primary Works,* p. 419.
[14] T. W. Manson, *The Church's Ministry,* p. 27.

in the redemptive work of Christ. First we are reminded again of God's great act for the redemption of men, by which we receive assurance of his redeeming love. But secondly, we are reminded that our trust in his promises is not something which can be appropriated selfishly for our own salvation — it must lead the Church on to dedicate itself in service to others by the consecration of time, talents, and means: it makes a total claim upon the life of the Church. As P. T. Forsyth has said, "The great sacrament of Christianity is the sacrament of the living and preached Word of Reconciliation, whether by speech, rite, or work. The elements may be anything; the Word is everything, the active Word of God's act, Christ's personal act met by His Church's."[15]

(c) Is ordination, then, a sacrament? Protestants have always been unwilling to regard any rite as a sacrament that does not have the scriptural warrant of our Lord himself. Luther would strenuously deny it on the grounds that there is no scriptural warrant, and in his view the act of ordination contained no gospel promise; therefore such ceremonies "are merely employed to prepare men for certain offices, as in the case of vessels or instruments."[16] In other words, ordination was to him an indifferent matter which might (or might not) be employed to distinguish a particular function, but without any other significance.

We must adhere to Luther's fundamental claim from the New Testament that baptism and the Lord's supper (Luther at first also included penance) were used by Jesus in a special way to proclaim the nature of his death and sacrifice. Their uniqueness is in this use he made of them. Yet, although we may hesitate to regard other actions and other symbols as sacraments in this specific sense, it is clear that there are many actions of the Church that are truly sacramental, in the sense that they declare the living Sacrament that is Christ, the Word, himself. Confirmation was not regarded by Luther as a sacrament for reasons that were important in his day, but insofar as confirmation declares Christ's redemptive love and ratifies that which was proclaimed in baptism, it *is* sacramental — it partakes of a sacramental character. The celebration of marriage was not a sacrament to Luther for good reasons, and yet can we say that Christian marriage

---

[15] *The Church and the Sacraments,* p. 141.
[16] *Luther's Primary Works,* p. 392.

knows nothing of the sacramental character? In Thomas Hardy's *Far from the Madding Crowd,* when one of the younger men is asked why he has to hurry away from what looks like a very promising stag party, he replies, "Well, ye see neighbours, I was lately married to a woman, and she's my vocation now." The circumstances were dubious but the sentiments commendable, and possibly significant. The apostle tells husbands to love their wives "as Christ also loved the church and gave himself up for it, to consecrate it" (Eph. 5:25, NEB), and did he not show in this that there must always be a sacramental element in the way in which Christian husbands and wives are to treat each other? The last offices of death are not a sacrament in Protestant churches, and yet when Christians gather to give thanks to God for a loved one within the family of the Church, few actions of the Church are more redolent of the great work of Christ or recall more triumphantly his victory over sin and death.

So it is with ordination. Through one life this act speaks to the Church of Christ's work of reconciliation, and calls the Church to recognize its own part in the redemptive ministry. Again I am forced back to P. T. Forsyth, who said these things so very clearly at a time when there were few in Anglo-Saxon Protestantism prepared to listen. "We can never sever that great impressive idea of a real Sacrament from the idea of the Ministry," declared Forsyth, and then a little later he went on to say, "In the sacrament of the Word the ministers are themselves the living elements in Christ's hands — broken and poured out in soul, even unto death; so that they may not only witness Christ, or symbolise Him, but by the sacrament of personality actually convey Him crucified and risen. This cannot be done officially. It cannot be done without travail. A Mother Church must die daily in bringing the gospel into the world — and especially in her ministry must she die. There is indeed a real change in these true elements. Their transubstantiation is a constantly renewed conversion."[17]

One can argue about Forsyth's terms. Some will not like what appears to be an over-concentration on the sacramental function of preaching, and others might very well question whether he claims too much for the Ministry in terms of its sacrifice. I would only remind the former of what Forsyth said previously

[17] *The Church and the Sacraments,* pp. 140, 141.

about the one "great Sacrament" that can be mediated "by speech, rite, *or work*," and perhaps we have to remind the latter that he is describing the Ministry as it should be and not as it so often is. His essential insight is that the Ministry, and hence ordination, is sacramental as it points the Church to the reconciling Word of God, Christ. And although within the classical view of the Protestant Ministry the functions of ministry often reach a high point of expression in preaching — Richard Baxter preached "as a dying man to dying men" — yet we must not forget that the word of the preacher is finally authenticated as it becomes a text expounded through a life of witness and service.

That means sacrifice; and that is a subject about which it is difficult to speak without lapsing either into platitudinous nonsense or into the worst kind of spiritual pride. Even Forsyth's words about the "sacrifice" of the preacher "broken and poured out in soul, even unto death" seem rather too much to claim for even the best of sermons. Furthermore, let us be honest and admit that the life of a Minister, while it does not bring in the highest material rewards, compares very favorably with many other occupations, and often the pill is quite thickly sugared with tasty perquisites such as a free membership in the country club and a generous 10 per cent discount. If this is sacrifice there are many who could bear it.

Perhaps our difficulty with the word is that in our minds sacrifice is almost inevitably linked with suffering, whereas they must not be confused. The association is obviously a legacy from the time when sacrifice meant the "blood sacrifice" and the giving up of life. There is a real sense in which two people who are in love and who give themselves up to each other in marriage may truly be said to enter into the meaning of sacrifice, and yet there is no obvious suffering in their joy. It is the giving up of a life completely in the service of another that is surely the basic principle of sacrifice, and the question how far suffering is involved becomes secondary and even irrelevant. When we pray in the Communion service, "here we offer and present unto Thee ourselves, our souls and bodies, to be a reasonable, holy and living sacrifice," [18] we do not mean that the congregation is going to fulfill its oblation to God in a masochistic orgy, but

[18] Order for the Celebration of the Sacrament of the Lord's Supper or Holy Communion, *Book of Common Order of the Church of Scotland,* p. 120.

that here we offer again to God our lives, our capacities, all our spiritual and material potential. This is the prayer that is prayed by every Christian, and this is the kind of sacrifice into which the Minister enters and which he helps to objectify for us in the act of ordination.

Of course, we *may* be called to suffering as an outcome of this act of self-offering. To commit oneself absolutely to anything or anyone necessarily involves that possibility, but the heart of sacrifice in the Christian life is not the extent of our sufferings or deprivations but the completeness of our commitment to God. Here again, as in so many other aspects of our vocation, a false understanding of the terms can lead us into hypocrisy by claiming too much for ourselves. Sometimes sacrifice comes to a head in poignant suffering, a martyrdom that is clear and visible to all the world, and if that test comes, the Christian prays that he may be given the grace to accept it for his Lord, but most of the time it is small pains and a big commitment. Sacrifice may mean going to the same factory for thirty years for the sake of a family; sacrifice may mean accepting or refusing promotion for the good of the cause; sacrifice may mean the loneliness and responsibility of high office, just as it may also mean the loneliness and drabness of lowly faithfulness; and occasionally sacrifice will mean that a John Fitzgerald Kennedy goes unwittingly to Dallas. Sacrifice can be all these things and many more.

The Ministry too is concerned with sacrifice, with dedication, with commitment. The Minister is involved with these no less and no more than other people in their vocations, but the sacrifice which he is called upon to undertake is specifically related to the service of God in his Church. All other things should be secondary to every Christian, it is true, but in the Minister's vocation the nature of the Christian's self-offering to God stands clear by the very setting in which he is called to work. His "sacrifice" is no greater and no less than that of many of the members in his congregation, and certainly in twentieth-century America we cannot claim that many Ministers suffer greatly, and yet in the character of his commitment to God in the service of the Church he becomes an example of the way in which the Church offers herself to God in the service of the world. This is preaching that is lived (or living that is preached), and it is given to the Church and for the Church. Sacred oratory may be a great gift, and Christlike service an even greater gift, but finally all the gifts of the Ministry, in the pulpit, at the altar, or in the study, home, hospital or street are given to the Church so that through them the Church may recognize its own ministry in the world. For behind the Minister and behind the Church stands the figure of the great Shepherd of the sheep, who is also the Saviour of the world.

III

ELECTION AND CALLING

When Max Weber investigated the origins of Western capitalism, he laid the blame mainly on the Protestant doctrines of Election and Vocation. We may question the use he made of his facts, but we cannot question the insight that in Protestant thought election and vocation are intimately related. Indeed, in the writings of John Calvin we find the clearest expression of Christian vocation in the places where we also find the strongest doctrine of election.

The two ideas go together. The Christian's vocation in this life is simply the fulfillment and the response he makes to that divine choice that has selected him for God's special purpose and greater glory. We cannot help asking questions about God's choice of particular people, whether we think of it as choice for salvation or to do a particular piece of work for him in the world: what does it mean to be "elect" or to be "called" or "chosen"? The Bible constantly repeats the theme of special choice. This is the way the God of the Bible works. He chooses particular instruments who are called to personal obedience and special responsibility — the family of Noah, the seed of Abraham, the tribe of Jacob, the nation of Israel, the house of David. Even within this chosen people he selected the individuals to exercise leadership, and who in exercising it were called to fulfill it in a way that would reflect God's own nature and the nature of his purpose for the human race — the intercession of Moses, the obedience and the penitence of David, the witness of the prophets, the sacrifice of the Remnant and of the Suffering Servant. All of this history found its epitome in Jesus of Nazareth, and it underlines God's primary choice of the human race to be the vehicle of salvation and the apostle of reconciliation to the whole cosmic order. He works by calling people into special vocations. And yet we are left with the question whether this does not run counter to all that the Bible affirms about God's impartiality and providence. Does election mean favoritism?

1. *Election to What?*

Here we must point out that the Church is most likely to err when it separates the ideas of election and vocation, for a doctrine of election implies "election to salvation" and hence to honor, but vocation emphasizes a calling to special tasks and responsibilities. We do justice to both ideas only as we see that they are really the two sides of a single coin. Israel considered itself to be an elect people, a people of God's special choice, and yet the whole story of the people of Israel shows that the "honor" for which the nation was chosen was very different from the ideas of national glory that the nation entertained about itself. It was, in fact, a glory that could be realized only through the recognition and acceptance of a special vocation. Israelites might dream of their national destiny in terms of the Davidic grandeur, but God had sowed a seed in the Davidic line which would make David's throne pale by comparison. The crown of this dynasty would be of thorns, and the supreme pattern of its kingship would be that of the Servant. The lesson of Israel's prophets was that her "election" would come only through the acceptance of her vocation to be the servant of God, but the lesson of her history was that she confused election with vocation and mistook the glory of being God's people as the mark of her vocation. She claimed the honor but she ignored the service.

Often the same has been true of the Church. We concentrate upon the fact that the people of God are elect to salvation, as if they are somehow better than other people, more worthy of respect and honour. When Jan Coggan in Thomas Hardy's *Far from the Madding Crowd* declares that "chapel folk" [i.e., nonconformists] have better chances of getting to heaven than other people because "They've worked hard for it, and they deserve to have it, such as 'tis," he not only expressed the grudging admiration of the world of the pub, but he also hints at the way in which the chapel folk have too often viewed their own chances. The garments of salvation may have a more sombre coloring than other forms of dress, but they are often worn with no less pride by the "saints," and with no less expectation that they will be recognized as status symbols not only in the Kingdom of God but also nearer at hand.

Yet a Christian is elect to salvation not by his own efforts but solely as he accepts the act of God's grace in Jesus Christ. He reveals his place in the kingdom not as he flaunts his own goodness before men, as if goodness or piety were the credentials of membership, but as he recognizes that salvation is a vocation to which Christ has called him in this world. Salvation is a ministry written in terms of the One who is the source of all ministry, and the way to the glory of the resurrection always passes across the hill of Calvary. You claim to be elect? Then you will need to work out your salvation with fear and trembling, for you are elect to a cross of sacrifice.

2. *A Minister's Call*

All that we have said about Israel and the Church must be said about the ordained Ministry. Ministers are called, chosen by God and given to the Church for leadership, and among frail humans there is always the temptation to claim the wrong kind of esteem for having been so chosen. A Minister is chosen for service and to lead the Church into the meaning of its own ministry. An erroneous view of the Ministry will therefore almost inevitably lead the Church into a wrong view of its own vocation; but equally, an erroneous view of the Church in terms of worldly honor or satisfaction in its own assurance of salvation will almost inevitably call forth the wrong kind of leadership. Just as Israel's expectations of power and empire caused it to look for the wrong kind of Messiah and closed its eyes to the Christ of God, so a Church that concentrates upon its own salvation will not recognize that it is begotten of God in and through the Cross. It is "saved" that all men may find redemption.

Only a doctrine of the Church that has a doctrine of *ministry* at its center will remain close to the gospel, for the temptation to spiritual pride and moral kingship can be just as destructive of the Church as Israel's imperial ambitions and exclusive claims were for her mission in the world; and if church history is a reliable guide, the distance between spiritual pride and worldly pomp is very small. In the same way, only a doctrine of the Ministry that recognizes its focus in the corporate ministry of the whole Church will avoid the temptation of making its pastors and priests a class apart and thus falling prey to a false aristocracy of the spirit. We are all elected to ministry, to service, to the obedience that in the end must be ready to embrace the Cross.

Ministers are given to the Church that we may all come to a deeper understanding of what "the cross" may mean for us in this twentieth century, so that we may delve deeper into the meaning of the service that we offer, so that we may explore the ever new ways in which the Christian community can minister to the world's need. These are the Ministers we need, and this is why the Ministry is necessary.

A Minister should lead the Church into the meaning of its own ministry. He is no different from other Christians except in the fact that he has been chosen to lead them into what they as a body are becoming. He has not arrived any more than they have arrived at the place where they are to stand. They do not follow him, but he points them, and they point him, to Christ who beckons them all. The Minister, then, should not hold himself apart from his congregation or laud his own office, for to do this would be to invalidate the very charge to which he is committed. He should not seek to maintain distinction between his own spiritual status and that of his fellow-members in the body of Christ, but on the contrary he should rejoice in every sign of their growth, for this is the reason behind his Ministry. He is called to present them with an example of what the Church itself is called to be, and yet he must always point beyond himself to the One who alone is worthy to be called Minister. A Minister is one whose glory it is to minister, and who asks no other honor but that of being obedient to Christ, the great Head of the Church.

The glory, then, that a Minister should recognize is very different from the honor and deference he is often given by society, or even by the members of his own congregation. All the arts that he possesses and all the graces that are his must be directed towards breaking down these false ideas of the distinction or esteem that is due to him, for only by breaking these down can the Church begin to recognize the true character of the "glory" that is her own. Together with the rest of the Church the Minister is on a pilgrimage to Christ, and he is just as much a member of that pilgrimage as the humblest member in his congregation. The object of his work is that they may all reach the point where their individual ministries are nothing and where the ministry of Christ is all in all within the Church.

A Minister should flaunt no gifts of his own, for he should be the first to realize that he has no gifts of his own. He should certainly not flaunt a mock modesty or humility. "But under your bushel, Joseph! under your bushel with 'ee!" exclaims Joseph Poorgrass unctuously, "A strange desire, neighbours, this desire to hide, and no praise due." And then he adds complacently, "Yet there is a Sermon on the Mount with a calendar of the blessed at the head, and certain meek men may be named therein."[19] Nothing is so obviously and nauseatingly spurious as false humility, which is probably the final and most impregnable refuge of spiritual pride. It is not our gifts, even our imagined virtues, that our ministry is to set before men, but God's grace in Jesus Christ.

3. *Christian Vocation and the Secular*

We must turn to something that may appear to be very far afield from ordination and the Christian Ministry, but I believe it may be increasingly relevant as we begin to review the vocation of the Ministry in relation to the general vocation of being a Christian in the world.

Max Weber, the sociologist, in *The Protestant Ethic and the Spirit of Capitalism,* developed the thesis that there is an essential relationship between the Protestant idea of vocation, calling, and the development of Western capitalism. Luther destroyed the medieval division between the religious and the secular by recognizing that all Christians had a particular calling (*Beruf*), and Calvin tied the idea of vocation to a system of ethics in which frugality and hard work eventually became the justification for profits and commercial success.[20] The "Weber thesis" has been argued backwards and forwards for many years, the basic issue usually revolving around the question whether Protestantism in general and Calvinism in particular are to be blamed for the rise and expansion of capitalism in Western Europe.

Leaving aside the rights and wrongs of the historical arguments *pro et contra,* I suggest that the time may have come to look at the Protestant and Calvinistic view of vocation from a different and slightly more positive angle. We grant the probability that

[19] T. Hardy, *Far from the Madding Crowd.*

[20] The reference, of course, has to be generally to Weber's book, but a similar view may be found in R. H. Tawney's *Religion and the Rise of Capitalism.* A useful, interesting synopsis of the Weber thesis and the theories that have gone into orbit around it is to be found in *Protestantism and Capitalism,* ed. Robert W. Green (Boston: D. C. Heath, 1959).

Reformation ethics, even if it did not bring capitalism into being, certainly provided a "climate" in which it was able to develop. We grant too that the profit motive cuts across much in New Testament ethics, and that when it is freed from moral restraints or is allowed to be exercised without responsibility, it leads to inevitable exploitation of material and men. We concede that when the stimulus of the Industrial Revolution was added to the demise of church discipline in later Calvinism, it led to vicious exploitation of the individual.

On the other hand, every argument that links Protestantism or Calvinism to capitalism through this concept of "calling" is evidence of the movement's real concern to baptize the secular, and to give the Christian a real sense of vocation *in this world*. When Oliver Cromwell, a good Calvinist, spoke of preparing his son for "public services, for which a man is born," he was expressing this same concern in relation to the Christian's responsibilities in politics. The same ethic which, for better or for worse, helped to produce nineteenth-century capitalism with all its horrors, also helped to produce the democratic state with all its hope. Furthermore, the very interest that was expressed by Dietrich Bonhoeffer for a new Christian ethic that would be frankly "world affirming" and which would develop a concept of "holiness" in the acceptance of this world as it is, can be seen to have been a major concern of Protestantism from the beginning. Whether or not we approve of the way in which individual Christians worked out its implications in business life, there was in this idea of vocation a real attempt to claim the world for Christ and to understand the world as essentially good. Yet such is the fear of admitting any taint from Max Weber's accusation, that in an issue of *Laity* devoted to tracing the Church's assertion of the Christian responsibility in and for this world, not one of the contributors mentioned the Weber thesis![21]

This suggests that Bonhoeffer's concern is not a very new one but a very old one. It may point to a very significant line of exploration for church historians and for those who study Christian social ethics; but it also contains a built-in warning. To be

[21] *Laity*, No. 9, June, 1958, "Towards a New Christian Style of Life?" As one of those who contributed, I admit my share of the blame. On the other hand, I have tried to make amends recently in an article "Weber and Calvinism: The Results of a 'Calling,' " which will appear in *The Canadian Journal of Theology* in January, 1965.

"world affirming," to have a kind of "worldly holiness," is good. It is an essential part of the gospel, and in particular it contains within it the logic of the incarnation; but this, like any other interpretation of the gospel, can be abused. To develop a doctrine of the Church based solely on the "theology of the laity" and a system of ethics centering wholly in the secular, without any reference to the wholeness of the Church on the one hand or the eschatological dimension of Christian life on the other, would probably result in something quite as demonic as capitalism made of the Calvinist view of vocation. The Spirit that breathes in the Christ of the New Testament must be paramount for the Christian in whatever calling he finds himself, and although the New Testament ethic has to be reinterpreted in different times and different circumstances, no doctrine of the Church that falls short of it and no system of ethics that contradicts it can ever be truly Christian.

This ends our digression, for this brings us back to our main subject. It emphasizes that the interpretation of a Christian's vocation, whether it be in the service of the Church, or in business, politics, or any other field of the secular, must be informed by and conformed to the primary vocation of ministry as revealed in Jesus Christ. Without this, when "the world" becomes simply a preoccupation of the Church and not the object of its total ministry in the Spirit of her Lord, then concern with the secular can become capitulation to the secular spirit, and this in turn leads even to the exploitation of the world and those within it for whom Christ died. Only a Christian community with an understanding of ministry at its center can keep Christians true to their Lord and faithful in their mission. The answer to clericalism is not anticlericalism or laicism but ministry.

IV

THE SERVICE OF ORDINATION

Services of ordination among the Protestant denominations may exhibit many differences. The ordaining authority may be principally the congregation, the local association of churches and ministers, the presbytery, the conference, or the episcopate. Our interest at the moment is not in the differences, but to determine those elements that are common to all.

The context of the service is worship. It is a service of praise to God for what he has done. We all believe that the Church is doing something in this act, and yet that which is being done in the service does not initiate something new but recognizes that which has already been accomplished by God. Behind all the forms which Protestant churches may use to ordain their Ministers, this at least is common to them all — we give thanks to God for what he has done first of all in Jesus Christ, and for that which he continues to do now through the living Christ in the life of this man and in the Church. Other things may be of interest or even important — this man's faith, for example — but they should never usurp the place of that which is primary, our offering of praise and thanksgiving for God's redeeming work. We recognize that God himself gives us the gift of leadership in the Church, and in the calling of a man into this service we are again the recipients of God's grace; for to be a true Ministry his calling must find its center in the life and work of our Lord, the great Minister of the Church. "Therefore with angels and with archangels, and with the whole company of heaven, we laud and magnify thy glorious name; evermore praising thee and saying, 'Holy, holy, holy, Lord God of hosts, Heaven and earth are full of thy glory: Glory be to thee, O Lord most High." The service is the service of ordination, but the theme is that of eucharist, thanksgiving.

1. *Our Faith and the Faith of the Church*

The Church witnesses to Jesus Christ, and the leadership that God grants to the Church is above all things else leadership in witness to the gospel. Ministers set before us week by week, through the declamation of the pulpit and the drama of font and communion table, the historic Faith of the Church. They are ordained to be Ministers of the Word and Sacraments to us — witnesses to the Christ whose life becomes Word and Sacrament to us. The dominant note of the ordination service, from the call to worship or the opening hymn to the benediction, is this Faith of the Church in Jesus Christ, its Lord. "The Church's one foundation is Jesus Christ her Lord" — this is where our Christian Faith has its center, and it is to this Faith that the Minister leads the Church as his primary responsibility.

Therefore within the context of worship the Church's Faith is the first and most important theme of the ordination service, for when God sends his gift of leadership, it is leadership in witness to the apostolic Faith. Whether or not it is expressed in the formal recitation of the ancient creeds, it should be the dominant note of the whole service, for it is in the events of salvation that we find the heart of our praise. True, there is place for a Minister's individual insights into the gospel under the guidance of the Holy Spirit; true, the language of the creeds must be constantly reviewed and often revised to do justice to the truths they try to express; true, the Church has to search out new ways to present the ancient Faith, and new terminology with which to challenge each succeeding generation. However, it is not a new faith but the apostolic Faith that the Church is committed to proclaim, and the Church has the duty in love to examine the fidelity of any person who presents himself for ordination. As a Minister he will have the responsibility of assisting the Church to interpret the gospel for our contemporary situation, and if he is to perform this high responsibility, the Church must assure itself that he will "contend for the faith which was once delivered unto the saints" (Jude 3). This is not a matter of the personal preference to the ordaining authority; it is its responsibility to the whole Church of Jesus Christ.

This may sound like a conservative defence of "the old time religion." It may or may not be held under this name, but often what is represented as "old time religion" is often less like the apostolic Faith of the New Testament than a sentimental memory of how that faith was interpreted during nineteenth-century revivals or in seventeenth-century creeds. Fundamentally the Church needs to know that the man who is called to be a Minister will preach the Faith of the Church and not some stilted version of his own or any previous age; and there is no better way for the Church to do this than by living close to the gospel itself. Even the early Church knew the same problem. "But do not trust any and every spirit, my friends," warned the apostle, but "test the spirits, to see whether they are from God, for among those who have gone out into the world there are many prophets falsely inspired. This is how we may recognize the Spirit of God: every spirit which acknowledges that Jesus Christ has come in the flesh is from God, and every spirit which does not thus acknowledge Jesus is not from God" (I John 4:1, NEB).

This particular advice was probably written in the face of the Docetic heresy that was making its appearance, but the author knew that the distinctive center of the Christian gospel was in the reality of the incarnation and of God's redemptive purpose in Jesus. We know the dangers which arise when the Church tries to make its own present understanding of the Faith a test of orthodoxy. At one time or another a literal view of Scripture, or a particular view of atonement, or of church polity, or even whether the church is to employ organs in its worship, has falsely been made a test of the Faith. There is no infallible way to "test the spirits" except by allowing that Spirit which was in Jesus himself to rule in our hearts, by staying close to that love and care for the brethren which animated the ministry of the apostles. The whole life of the Church is a struggle to understand and to be faithful to its historic Faith, but it cannot abdicate this responsibility to anyone else.

In an interesting little book, *The Call,* written from the standpoint of a British Congregationalist, C. E. Norwood claims that the "power to appoint pastors is conferred by Christ upon the local church." But he continues, "Its members do not rely upon their own powers to discern ability and to weigh character. They are to choose the persons who have been appointed by the Holy Spirit. Much of our trouble today," the writer suggests, "may be traced back to the fact that we have largely lost effective belief in the Spirit who appoints men, and whose appointment may be discerned by the Church."[22] Presbyterians, Methodists, and others may very well wish to question the Congregational presupposition about the local church's authority, but we would all agree with Norwood's basic contention that the real choice of a Minister is by the Holy Spirit, whatever the agency used. In calling a Minister the Church, whether through the local congregation, the presbytery or by whatever means, must be sensitive to the Spirit, and must be open to recognize fidelity to the gospel in the man. We do not worship God in the abstract, but the God who acted in certain historic deeds for the redemption of the world in which we live, the God who in Christ did something unique at a particular historical time and in a specific geographical place. It is within these events that the Church discovers the meaning of human life and destiny and the promise of final victory over sin and death.

It is a Faith to sing about, and this is the time to start sing-

[22] C. E. Norwood, *The Call* (London: Independent Press, 1949), p. 11.

ing. Indeed, perhaps it would mean more to us if we sang it, rather than recited it. Bernard Manning used to say that Congregationalists sing their creeds in their hymns. With the remarkable heritage of Martin Luther, Isaac Watts, and Charles Wesley behind them, all Protestants should want to sing about their Faith. The reading of Scripture and the preaching of the Word undoubtedly provide the doctrinal center in the service of ordination as for every service of the Church, but in glorious exposition of these spoken utterances there is the opportunity for the music of the Church to reveal its true *métier* — not to be the jam in a somewhat didactic sandwich, but the voice of the congregation lifted in praise to Almighty God. Here is the chance to sing the *Te Deum* as the great choral expression of the Faith, here is the occasion for the choir to sing an anthem on the theme of Pentecost, here is the opportunity for the congregation to sing the great hymns of faith, rather than the mawkish little lyrics of individual piety. Above all else, it is the Church's faith we proclaim, and only in a derivative and secondary sense is it our own.

Of course, it must be our own as well. This historic Faith of the Church has little significance unless it is also shown to be ours: it must be related to the Church of the present, and the relationship made manifest through the faith of the man who stands before us as an ordinand. In some churches the theological examination of the candidate and his "Statement of Faith" is presented some weeks before the service, and it is right that this should be so. But this invests with a special solemnity the questions that are put to the ordinand in the name of the Church, for here in summary we lay before him and the congregation the doctrinal heart of the gospel which he is to serve. Even if only briefly, there should be a place in the service where he rehearses again the steps by which he has come to this place and this hour. We need to see the veil pulled aside from personal experience and to have revealed to us the effect of the historic Faith upon one man's life: we need to see how the Faith comes alive in faith.

For the Church's Faith is not simply a series of narrow dogmatic propositions about God and Christ, however sublime and time-honored the form of them may be, but to become alive in the Church it must find its home in the individual Christian: "The Faith," as the historic body of Christian doctrine, remains dead in its creeds unless it is caught and mediated through *faith,* the active response in trust to that which a man believes. We need Ministers who accept the content of the historic Faith, but who do not allow it to become petrified within its historic forms, and because of this we need this man's Christian experience, this man's insights and understanding of the gospel. Our Ministers are called to proclaim the apostolic Faith of the Church, but it is a Faith that has been transmitted down the ages through "men of faith" in the midst of a believing Church.

Both these aspects of faith, the Faith that is the essential doctrine of the Church, and the faith that is the personal trust of the Christian, are brought together for us in the ordination prayer and the "laying on of hands." The prayer will celebrate the great themes of the Faith, for that is the very setting of our worship, but when we gather around the newly ordained Minister and place our hands on him, we call to mind the Ministries by which this Faith of the Church has been mediated from the time of the apostles until now. We set this man within this succession. In most Protestant churches few claims are made to special grace through this act, for this servant of God can receive no grace greater than he has already received through the redemptive work of Christ and the assurance of his Spirit; but within the ancient form we do recognize that the man before us has been chosen by God for the ministry of Word and Sacrament in the Church, and that God's choice and the Church's joyful acknowledgement makes him one with the company of those who have exercised like ministry in the Church through time.

The Church exists not only in time, however, but also in space, and often in a service of ordination the "right hand of fellowship" is offered on behalf of the local family of congregations to which the new Minister will belong. It is a simple way of stressing the wider unity in Christ which we experience here and now. How impoverished it is made by the fact that the recognition is limited to those within a single denominational family! What a difference it would make if at every ordination the representatives of each Christian denomination in the vicinity could come forward to extend the right hand of fellowship in the name of Jesus Christ, the Head of the Church!

2. *The Call of God and the Call of the Church*

The context of the service of ordination is the worship of the God who redeems us, and this context comes to one clear focus in the proclamation of the apostolic gospel. But there is another focus in relation to the ordinand — his "call."

Essentially, God calls the man. The Church does not create a Minister by ordination, it simply recognizes him. "You did not choose me," said Jesus to his disciples, "I chose you" (John 15;16), and as one reads or hears the Statements made by young ordinands, one is often impressed by their growing consciousness of divine leading, despite the almost pathological anxiety in these days not to say anything that might sound supernatural or "pious." Even those who in their seminary "bull sessions" were protesting a few months ago that they felt no such thing as a divine call, and asked simply to be allowed to "do a job" in the Church, find more often than not that the pieces of their life have fallen into a pattern that they did not design — a pattern which fills them with something akin to awe as they discover themselves at this time and place.

Theological students today are trying to be honest. They are a good deal less ready to claim a divine call than some of their predecessors, for they are all too conscious that their vocation may have been the result of many mixed motives and a set of comparatively mundane circumstances. They do well to be sceptical, for this is another subject on which parsons can be guilty of the most pretentious and saccharine hypocrisy. The motives of a young man offering himself for the Ministry may be many, and not all are as pure as the gospel he professes; if we react violently against any claim to divine leading in the matter, it is because we are all too conscious of the subtleties of our own hearts. And yet when we reach the point of ordination, we have arrived at this time, this place, to be a Minister of Jesus Christ to this congregation; and to say that this progression within our own life falls outside the scope of God's activity and concern is to deny that his Holy Spirit has had or could have any purpose in us despite the subtleties of our hearts. It comes very near to denying that Christ is truly Head of his Church. If the nature of this Ministry is truly understood, to say that we have been called by God for this service is not a boost to our self-esteem, but something to be accepted with fear and trembling.

In 1804 the Church meeting at Carr's Lane in Birmingham, England, sent a call to a young student from Gosport Academy, John Angell James. The letter said, "We bless the Great Head of the Church, to whom all events are known, and who sees the end from the beginning, that he has deigned to favour you with such abilities for the ministry, and we hope with a view that you should exercise that ministry in Birmingham. We have long been praying, and we hope sincerely, that God would in His providence direct us to such a man as He would own and bless among us, for the conversion of sinners, for the edification of His saints, and the building up of the Church in this place in particular; and we cannot help thinking that your being sent among us was in answer to our prayers."[23] Such a letter might be nothing more than pious hypocrisy if the authors did not really believe what they were saying, or if believing they had proceeded to select their candidate by very different canons. We cannot avoid the possibility of hypocrisy whenever we seek to express the Faith. The answer is not to deny the Faith but to treat it more seriously — in particular, to treat with very great seriousness the fact that "the Great Head of the Church, to whom all events are known, and who sees the end from the beginning," can and does call men into the service of his Church.

The Church has an indispensable place in the call of a Minister, but often in a Free Church setting it is emphasized so much that it obscures the primary call of God himself. When this happens the act of ordination becomes simply a solemn and somewhat pompous way of installing a new paid executive, a status symbol that invests this office with a peculiarly impressive but unwarrantable dignity. It appears to me that a good deal of the honest questioning about ordination today arises here, from the secularized way in which churches understand their part in the Minister's call.

If a church chooses its Minister in an essentially *secular* way, concentrating upon his qualifications to enter a profession, then we are bound to ask why such an office should be honored by a ritual of particular solemnity. In secular life we give this kind of recognition only to those offices that have special honor and dignity among us — such as the inauguration of a President (or the coronation of a King), but the other offices in society do not get this red carpet treatment, nor do those that hold them expect it. If the service of ordination serves no other purpose in the Church than this, then there is no justification for ordaining Min-

[23] Quoted by C. E. Norwood in *The Call*, p. 25, from R. W. Dale's *The Life and Letters of John Angell James*.

isters any more than any other vocation in civil life; for there can be the serious danger of investing the office with a spurious status that is fundamentally opposed to the servant status of the gospel.

Ordination is justified only if its meaning pertains not to the office or job of being a "Minister," but to the essential nature of *ministry*. It is important not because it gives an aura of special dignity to the office, but only because it re-presents sacramentally to the Church the nature of the Church's own corporate ministry. We seek its justification not primarily in what it does for the Minister, but in what it means to the Church, both Minister and people.

If churches get Ministers who have difficulty in seeing the Holy Spirit's guidance in their own call, it may be because they have given up the responsibility of being vehicles of the Holy Spirit's purpose. The Church does not act through its ordaining agents by its own authority as a human institution but as an instrument of the Holy Spirit, and a secularization of the Church at this point is not a form of modesty but a limitation on God's power to act in and through us. The Church has the necessary task of recognizing and accepting God's gift of Ministry, and when it does the act of ordination becomes the Church's "Amen" to the Holy Spirit's hymn of praise.

3. *Mutual Ministry*

If I were writing to a predominantly Congregational constituency, this is where we should have to mention the Church Covenant, for it is particularly in the sense of a people covenanted together under God that Congregational churches[24] have historically tried to establish the truth that Minister and people are *together* in the ministry of the Church. Whether or not our denomination owns a particular idea of covenant in local congregations, however, the truth still stands. Minister and people exercise a mutual ministry towards each other. If it is true that the Church needs the witness, encouragement, and pastoral care

[24] Historically, Congregational writers (in England, at least) have made a clear distinction between a "church" of covenanted members, and a "congregation" which included not only the members but also adherents and uncommitted worshippers. For historical reasons the word 'parish' was not used, since it was associated almost exclusively with the parochial organization of Anglicanism.

of its Ministers, it is equally true that the Minister can be sustained only by the witness of the Church, the encouragement of his fellow members, and the pastoral care of the whole fellowship in which he is placed. This will not convince any clergyman who has not himself felt the sustaining power of a congregation which understands its ministry towards him. If the act of ordination is to fulfill its proper function within the Church, this pastoral relationship of Minister to people and of people to their Minister should be made clear. It is a mutual ministry sustained by the essential ministry of Jesus Christ.

There will probably be sufficient stress upon the responsibilities of the pastor to his people, but ordination is essentially the re-presentation of the Church's *own* ministry. Here the very context of the service presents us with the historic Faith, and is related to the primary task of proclamation; here through the personal faith of one representative man we see the Church constantly wrestling with the need to relate this Faith to its own experience of Jesus Christ; here we are presented with the pattern of the Church's own life of service as one representative member becomes the Minister of this community. The gospel of reconciliation is set before us *all,* not as the exclusive call to this Minister but to the whole community as a lifelong commitment. At every point in the service, as we stress the relationship between the pastor and the congregation, we accent the ministerial relationship of the Church to the world. The world is the Church's concern just as this congregation has become the concern of this Minister, for as Forsyth said, the Ministry "has not to be directly effective on the world so much as to make a Church that is."[25]

All the strands come together when the sacrament of the Lord's Supper follows the act of ordination,[26] or in the first Communion that pastor and people take together. If there is any spiritual and liturgical logic in what ordination should mean, it is to be seen in this sacrament, for at the Lord's table both the Church and its Ministers come to the source of their common ministry as in the symbols of broken bread and poured out wine

[25] *The Church and the Sacraments,* p. 131.
[26] This is a commendable feature of the Service of Ordination proposed in the United Church of Christ. Cf. *The Manual on the Ministry* (published in *The Minister's Quarterly,* New York, 1963), pp. 26-29.

they take to themselves the assurance of God's grace and forgiveness in Jesus Christ. But in the same act they accept the pledge and in turn offer their own lives in the service of the One who is Minister to us all. Here having received the promise of our Lord's continuing presence in the benediction, the members go out to fulfill in the world the quality of witness and of ministry that they have shared in the Church.

Certainly we ordain individual Ministers to service in the Church, but we have missed the significance of what we have been doing if the meaning of this act ends with our solemn recognition of their function in our midst. Far beyond his individual call, this Minister represents the Church, and as he receives his charge, the Church hears again the charge to go into the world and proclaim the gospel, and the promise that our risen Lord will be with us until the end of time.

4. *Ordination and Christian Unity*

The preceding paragraph would have been a very agreeable note on which to end this chapter. But although it is probably where we should end — with the place at which the Church takes up its mission — we cannot, because there is still the unfinished business of the Church's disunity. Forsyth pointed out nearly fifty years ago that the more we think of the unity of the Church, the more significant we discover the Ministry to be,[27] and this not because of pressures from the "catholic" branches of the Church, but because from the first the Ministry has had a special responsibility to the Church for maintaining the historic Faith. Protestants properly raise questions about this concern and the tendencies which produced first the monarchial episcopate, then the patriarchates, and finally the papacy. The answer to the trend towards ever more exclusive clericalism, however, is not to dismiss the problem (as if the Ministry and the Faith entrusted to it were unimportant) but to present an evangelical example of Ministry that is both loyal to the Faith and which also refuses to become a separate caste. The need is for a Ministry committed to both the freedom *and* the content of the gospel, Ministers who will defend the freedom as an outcome of, and not as a reaction from, the gospel. Forsyth, writing about churches at the beginning of this century, declared that the evan-

[27] *The Church and the Sacraments,* p. 133.

gelical Ministry should be a protest against the relativism and individualism that disregard the churches' disunity, because the Ministry "is the trustee specially charged with this one positive gospel; therefore, it is the most effective agent of the one Church." He went on to plead that in the Free Churches at least there should be mutual eligibility of Ministry, and for the basically theological reason that the Ministry should be *par excellence* representative of the Church's unity; for beyond its representative character, by its very proclamation of the gospel of reconciliation, the Ministry "sets *up* the Church's unity, and not only sets it *forth*."[28]

Fine words from a Free Church theologian, but what has been done about it? Little enough up to the present, although we must not underestimate the giant strides taken by the ecumenical movement in this century that make it probably the only movement in the modern church to keep pace with the expansion of technology and science. We have gone a long way towards recognition. On the other hand, we have to admit, at the practical level, that Ministers are still ordained into truncated, twisted, rival editions of what the Ministry should be. The Ministers who should represent, and help to call into being, the One Holy Catholic Church of Jesus Christ, become the representatives and the agents of partial, schismatic, and unreconciled denominations, be they Catholic, Orthodox, or Protestant in name. Some years ago, writing of the ecumenical situation in Britain, I ventured to suggest that as a first step towards mutual recognition representatives of the various Christian denominations might be invited to share in each act of ordination.[29] If this principle were adopted among denominations that have little theological reason for refusing to recognize each other's form of Ministry, it might help to separate the ecumenical men from the denominational boys.

The Minister should be the representative in the local congregation of the One Great Church of Jesus Christ. The unwillingness to recognize another church's ordination may sometimes be due to legitimate doubts as to whether this other Ministry really

---

[28] *Ibid.,* p. 134.
[29] "British Churches and the Ecumenical Future," *The Ecumenical Review,* VIII (Jan., 1956), 186. I was interested to see that the same suggestion has been made much more pointedly by Walter D. Wagoner in *Bachelor of Divinity,* pp. 151f.

seeks to maintain the historic Faith. But it can also be due to our unwillingness to recognize the essential ministry of Christ in any garb but the one we wear. When that happens, we are very near to sin against the Holy Spirit; and if the churches in our day are being saved from that, it is only by the grace of God.

V

CHARACTER INDELEBILIS

In an address to seminary students the Reverend Gwenyth Hubble pointed out the reluctance of young modern Christians to offer themselves for a lifetime of missionary service.[30] Something has happened within postwar Western Christianity, whether under the influence of such enterprises as the Peace Corps or not, which makes the present day young Christian unwilling to consider the call to missionary service as a total commitment. A stint of three years, or five years possibly, is regarded as reasonable enough, particularly when it promises the glamour of foreign travel with all expenses paid, but a lifetime of service is too risky, too full of insecurity, too final.

Perhaps the same attitudes are beginning to filter through our concept of the Ministry. Recently I read the letter written by a young Minister to his congregation, in which he declared that he was "leaving the Ministry." The motives, which in his case appear to be laudable, need not concern us, but the question we must ask is whether what he claimed to be doing was in fact possible. A Minister may leave his work in a parish to enter so-called secular employment, many more may leave it in order to become teachers, to engage in church administration or to become peripatetic evangelists, but do they "leave the Ministry"? Do they negate their ordination?

Many would say that they do, and some would probably question whether that is very important. The old Puritans would certainly have answered with an unequivocal "yes" to at least the first part of the question, for on the basis of their rigorous attempt to reproduce the New Testament ecclesiology they recognized that the Ministry was essentially given to the Church; and for them the Church was primarily expressed in and through

[30] "The Way of Obedience," *The Hartford Quarterly,* III (Spring, 1963), 99ff.

the local covenanted congregation. The early New England divines even insisted on a pastor being re-ordained when he moved from one parish charge to another.

The Puritans were, of course, reacting to views of the Ministry that not only tended to disregard the local parish, but which had also inherited the medieval distinction between those in holy orders and those who were not. The Medieval Church had been full of those who performed offices that were not in the slightest related to pastoral functions, but who claimed full benefit of clergy and whose ordination was thought to raise them far above ordinary Christians. The Puritans insisted that a Minister must exercise a *ministry*.

On the other hand, few today could go as far as the Puritans went in their reaction, for at this point they seem to have taken too narrow a view even of what the pastoral Ministry should mean. When a Christian is ordained to the Ministry of the Word and Sacraments, it is principally not something which he performs, but it is something which much more fundamentally he *accepts;* and if he is conscious that this is a charge which he has first accepted from God, can such a man ever walk out of his Ministry unless he is prepared to reject Christ? If he is still trying to obey the call of Christ, if he is still ready in word and action to proclaim the gospel, if he is still motivated by pastoral concern and care for the brethren, surely he is still "in the Ministry," whatever functions he may undertake.

The young Minister I cited earlier is a case in point. He felt that he was called to give his Christian witness within a frontier situation of the Church, but he made it quite clear that this was just as much a call to him as was his call earlier to serve that particular parish. Of course, he may have been mistaken, and we cannot prejudge the case. But the point I would make is that insofar as a man's motives are those of the gospel, insofar as he is not an apostate to Christ, that which his ordination represented once to the church and himself remains, even though he may be called to exercise his ministry in work that is very different from that of the normal pastorate: his commitment to witness, to service and to pastoral concern is not less than it was, although the constituency to which it is offered may be very different.

To approach the issue in another way, ordination intensifies and objectifies the commitment that is inherent in the sacramental action of baptism and confirmation. It does not begin with something that we do, but with something that is done for us. Only then does our response become important, but once that response is made it is total — it has no reservations, because the gospel knows no reservations. In obedience to the gospel one may seek many different forms in which to express the Ministry to which he is *now* committed, and some of them may well be unconventional, but he cannot go back on the commitment without turning back on Christ himself. If a man is ordained, his call to pioneer for the Church remains for as long as he remains a Christian.

Ordination reaffirms and objectifies that which the baptism of every member implies, a total commitment in the service of Jesus Christ; and total commitment cannot be any more than that total:

> *Never further than Thy cross,*
> *Never higher than Thy feet. . . .* [31]

Ordination takes its character from baptism, and because it takes meaning from this sacrament, it must also share to some extent in its indelible character, not in such a way that it removes the ordained person from the common ruck of Christians, but in the sense that in this man the Church publicly affirmed again that it was under God's grace in Christ and declared once more its mission to serve. A man may legitimately feel that his ministry ought no longer to be exercised within the boundaries of the Church's own pastoral Ministry, but he cannot deny that he is called to ministry and even, by God's grace, to leadership in ministry. Because of that which was done at his ordination with the concurrence of the Church, he will personify to his fellow members for as long as he lives the commitment that the Church is called to make. His Ministry may now be exercised within the general ministry of the Church and not within its particular Ministry of church life, but it remains true that the Church at one time recognized this man's gift in Christian leadership. He cannot leave this Ministry without leaving Christ. You may leave a profession, or retire from it, but you can no more leave or retire from Christian commitment than you can from the Christian Faith itself.

---

[31] Elizabeth Rundle Charles (1828-96), in the hymn "Never Further from Thy Cross."

It has been my contention that within the framework of the visible Church ordination represents to the Church in terms of service the Church's own ministry to the world, and that it is a ministry which is at once apostolic in its witness and total in its commitment. Within the context of the Church an ordained Minister cannot help being a "marked man," although that mark does not relegate him to a separate caste from his fellow members but rather identifies him more closely with them. Whether he fulfills his Ministry in the pastorate, in thought, in administration, or in teaching, the keynote will always be service, for that is the nature of his ministry to the Church. Outside the context of the Church the mark may or may not be recognized. There is no reason to claim that it should be acknowledged — except by the man himself; for the mark is a cross, and the cross makes no claim for itself but the right to serve.

chapter six

Authority in the Church

I

AUTHORITY AND CHRISTIAN DIVISION: THE DILEMMA

You will probably want to put this chapter into parentheses. Its relationship to ordination and the Ministry may initially appear to be somewhat tenuous, but I must ask for the reader's patience. I include it because the subject is central to any discussion of the doctrine of the Church and is therefore bound to affect our understanding of the Christian Ministry. I also include it here because I feel it is in danger of being overlooked in the present ecumenical debate. But first let us look at the problem, and perhaps the best way into it will be by way of an illustration.

While returning to New England after a camping trip in the Far West, as we travelled through New York State, I became aware of the interesting variety of spiritual solace offered to the traveller. Large billboards urge America to "Attend and Support the Church of your Choice." The philosophy based on the widest possible diversity of reputable brands mixed with discreet competition is then maintained by the battery of welcoming signs which greet you as soon as you pass any town line. "The Episcopal Church Welcomes You," featuring the arms of the diocese — a sign that holds evident charm for those who favor blazers and college crests; "WORSHIP AT THE METHODIST CHURCH" — designed to present a large-lettered Public Image; "St. Blank's

165

Catholic Church" — presented with a large Chi-Rho symbol to remind you where Christ is truly to be found, or a more psychological approach, "Seeking Peace? — The Catholic Faith." I must admit I could not refrain from an inward cheer for the churches of Middleville, New York, for setting up the following notice:

The Churches of Middleville welcome you.

Episcopal

Catholic

Methodist

I wonder whether any of the churches in the towns we passed had ever pondered the fact that the tacit rivalry of their notices relativized all the absolute claims they make for the Christian Faith. As Forsyth once remarked, a characteristic of Christianity in our century is that religious certainty has given place to "what helps."[1]

It has been the search for certainty, or, to put it in another form, the question of authority, that has been a primary cause of the Church's division. What is our authority for the gospel we confess? How does it become authoritative for us, and by what means do we believe that it has been authoritatively handed down to us? The question of authority remains at the very center of the ecumenical problem: if we could agree at this point, there would be little doubt that other questions would be relatively easy to solve. Our answer affects the form of the Church we accept, and our church polity governs the place given to the Minister. It controls whether or in what way the ordained Ministry is to be considered as itself the only, the main, an important, or an irrelevant seat of authority in the Church.

While the subject demands a full-scale treatment in itself, I think we can see that the churches have given three different answers to the problem of authority, concentrating on one or another channel of grace that has guided them through their history. All churches recognize that the authority of Jesus Christ comes to us through the Holy Spirit, but the *locus* of the Spirit is understood as being either the Church, the Bible, or the Christian conscience, and although few churches rule their life so rigidly as to make their appeal exclusively to one or the other, most

---

[1] P. T. Forsyth, *The Principle of Authority,* p. 35.

churches come down mainly at one of these points in theory and practice.

1. *The Church*

The "Catholic" branches of the Church have tended to emphasize that the final seat of authority for the Church is the Church itself. They have emphasized that the Church brought the books of the New Testament into being, that it judged and authorized the canon of Scripture. Because of the special responsibility of the Ministry in maintaining the purity of the Faith, however, these same branches of the Church have tended to interpret the "Church" as the clerical hierarchy, which controls the sacred tradition and is the special repository of the Holy Spirit's power and guidance. The tendency in such churches is for the hierarchy alone to be charged with responsibility for the Faith of the Church and interpretation of the Scriptures.

Of course, there are differences among these "Catholic" branches of the Church. There will be serious differences of emphasis between Roman Catholics, Eastern Orthodox, the Monophysite churches of Syrian Orthodoxy, and Anglo-Catholics, but they do not differ so much in the primacy they give to the Church and its hierarchy as on what they define as the true Church and the true hierarchy. If there are radical points at issue between Episcopalians and the Papacy, they arise less from the episcopal structure of the Church, than from the question whether authority is vested in the Bishop of Rome or in the bishops individually and collectively.

Our difficulty with this view of authority in the Church is basically that the Church (and its bishops) can make mistakes, and there is little way of either admitting the mistakes or of correcting them. Although it can be readily admitted that the church which puts matters into the hands of sage and wise elder statesmen will make fewer mistakes than one which seems to identify *vox populi* with *vox dei,* yet mistakes do happen, wrong interpretations are given, regrettable actions are perpetrated, accretions do occur in the course of centuries; but if you regard the hierarchy or ruling agencies of the Church as infallible, there is no way of retracing the steps other than the way of complete repentance. The difficulty of such churches to amend or revise their liturgy to meet the demands of succeeding generations is a case in point, and the changes we are witnessing in the Vatican Council are an indication not only of the difficulty involved but even more of the Holy Spirit's real work in the Roman Catholic Church today. The fundamental criticism of placing all authority in the Church itself is that too often it has ruled out the possibility of repentance for the Church itself, and this has meant that whereas the Church is called to service, she has often presented an arrogant face to the world.

Furthermore, the concentration upon the clergy as the real seat of the Holy Spirit's power has reduced the faithful to passive subservience. The Lay people of the Church are expected simply to accept what the clergy tells them, and to be in all things obedient to the voice of the Church expressed through their clerical mentors. This has minimized the responsibility of the individual Christian to be a "defender of the faith," to understand that Faith up to the limit of his human capacity, and to be at all times a witnessing apostle.

On the other hand, we should point out that this view of authority does maintain the vitally important truth that the Holy Spirit continues to guide the Church in every age. Often to the Protestant it appears to be just the opposite, for the rigid and often excessively conservative control of episcopal greybeards very frequently stifles new thought and is content to remain with ancient creeds and outdated forms rather than risk the Church to any review of its faith and practice. It must be said, however, that a view of authority that concentrates on the living Church, whether expressed through councils or papacy, is able to review its position, in contrast, for example, to the essential conservatism of those Protestants who think that the essence of good churchmanship is to reproduce within twentieth-century America the Church of the first century.

Of course, it may be better to reproduce the Church of the first century than to reproduce the Church of the twelfth century, and if we are talking about spiritual values and not the adiaphora of life and polity, we will have to go back to the Gospels. We are not able to "advance" in essentials on the Church of St. Paul's time. Much of the restorationism of the Reformation and of the sixteenth-century Puritans was a necessary recall of the Church to the Rock on which it had been founded. Nevertheless, restoration for its own sake, the literal reproduction of every iota in the New Testament Church, is fundamentally faith in a dead and not a living Christ: it is a denial of the Holy Spirit's power in the Church *today*. The view of the Church which believes every generation to be guided by the Spirit through its Ministers, or through a particular Minister, while it can be terribly abused, is nevertheless an expression of the faith that Christ can and does guide his Church today by the gift of the Spirit as he did at its inception.

2. *The Bible*

Protestants generally have appealed to the Bible as the final seat of authority in the Church. It was the classic claim of the Reformers over against the abuses they saw in the sixteenth-century papacy. Their concept of the church was to be found in the "Word of God," and as they were pushed more and more to establish authority for their actions against what had been the unquestioned authority of the Pope, the "Word" of God tended more and more to become identified with the words of the Bible itself. In reply to the "Catholic" contention that the Church authorized the canon of the Scriptures, Protestants assert that it was the gospel recorded in the Scriptures that brought the Church into being, and which continues to bring it into being. Catholic and Protestant are both right in what they assert, and wrong in what they deny, for our Lord is representative both of the Chosen People and also of the gospel to which these people witness.[2]

A position centered exclusively on Scripture, however, does deny any authority outside the pages of Scripture. The difficulties of such a position are obvious. All parts of Scripture are not literally consistent with each other, and the books of the Bible are not universally clear and unequivocal to the reader. It seems to have been the belief of the first Reformers that as soon as the words of the Scriptures became available to everybody through the use of the vernacular, their claims would be vindicated and the unity of the Church would be reasserted as a kind of *consensus fidelium universalis*. They were wrong. Our different forms of the Church and of Christian doctrine are the result of sincere differences of interpretation which all claim to be biblically based. Each denomination of Christians has found it necessary to set its own standards of authority to control "irresponsible" interpretation of the Scriptures — either a consensus of scholarship (which appears to be the answer of moderate liberalism), the ancient creeds and Reformation confessions (the answer of ortho-

[2] *Supra,* Chapter III.

dox Lutheranism and Calvinism), the strict letter of a particular version of the Bible (as in fundamentalism), or the individual conscience (as in the more extreme forms of liberalism). It is clear that where there is no effective ecclesiastical discipline, reliance upon Scripture alone tends to produce either rigid adherence to the letter as in fundamentalism, or else disappears entirely in the complete relativism of private interpretation.

At the same time we must assert that there can be no concept of authority in the Christian Church which does not start from the truths that the Scriptures proclaim and the facts about Jesus Christ that they expound. Because the Christian Faith is founded in the events of a specific historical situation, it must find its basis, and to some measure its authority, in the historical record of those events.

3. *Individual Enlightenment*

In one sense this is simply the private interpretation which we have referred to above, but in its best expression what we have in mind here is not quite the same as the private interpretation of an individual. We are thinking of the guidance of the individual by the Holy Spirit, which probably found its best expression in some of the more spiritual radicals of the Reformation and in early Quakerism. There is a good example of this in Margaret Fell's description of her own conversion by George Fox in Ulverston Church. She described how George Fox had stood up in the church and had declared that Christ was the Light of the world who lighted every man, "And then he went on and opened the Scriptures and said, 'The Scriptures were the prophet's words, and Christ's and the apostles' words, and what, as they spoke, they enjoyed and possessed, and had it from the Lord': and said, 'then what had any to do with the Scriptures, but as they came to the Spirit that gave them forth? You will say, Christ saith this, and the apostles say this; but what canst thou say? Art thou a child of Light, and hast thou walked in the Light, and what thou speakest, is it inwardly from God? etc. This opened me so," declared Margaret Fell, "that it cut me to the heart; and then I saw clearly we were all wrong."[3]

What George Fox was speaking about was not simply the will

---

[3] Margaret Fell's account of her conversion, quoted by Howard Brinton, *Friends for 300 Years* (London: Allen & Unwin, 1953), pp. 15f.

of an individual to judge matters as he pleased, but the inner promptings of God's Spirit, informed, instructed, and corrected by that which he found in Christ and in the prophets and apostles.

It is clear, however, that even with the sincerity of the early Quakers, this subjective view of authority reduces Christianity to a number of individually held interpretations that could very well be contradictory. Whose "inner light" is ultimately to be preferred against another's? It was a question that was soon to trouble the movement, as in the case of poor James Naylor.[4] Even if I try to be open to God's Spirit, I may mistake his voice, I may misinterpret his will — in short, I can be wrong. Indeed, when the interpretation of the individual becomes the highest form of authority, the doctrine of the inner light very soon develops contradiction, for its inherent subjectivity produces two forms of individualism that are about as far from each other religiously as they can be: pietism, which reduces the Holy Spirit to religious "feelings," and rationalism, which virtually gives priority to reason.

At the same time we must recognize that no view of authority in the Church can ignore the place of the Holy Spirit within the individual Christian without taking away his responsibility before God. Even within the most authoritarian church or in accepting the most literal interpretation of Scripture, I cannot evade the fact that I have to make a choice that is implicit if not actual. Finally *I* must decide, and the responsibility for having made the choice is properly my own.

Here then is our dilemma in the question of authority in the Church. The Holy Spirit works through each of these channels of grace — the Church, the Scriptures, and the individual Christian — and the "Word" to which he witnesses in each is the same living Word of God in Jesus Christ. We cannot separate them, or rely upon one to the exclusion of the others, because it is the

---

[4] James Naylor (1618-60), an early Quaker who almost rivalled George Fox in influence during the first years of the movement. However, in 1656 he allowed himself to be persuaded by some of his more unbalanced women disciples into an entry into Bristol that closely parallelled our Lord's entry into Jerusalem. His doctrine of the "inner light" permitted him to identify rather too closely his own inner light and the spirit that was in Jesus. He was convicted of blasphemy by Parliament and viciously punished.

same Christ who speaks through them all. It has been seen that even in denominations which pride themselves most on being free from "tradition," we can make no clear distinction between *the* tradition (the gospel) as we received it in the historical record (the Scriptures) and as it is interpreted, lived, and experienced through the faith of the Church. Neither can we clearly separate the decision of the individual from the mind of the church community in which he lives and worships. Somehow the channels by which the authority of the Holy Spirit comes to us have to be seen not in opposition to each other, but as complementary witnesses to the one Word of God.

II

AUTHORITY AND CHRISTIAN DIVISION: TOWARDS AN ANSWER

We must start with the premise that final authority for the Christian and for the Church is in the living will of Christ, i.e., what our Lord wants us to do here and now. The Holy Spirit does, however, come to us by several channels. In particular, Christ's will does become manifest to us through the pages of Scripture, through the witness of the Church in time and space, and in the innermost heart of a Christian as he faces the truth in Christ and the truth about himself. It is not a different Spirit or a different Christ that speaks to us through these witnesses, but it is the same Word of God that we see manifested in the gospel story, and the answer to our problem of authority is therefore not to set off Bible against Church, or Church against a Christian's conscience, but to discover their proper relationship. We have to remember that in each case God risks his truth to earthen vessels, and because the vessels are earthen, Church, Scripture and the Christian conscience come under the judgment of the Living Word that they possess, and by which in turn they must be possessed. If we are seeking the truth that is to be revealed by this living, contemporary Christ, then we are not primarily concerned with the defence of traditional standpoints. When Scripture and the Christian conscience recognize that the gospel is Christ himself, they can and do judge the failures and the sins of the Church, because they stand under the judgment themselves. This was Luther's position. It was not the principle of *sola scriptura,* but the reality of the living Word that spoke *through*

Scripture and to which the Spirit in Luther's heart responded. When the Church and the Christian conscience are informed by the truth that is in the Living Christ, they can judge the letter of Scripture, as in fact they have on the issue of fundamentalism. But equally when it is clear from the Scriptures and from the history of the Church that my personal whims and prejudices are being judged by Christ, I must be ready to listen and to accept the judgment.

This leaves a number of questions still uncertain. Can the "Church" ever be equated with a single denomination or is it best represented either by its scholars, its Ministry, or the *consensus fidelium?* Is there such a thing as "invincible prejudice," where an individual persuades himself that he has the truth of Christ when in fact he is maintaining his own stubbornness? How are we to discover the Word of God that is contained in Scripture within and yet beyond the text? There is no easy answer to these questions, and perhaps there will never be an infallible answer to them within our human situation. The essential fact which we must keep in the forefront of our thinking is that we are concerned to discover the contemporary will of Christ for his Church in its present situation.

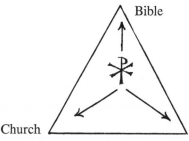

Perhaps the problem may be illustrated in the above diagram in which the Chi-Rho may represent our Lord in his risen power. The Holy Spirit comes to us through the Bible, the Church, and through the Holy Spirit in the Christian soul. When the Church has to make a decision affecting its faith or morals, it must go first of all to the Scriptures, but it has other witnesses to the Spirit of its Lord — the expressed interpretation of the Faith in the fathers, the creeds and confessions, in life of piety and worship, and it also has the thought of the Church through its thinkers and scholars and the experience of the faithful here and now. The Church cannot afford to ignore the understanding of Christ in past ages, any more than it can ignore the scriptural record or the contemporary witness of its own inner life: as Forsyth pointed out, if you are going to decide these matters by simply counting noses, then "the real spiritual majority are the dead."[5]

However (and I hope this is not simply Protestant prejudice), there is a certain primacy which belongs properly to the Bible which must be recognized. It is not the case, as it has been some-times represented, that the letter of Scripture is infallible where Church and conscience are not, but Scripture has the primacy because of the historical facts on which our Christian Faith is founded. This we cannot escape. The Church may have weighed the evidence and judged the truth of the scriptural writings and made its decision in the selection of the canon, but presumably it judged those writings for their truth in respect to the gospel. Insofar as the present books of the New Testament represent the reflection of the Church, they represent not merely factual rec-ord but also the judgment of the early Church about the *meaning* of that record. When we read the New Testament writings, we are brought face to face not only with our Lord's earthy life, but also with the meaning of that life as it was understood by the early Church under the guidance of his Spirit, and we are forced to realize what decision the Church made upon that life. This gives the New Testament a unique authority for the Christian and for the Church in every age, for in the first centuries of the Church's existence these were the writings that the Church believed did most justice to what it knew and had experienced of the liv-ing truth in Christ.

The Scriptures are in this sense primary. They are the start-ing-point. They provide the fixed point of reference to which we may constantly turn in order to get our standards adjusted. But they do not represent the place where we are to settle forever, for their times are not our times; they do not stand at precisely the point where we stand, neither do they trace the way by which we have reached this point in the twentieth century. We need other witnesses — those from church history, those from the Church as our great contemporary, and the "Amen" from our own heart. To

<hr>

[5] *The Principle of Authority,* p. 10.

the extent that they are all guided and instructed by the Holy Spirit, they all witness to the one Christ.

Perhaps the Church will never completely resolve the problem of authority, and possibly we are not intended to in this life, for it would seem that if we were assured of an absolute certainty in the Faith, there would be little need for personal faith. Perhaps the truth for the Church on earth is to be found not in the finding but in the quest. In this quest, however, it is essential not to confuse the channels of God's grace with that grace itself, but to remember that Christ is the Head of the Church and its only final Authority. Other institutions and instruments may be channels of his grace to us, but they are important only as they reflect his will, and if they can do that in any measure, they are in agreement and not in opposition to each other.

What then is the relationship between Scripture, Church, and the Christian conscience? For me, it has to be put in some such statement as the following: final authority is to be found in the living Christ (the Word of God), as revealed first in the historic record (the Bible), to whom the faithful in all generations (the Church) bear their historic witness, and to whom in the gift of the Holy Spirit the Christian gives the assent of faith.

What certainty is there in this? The answer must be in the form of a paradox — none at all, but also all you need.

Certainty of the kind known to science is assuredly not possible. Even if there could be universal agreement on what is meant by the terms 'Church,' 'Scripture', and 'Holy Spirit', there would still be areas of choice and therefore of doubt. The individual or the church making its ethical or doctrinal decisions is still forced to weigh not the relative merits of two practical alternatives, but the relative truthfulness and faithfulness of more than one reputable witness. Such a formula keeps squarely upon those who make the decision, whether Church or individual, the responsibility to weigh the issues up to the limit of their spiritual capacities. The onus of decision is on us. That is why we need Ministers to lead us and persuade us and not spiritual directors to tell us. For the Minister is an instrument of God's Word, an interpreter of the Scriptures and of the witness of the Church. A Minister should never presume to tell *you* what God wants of you in your situation, but he can help you to reach your decision: he can explain what the Bible says, he can describe what the Church has said through its thinkers and done through its saints, he can help you to see what the Spirit of Christ would have us do today. He can show you that the Church can help you stand on your own two feet before God; it will surround you with its Faith and its prayers, but it will never usurp your decision.

And this is all the certainty you need to make the response of faith. Absolute certainty in this life would remove the need for faith. But if God had felt it necessary to give his servants the kind of certainty that made faith unnecessary, would he be the God and Father who risked sending Jesus Christ into the world to call forth a free response from us? Surely it is closer to the God we see revealed in Jesus Christ that he would expect us to trust, and not to trace the proofs. In the last resort there is no proof or certainty for the Christian or for the Church other than to put faith in this kind of God shown to us in Jesus. Could God have it otherwise without detracting from his own nature?

The foundation for the authority that we claim, and that which defines its character, is *Christ made contemporary*. The answers are not to be found in any infallible form of the Church, any infallible hierarchy; nor are they to be found in any infallible book of answers, whether we are tempted to turn to the literal text of the Bible or to the canons of the *Codex Juris Canonici*. We are sent back at every point to the historic figure of our Lord himself, so that through the *magnalia christi* of the Scriptures and church history he may become our Great Contemporary.

This subject of authority may appear to be a long way from our main interest in the Ministry of the Church, but it is important at this point because throughout long periods of church history the clergy have claimed special powers and exercised special functions in respect to it. "The confusion in modern Christendom about the meaning of the ministry," wrote H. Richard Niebuhr, "makes itself evident in uncertainty about pastoral authority as well as in the vagueness present in thought about pastoral functions."[6] The judgment is just, and if we are not going to make the confusion worse we have to decide whether, or in what sense, the Ministry may be regarded as a special vehicle of authority in the Church.

We shall come to the heart of this if we consider the Minister's particular responsibility in proclaiming "the contemporary Christ." This is where the Minister must present his credentials.

[6] *The Purpose of the Church and Its Ministry,* pp. 72f.

At this point, however, we must note that to bear authority is not only a matter of carrying the right credentials, but it also has a good deal to do with the way in which the credentials are borne and their authority exercised. If, in the words of St. Paul, we are ambassadors for Christ, then the way in which His authority is exercised has a very special relationship to the kind of credentials that are presented, and it is to this that we now turn.

III

A Historical Interlude

Any reader who is not too interested in history may pass directly to the fourth section of this chapter, and I promise that he will lose nothing more than an illustration of the argument.

What is hypocrisy? We sometimes forget that those who conducted Inquisitions were "Christians," people who were undoubtedly sincere in their faith, and saw nothing inconsistent in what they were doing. As I have said elsewhere, "Every Inquisition that has been launched has been promoted on the assumption of the Church's God-given authority."[7] This fact ought to be given far more attention than it has had in the past and by theologians as well as historians, for it should raise some radical questions about the nature of the authority that the Church claims from her Lord.

The usual argument in Church history seems to have run something like this: Christ has given absolute authority to the Church (sometimes identified with the clerical hierarchy) through St. Peter (Matt. 16:17-20, cf. 18:15-19). Therefore to disobey the Church is to disobey the will of Christ, and to disobey Christ is to disobey God. But God has also given power to civil rulers for the punishment of those who do wrong and the reward of those who do right (I Pet. 2:13-14), and hence Christian rulers have a special responsibility to maintain the ethical and doctrinal standards set up by the Church and to punish anything contrary to these standards in belief and behavior. The Church has defined what is punishable, and the State could be relied upon to do the rest, whether the sin is that of heresy or immorality.

Historians have recognized that this chain of logic was broken

---

[7] *An Apologeticall Narration* (Boston and Philadelphia: United Church Press, 1963), p. 124.

first in the radical groups of the Reformation by their insistence upon the separation of Church and State. Liberty of conscience was given a theological basis by such radicals as the Anabaptists of the Reformation, the Separatists, Roger Williams, or the Independents of Cromwell's army, so that with the arrival of scientific rationalism at the end of the seventeenth century it was able to take root and flourish. Inquisitions became *demodé*.

We have often not recognized, however, that although the new doctrine of the separation of Church and State cut the chain of logic that produced religious intolerance, it often left the Church with its concept of authority intact. While it is clear that opinion is divided, for example, in the Roman Catholic Church on the issue of religious liberty and its limitations,[8] as recently as 1948 a responsible Roman Catholic writer could write the following:

> The Catholic Church being convinced, by reason of her divine prerogatives, that she is the one true Church, claims for herself alone the right to freedom, for this right may only be expressed by truth, and never by error. Where the other religions are concerned, she will not take up the sword against them, but she will ask that by lawful means, worthy of the human creature, they shall not be allowed to propagate false doctrines. Consequently, in a State where the majority of the people are Catholic, the Church asks that error should not be accorded a legal existence, and that, if religious minorities exist, they shall have a *de facto* existence only, not the opportunity of spreading their beliefs. Where material circumstances — whether the hostility of a Government or the numerical strength of the Dissenting factions — do not allow of this principle's being applied in its entirety, the Church requires that she shall have all possible concessions, confining herself to accepting as the least of all evils the *de jure* toleration of other forms of worship. In other countries the Catholics are obliged to ask for full liberty for all, resigning themselves to living together where they alone had the right to live. The Church does not in this way give up her thesis, which remains the

---

[8] See A. F. Carrillo de Albornoz, *Roman Catholicism and Religious Liberty* (Geneva: World Council of Churches, 1959).

most imperative of all laws, but adapts herself to the hypothesis, which must be taken into account on the material plane.[9]

In view of the remarkable change in the attitudes of the Roman Catholic Church in many parts of the world, it would be unfair to regard the above as its official position. Even before the Second Vatican Council the situation was ambiguous. I cite the above passage not to attack Roman Catholicism, but in order to show that far more basic than the relation between Church and State is the very nature of the authority which the Church claims she has from Jesus Christ. You may destroy the legal grounds for persecution or suppression by cutting the authority of the Church from the power of the State, but if the nature of that authority remains coercive in spirit, you have not destroyed the persecuting heart.

Here I would direct attention to the much-abused Puritans who wrestled with this problem. To Americans who have never compared the story of religious intolerance in New England with the massive proportions of persecution and inquisition in Europe, it may come as a shock to hear the Puritans commended. The issue of the nature of authority in the Church came to a head in the debates within the Westminster Assembly in 1644 between the Puritans of Presbyterian persuasion and the Puritans of Congregational views, who were the English counterparts of the New England divines. These latter, together with their co-religionists in New England, insisted that there were two different kinds of authority: "magisterial" authority based upon force, which is the prerogative of the State, and "ministerial" authority based upon persuasion in the gospel, which is appropriate in the Church. "Church government," wrote John Cotton on one occasion, "is not an authority but a ministry."[10]

Now let it be admitted that it was remarkable what they sometimes tried to pack into that concept of "ministerial" authority. The Minister of a Puritan congregation in New England could become as much of an autocrat as any English prelate; through the Eldership the "democratic" tendencies of the congregation

---

[9] Fr. F. Cavalli, S. J., in *La Civilta Cattolica,* April 3, 1948, as quoted in *The British Weekly,* June 3, 1948.

[10] In his "Foreword from New England" to John Norton's *Responsio* (1648), as in *The Answer* (a translation of the *Responsio,* by Douglas Horton; Cambridge, Mass.: Belknap Press, 1958), p. 15.

were controlled, and it has been pointed out that social pressures might be employed to do what more direct pressures achieved in Europe.[11] On American soil they even went back on their own principle and used the State to persecute out of existence Separatists like Roger Williams, Baptists like John Clark, and Quakers like Mary Fisher and Ann Austin, although it should be noted that it was often against the protests of their brethren in England.[12] Nevertheless, the question has been raised — what is the kind of authority that is appropriate to the Church? — and although in giving their answer they allowed themselves all sorts of latitude, often straining at a bishop but swallowing a Cotton, yet the English Independents insisted that to be true to the gospel the only authority which the Church could properly claim was "ministerial" in its operation and in its intention. To use a phrase which occurs often in their writings, the government of the Church must be "according to the mind of Christ," and the English wing of the movement very soon began to see that it was not according to the mind of Christ that people should be persecuted for their conscientious beliefs.[13] As one of their members in the Westminster Assembly wrote, "The only way the Church hath to keep downe errors or heresies is spirituall," for the "vertue of spiritual power works not upon the outward man but by its prevailing upon conscience."[14]

IV

THE AUTHORITY OF THE SPIRIT

Throughout a good part of church history the Church has argued that because Christ gave his authority to the Church, it therefore has the right to enforce its own will over all others. With the certainty of our Lord's own authority to justify it and with a doctrine of infallibility to back it, the Church conducted crusades against Moslems and Waldensians, initiated inquisitions

[11] Perry Miller, *Orthodoxy in Massachusetts,* 1630-1650 (new ed., Boston: Beacon Press, 1959), p. 192.

[12] See the quotation from Katherine Chidley's *The Justification of the Independent Churches of Christ, ibid.,* p. 279; the protests from Cromwell's army, Sir Henry Vane, and Sir Richard Saltonstall, *ibid.,* pp. 280ff.

[13] This issue is traced in the historical Introduction to *An Apologeticall Narration,* ch. v.

[14] Jeremiah Burroughes, *Irenicum* (1646), p. 42.

and witch hunts, sanctioned the execution of heretics and reformers, and gave its blessing to "holy wars." We must emphasize that it did all this with a clear conscience, because its
leaders profoundly believed that the Church had been given absolute authority by Jesus Christ, and hence by God himself. All its
actions were based upon that.

The Church *is* given authority by Jesus Christ. We must assert
that just as firmly as any medieval pope, but we must also go
on to emphasize that Jesus Christ *is* the Authority — his nature
determines the nature of the authority entrusted to his Church,
his character determines its character, his Spirit defines its spirit.
To exercise the authority of Christ in a way that is entirely contrary to the Spirit revealed in the Jesus of the Gospels, is to
relinquish the very authority that the Church claims. To use
force as the Church has through the centuries, to coerce men
by torturing their bodies or by putting overt pressures on their
minds and spirits, is repugnant to the mind of Christ as revealed
in the New Testament, and it is a denial of the Creator who
respects the dignity of men in his creation as responsible persons.
To use such means to maintain authority is a flat denial of the
authority which the Church claims she received from Jesus
Christ. At this point the Church as an institution in history has
often made herself close to Antichrist. We must therefore establish this ecclesiological axiom, that *the authority given by
Jesus Christ to his Church is his authority only as it is exercised
in accordance with his revealed Spirit.*[15] Any attempt to enforce
the will of the Church upon men by means that are contrary to
the Spirit of Jesus the man, is contrary to the mind of Jesus the
Christ.

We can see that at the heart of our ecclesiology there is Christology, and at the heart of this there is theology. The nature of
the Church is determined by the nature of its authority, the nature of its authority is determined by the character of Christ
himself, and the nature of the One whom we recognize as the
Christ is determined by the very character of God himself. All
questions concerning the Church are at root theological. It
makes an almost infinite amount of difference whether one's concept of God is derived from that of Almighty Power or from that
of Invincible Love.

[15] Cf. *An Apologeticall Narration* (1963), p. 119.

If once the principle could be established that the Church is only true to its authority as this is used in conformity with the Spirit of Jesus, then it could revolutionize our church relationships.

(a) *It would govern our approach to the world.* The Church can claim no preferential treatment from the world, nor does its Christ-given vocation provide it with any occasion for arrogance. It is given to the world as a servant, to lead humanity into the service of its Lord and King. The authority is his, and its quality is the quality of the One who gives it. The disciples of Jesus Christ are to be recognized by the fruits of his Spirit within them, and when we consider the shameful acts of "Christian" history, there is little room in our institutional churches for anything but penitence. When we reflect upon the extent to which, since the time of Constantine, the sword has been a major weapon of evangelism, when we think of the ways in which the Church has used power pressures to force men into the Faith, thereby robbing them of the dignity that their Creator gave them, there is no place for pride. Although swords and faggots have gone out of fashion as the instruments of church extension, has the Church yet given up the mentality that would seek to force people to conform to its teachings, or do we not tacitly still pressure people into a commitment that they do not feel and which we do not exemplify? As Martin Buber realized, to bludgeon a person into some sort of theistic belief is not to bring him face to face with the living God of whom the Bible speaks, but it is to make him acknowledge an idol created by our own reason.[16] To pressure a human being by the sales techniques of psychological propaganda, to try to buy him by social services, to overwhelm him by the extent of our technical know-how, to win his allegiance to "our God," in fact, by any means that prevents him from standing before God as the responsible person that God created him to be, is fundamentally to be working against the God and Father of our Lord Jesus Christ who created this man in his own image. In our conversation with adherents of other religions and of no religion, the disciple of Jesus Christ must be prepared to listen and to face the truth from whatever source, for this attitude of openness alone will recognize the other's dignity as a created

[16] *Eclipse of God* (New York: Harper, 1957), pp. 4ff.

child of God, this alone will do justice to the God who is his Creator.

That is not to say that a Christian should be willing to place Christ somewhere in the general pantheon of human thought. We claim nothing for the Church or for ourselves, but we can and do claim everything for our Lord. His authority must be absolute over the Christian, but because his authority is absolute, Christians cannot treat those of other faiths in a way that denies our Lord's own Spirit. Perhaps what I am saying is that before the Church can be an apostle, it must show itself to be a disciple — a follower.

(b) *It would influence our ecumenical relationships.* The churches are still in rivalry one against the other. We use the ecumenical jargon that is in vogue, but one suspects that in this case "à la mode" means simply adding ecumenical ice cream to the old confessional apple pie. When a denominational executive wants to find reasons for planting one of his own churches where there may be already a plethora of churches, he will find them, and be able to express them in an impeccable ecumenical accent.[17] Like one of the distinguished members of the fallen angels, we can

> . . . *make the worse appear*
> *The better reason, to perplex and dash*
> *Maturest Counsels* . . .[18]

"Authorities" within the Church that usurp the authority of Jesus Christ can always find ways of justifying their will instead of his will, which lead into actions that are basically contrary to his Spirit. The odd thing about the denominations is that our rivalry is not for the things that count in the gospel — we do not rival each other in demonstrating the lòve that was in our Lord. We follow the fashions often because it is expedient to follow the fashions, and not because we have been motivated by Christian concern. To put the matter sharply, if I were an American Negro I would be tempted to be extremely cynical about the way in

---

[17] I am tempted to cite illustrations. A prize example is the description by one denomination of its mission to an area of the country already well-stocked with other Protestant churches. It is asserted that "from the start that mission has been confessional, it has been evangelical, it has been ecumenical." You *can* have your cake and eat it!

[18] Belial in Milton's *Paradise Lost.*

which denominations are now crowding onto the civil rights bandwagon, just as I am tempted to be sceptical about those who are crowding the cab of the Protestant-Catholic "dialogue" express train. Brother, where were you before President Kennedy and Pope John XXIII came along? Let us be honest, how far are the ethical concerns that occupy the churches today genuine concerns of the members, or to what extent are they sponsored by those who have a cold and calculating eye on the new trends of this age? I ask to be informed — I do not imply a judgment. But I do know that only when the denominations try to outdo each other in supporting the unpopular causes of the gospel, only when the front pages of our denominational magazines publicize what *other* churches have done, will they begin to be worthy of the name of Christ. By that time, however, they will be less anxious to claim any worthiness. "Why callest thou me good?"

Let me add a footnote to this which has more specific bearing upon the institutional forms of the ecumenical movement itself. In 1957 the North American Conference on Faith and Order at Oberlin called for "an ongoing study of the ecclesiological significance of local, state, and national councils of churches," but the subject had been a live one in certain executive circles of the World Council of Churches for some time, inspired in part by the fact that Roman Catholic theologians had given far more attention to it than Protestants or Orthodox. It appears that it had not even occurred to those working within the institutional forms of the ecumenical movement to ask how these forms were related to the doctrine of the Church, or whether there was any doctrine of the Church that could include them without either changing itself or changing them.

We now have the report of the commission that has studied this subject, and although it was not allocated a particular section at Montreal, it was very much in the minds of some of the participants. There was the niggling suspicion that although it may be entirely proper to ask questions about the "ecclesiological significance of councils of churches," we might be asking the right question for the wrong reasons. Were we trying to invest the conciliar forms of ecumenism, which we had come to trust and respect, with new status and authority? — for it must be realized that there is nothing of ecclesiological significance that does not carry with it something of the Church's divinely-given authority. Is it not significant that up to this point this question had *not* been asked, and that the councils of churches had been content to *serve* the churches? The strange fact about the modern ecumenical movement is this, that in this service such organizations as the World Council of Churches have gained an increasing place in the thinking of many people about the Church, so that most Protestants, and I think some Orthodox, in thinking about the Church — even their own church — relate themselves in some may to the W.C.C. The W.C.C. through its *service* has become an instrument of the Holy Spirit that the denominations cannot ignore — it speaks to us with an authority that is unlike "that of the scribes." If I question the present tendency to fit the W.C.C. and other councils into a doctrine of the Church, it is not because either the doctrine of the Church or the agencies of the ecumenical movement are unimportant — quite the reverse — but first, because I think it would imply a doctrine of the Church more static than the Spirit will have the Church to be; and secondly, because the New Testament seems to be telling us that the only ecclesiological authority that is of any significance is that which expresses itself through service; unselfconscious service, at that.

(c) *It would change our attitude to questions of church order and polity.* The basic issue for the denominational discussion is not whether Presbyterianism balances the principles of leadership and popular control more nicely than Episcopacy and Congregationalism, or whether Congregationalism is more "democratic," or whether Episcopacy is more efficient or more historic than the other two forms of order. The basic issue is to ask what is the *nature* of the authority that is exercised through the church courts of Presbyterianism, the bishops of Episcopalianism, or the assemblies of Congregationalism. In relating these three historic forms of polity to each other, we can no longer settle the matter by the length of the New Testament proof texts that one may present over another; we have to ask, how can we best maintain the authority of the living Christ in his Church? How can we be sure that the authority with which the Church speaks to its own members comes from persuasion in the gospel, "the mind of Christ," and is not ultimately based on sheer force? Our Lord's concern for his people is pastoral, and I am convinced that those Puritans had a true insight into the gospel when they insisted that the power of the Keys — its final authority — was given to the Church with a pastoral intent. The power of excommunication, that final exercise of spiritual authority, was to be put within the context of the Church's ministry, which was directed as much towards the reclaiming of the lost member as to the maintenance of the Church's own purity. This was the reason why some of them refused to give this power to any but the local church where the Word and Sacraments ordered the Church's life.[19] To their contemporaries they may have appeared to underestimate the authority of the Church in its wider aspects, but they were surely right to insist that this august responsibility is never to be divorced from the sacramental fellowship in which the rule of the Word of God is paramount. Although today we recognize the claims of the Church Universal upon us all, this principle remains: we are concerned not with enforcing the will of ecclesiastical administration, but with establishing the rule of Christ. Church discipline must be directed to the reclamation of the errant and the extension of Christ's kingdom. Presbyteries, bishops, and congregational assemblies may all be valid ways in which the Church tries to discover the mind of Christ, but they are valid only as they rest in the last resort not on the power inherent in the ecclesiastical structure but on the Spirit of the Shepherd. They must be pastoral in intent and method, for to coerce God's people by open or secret pressures contradicts the Spirit of Christ at the very heart of his body, the Church.

The reaction of many executively-minded people will be to throw up their hands in holy horror, for they will at once demand to know how on earth we could expect to get anything done in the Church! Let me reply first by saying that such a view of authority ought not to exclude good administration, for there are many decisions in the Church's life where practical efficiency can be, and indeed, should be the primary consideration: there is nothing in the New Testament to suggest that our Lord equates goodness with inefficiency. I am speaking of the spiritual authority which should be at the very heart of the Church's life, and which affects its fundamental concern about the Faith and those to whom the Faith is given. Here the concern must be pastoral, and any question of confusing these matters with a call to efficiency is irrelevant and dangerous. At the pastoral center of the Church's life the Spirit of Jesus Christ must rule, and God's concern for the individual soul must be supreme. Whether it is

---

[19] Cf. *An Apologeticall Narration* (1963), pp. 118-125.

administered through presbyterian, congregational, or episcopal forms of authority, it must in essence remain pastoral — the *episcopē* of the New Testament, and not the episcopate of later prelacy. To argue that such a view of authority is impractical or unworkable is not an option within the Church of Jesus Christ, for that would be the equivalent of declaring our lack of faith in the Spirit of our Lord.

(d) *It reveals a Minister's place in the Church*. All that we have said hitherto comes to its focus in the exercise of Ministry. The uncertainty of the Ministry about its authority in these days probably comes about because we are really looking for authority of the wrong sort. As Richard Niebuhr says, the priest of the past received his authority from the institution and from the functions that he alone was qualified to perform,[20] the preacher received his authority from the institution of the preached Word and from the function that he was qualified to perform, and similarly the evangelist gained his authority from his own unique *charisma* and from its effectiveness. In each case the authority sets the man apart and gives a certain kind of status.

It appears that the modern Minister is looking for that kind of public image — that little something that he can do which others cannot, that specialization which sets him apart from others, but which causes them to turn to him for professional help. We seek a public image to describe the qualifications of the Ministry, whether we find it in the concept of Family Counselor, Ecclesiastical Administrator, Public Orator, or Pastoral Director. What is this but saying that we seek to establish status? Is our authority in the Ministry basically justified by our professional competence in certain arts or sciences? Is the search for a valid public image simply a search to justify our respected position in society? What if the uniqueness of the Minister is not to stress the professional qualifications that make him different from the rest of the Church's members, but the ordination that emphasizes the unity of the Church in a common mission? If ordination represents to the Church the Church's own ministry, then the uniqueness of the Minister is to be sought not in a separate public image from that of the Church, but by becoming completely identified with the mission of his congregation.

This reveals the kind of authority that he will have. The pas-

---

[20] *The Purpose of the Church·and Its Ministry*, p. 72.

tor's authority rests upon the Holy Spirit, which through preaching, pastoral concern, administration, prayer, and sacraments
continually persuades men in terms of the gospel, and in doing
so reminds the Church of the character of the universal mission
to which it is committed in this world. The inclusive concept
must be pastoral and not professional, a constant concern for the
spiritual growth of every member, a reflection of and an exposition on the reconciling ministry of the Great Shepherd who
gave his life for the sheep. Some time ago I came upon a pa-
sage from Dietrich Bonhoeffer's *Life Together,* in which he discusses a Minister's authority in precisely these terms. It is written
so much to the point that I quote it in full:

> Jesus made authority in the fellowship dependent upon
> brotherly service. Genuine spiritual authority is to be found
> only where the ministry of hearing, helping, bearing, and
> proclaiming is carried out. Every cult of personality that
> emphasizes the distinguished qualities, virtues, and talents
> of another person, even although these be of an altogether
> spiritual nature, is worldly and has no place in the Chris-
> tian community; indeed, it poisons the Christian community.
> The desire we so often hear expressed for "episcopal figures,"
> "priestly men," "authoritative personalities," springs fre-
> quently enough from a spiritually sick need for the admira-
> tion of men, for the establishment of visible human author-
> ity, because the genuine authority of service appears to be
> so unimpressive. There is nothing that so sharply contra-
> dicts such a desire as the New Testament itself in its descrip-
> tion of a bishop (I Tim. 3:1ff.). One finds there nothing
> whatsoever with respect to worldly charm and the brilliant
> attributes of a spiritual personality. The bishop is the sim-
> ple, faithful man, sound in faith and life, who rightly dis-
> charges his duties to the Church. His authority lies in the
> exercise of his ministry. In the man himself there is noth-
> ing to admire.
>
> Ultimately, this hankering for false authority has at its
> root a desire to re-establish some sort of immediacy, a de-
> pendence upon human beings in the Church. Genuine au-
> thority knows that all immediacy is especially baneful in
> matters of authority. Genuine authority realizes that it can
> exist only in the service of Him who alone has authority.

Genuine authority knows that it is bound in the strictest sense by the saying of Jesus: "One is your Master, even Christ; and all ye are brethren" (Matt. 23:8). The Church does not need brilliant personalities but faithful servants of Jesus and the brethren. Not in the former but in the latter is the lack. The Church will place its confidence only in the simple servant of the Word of Jesus Christ because it knows that then it will be guided, not according to human wisdom and human conceit, but by the Word of the Good Shepherd.[21]

That says it. You will see what Bonhoeffer implies about the question of Ministerial status. How irrelevant and almost blasphemous that question becomes when we recognize from Whom we receive our authority as Ministers. If Ministers are called, as they are, to leadership within the Church, it can only be leadership in what it means to "put yourself last," for that is the only kind of leadership that is recognized in the Kingdom of God. No subject can be greater than his King.

Ministerial authority is demonstrated not only in what a Minister says but also in the way he says it and acts it, for it is not only a matter of the credentials we carry, but the credentials are finally proved by the manner in which we conduct the embassy. The only kind of ambassador whose credentials are recognized by the king is the one who reflects the spirit and purpose of the kingdom; and other forms of recognition are unimportant. This is the kind of commitment and leadership that the Church needs, and as Bonhoeffer points out, the yearning after any other kind is really lack of faith — not simply our lack of personal faith, but something much more serious, lack of faith in Jesus Christ.

The question of spiritual authority in the Church may seem to be a long way from any serious discussion of the modern Minister, and yet no subject is more central to the ecumenical necessities of our time and to the Minister's understanding of his own place in the Church. The failure of the churches to understand the essentially ethical character of the authority they wield in the name of Christ may be traced to the weakness of their hold on the doctrine of the Holy Spirit. The character of the Holy Spirit in the Church cannot be different from that of the risen Christ, and it is clear that any claim to the Spirit that pursues its objectives by means of torture, fire, and sword must be false.

[21] *Life Together* (New York: Macmillan, 1954), pp. 108f.

It is equally false in any who claim the exclusive possession of the Holy Spirit and deny it in others who sincerely profess the name of Jesus Christ.

It is a sombre thought that the Church has probably suffered more from false orthodoxy than it has from the vagaries of Socinus and his followers, for if the latter has stifled evangelical zeal and produced sterile rationalism, the former has produced a zeal which bears all the marks of Antichrist. Whatever else the trinitarian position should mean, it cannot mean that the Holy Spirit is different in character or essence from the Spirit which descended upon our Lord. Ministers are given to the Church to lead its members in the ways of this Spirit.

Therefore the authority of a Minister must be essentially *ministerial,* i.e., it must take its character from the Spirit that was in Jesus, to which the Holy Spirit within the Church testifies, and which he seeks to exemplify in us. This seems to be the point that was made by Canon Phythian-Adams when he pleaded that in thinking about the Ministry, "What matters supremely in the Gospel is that *our mutual personal relationships should be those of love,* at whatever cost to ourselves in humiliation, mortification, and longsuffering. But," he added sadly, "this does not simply occur to most of us at all."[22] Ministry means *ministry.* Undoubtedly professional competence, historical continuity, and doctrinal orthodoxy are important, and in some measure necessary to a Minister in fulfillment of his vocation, but his authority as a Minister can come only from the source of all authority, and must bear the indelible stamp of Christ's character. A Minister's authority must be judged by its fruits; and the fruits are the fruits of the Spirit.

[22] *The Way of At-one-ment,* p. 97.

chapter seven

The Historic Ministry

I

APOSTOLIC SUCCESSION

What are a Minister's basic credentials? We have been skating around this subject for a long time, but one almost apologizes for introducing it because it may suggest an unhealthy concern in the clergy to validate their own position. Yet we must give the subject some attention.

All Christian churches believe in apostolic succession. They may very well differ about the various forms in which apostolic succession is held, but without historical continuity beween the churches of the twentieth century and the church of the apostles it is impossible to be part of the Christian Church. Our gospel is a historical gospel; that is, it is based on events that were enacted in history by a historical person, and it has been conveyed to us through the ages of history by the agency of people and things that lived and existed in history. Saints, prophets, and mystics have sometimes thrown new light upon our understanding of that gospel, but their inspired thoughts were not new revelations but insights into that once-for-all revelation that God gave to us in Jesus Christ. Different churches may honor the insights of one or another leader in church history, but insofar as they are "Christian," the gospel that they profess does not abolish or supersede that original gospel of God's grace in Jesus Christ.

191

Churches have received grace by differing means, and most of them have arisen in history as witnesses to a particular instrument through which the gospel of God's love has become known and is extolled. This vehicle of *charisma* then becomes the principal means of authenticating its leadership, its Ministry. So the Church of Rome, recognizing the early primacy of the bishops of Rome and the blessings that came to the Church through their Ministry, has stressed a priesthood in communion with the See of Rome. Anglicans and other Episcopalians have recognized the historical continuity of episcopally consecrated bishops and a clergy that is ordained through this office. Presbyterians have tended to regard representative church courts — particularly the presbytery — as the means by which the historic gospel has been safeguarded and transmitted, although there are some who would claim for the Eldership very much what Episcopalians claim for the Bishop. This was apparently the position reached by John Wesley when he read Lord King's "Account of the Primitive Church," for it seems to have been the basis on which he eventually ordained and appointed Thomas Coke to serve with Francis Asbury as Superintendent or Bishop in America.[1] On the other hand, Congregationalists have always stressed the importance of the local covenanted or "gathered" church in the ordination of their Ministry; they recognize an "apostolic succession" through local congregations of believers.[2] We might go further, for despite

[1] See John Wesley's *Journal* for Monday 20th January, 1746, where he writes, "I set out for Bristol. On the road I read Lord King's account of the primitive Church. In spite of the vehement prejudice of my education, I was ready to believe that this was a fair and impartial draught; but if so, it would follow that Bishops and Presbyters are [essentially] of one order; and that originally every Christian congregation was a Church independent on all others." If Wesley was really persuaded by the noble Lord, then we would expect his system of church government to be an amalgam of episcopacy, presbyterianism, and congregationalism, for although Wesley was apparently convinced about the identity of the orders of bishop and presbyter, he certainly retained the idea of a functional episcopacy in his ordination of Thomas Cook for America in 1784.

[2] This suggestion appeared independently from American and English sources in 1952. Douglas Horton's *Congregationalism: A Study in Church Polity* (London: Independent Press), although published in London is, of course, by a very distinguished American churchman and historian. During the same year I had made the same suggestion in a pamphlet, *Congregationalism and the Ecumenical Movement* (London: Independent Press), p. 19.

what later developed in these movements, Pietism has historically claimed continuity through the evangelical experience, and Quietism through the influence of the "inner light." The early pietists did not think of their conversion experience as something which was suddenly given by God in the sixteenth century, but as something which linked them with St. Paul on the Damascus road, and in the same way George Fox thought of the inner light as essentially the Spirit that was in Jesus Christ and which was present in true believers in every age. All Christians recognize that channels of grace are given to the Church *in time,* that the Holy Spirit which linked the apostles to Jesus himself continues to transmit the gospel through men and institutions to the Church of each succeeding age.

Most Christians would also recognize that the channels of grace emphasized by other churches have been an effective means of grace to them. We may differ on where to place the priority, but there is increasing recognition that we have often been more right in what we have asserted than in what we have denied. Indeed, we begin to feel uncomfortable only when one denomination begins to claim that it alone possesses the Holy Spirit's chosen channel of grace to the Church; and our unease in the face of such exclusive claims is not any unwillingness to recognize that the Holy Spirit works in history by human agents, but because that very claim to exclusiveness seems to contradict the nature of the Holy Spirit. Such claims do, of course, tend to accent the material means of succession rather than the spiritual grace that is transmitted, but fundamentally our criticism is that they deny the humility which is the Holy Spirit's distinctive characteristic. They point to themselves instead of pointing to Christ.

Therefore, in looking for the Christian Ministry's credentials, let us remember that the Ministry has nothing of itself. It is given to the Church by Christ, and it is given so that it may become completely immersed in and identified with the Church's own ministry. We must look not for that which is distinctive, separate, but for that which is of the *esse* of the Church at the center of its life — the gospel of the living Christ. Beyond all the differences of emphasis, this is what all the channels of grace are supposed to transmit, this is the one thing that must be handed on for a church truly to be a part of the Christian Church. Its life centers in its fidelity to that gospel of God's redeeming love in Christ. There can undoubtedly be gatherings of Moslems and Buddhists, Humanists and Theosophists who may be more "Christian" in certain respects than many who call themselves Christians and belong to Christian congregations, but if we are trying to define what the visible Christian Church is, then we must affirm that a Christian Church is a church that confesses Jesus Christ, i.e., Jesus *as the Christ of God*.[3] Hopefully that confession of faith will be in word *and* deed, although we know that we constantly fail in both. The first epistle of John illustrates this relationship between faith and action, for the whole tenor of the epistle is that we deny the Faith when we fail to love our brother (I John 2:3-11, 3:2-12, etc.). At the same time, the writer also emphasizes the importance of testing the public confession of men, for "every spirit which acknowledges that Jesus Christ has come in the flesh is from God, and every spirit which does not thus acknowledge Jesus is not from God" (I John 4:2f., NEB). The fruits of the Spirit are important; indeed, they are the final test, but it is of equal importance to the Church that they should be acknowledged as fruits of the Spirit *of Jesus Christ,* derived from the confession of those who love their neighbor because they have first seen in Christ how God has loved them (cf. I John

---

[3] The need to make this kind of definition constantly befuddles the ecumenical issue, particularly at the local level. It is bound to arise whenever we attempt to define the basis of membership in a "Council of Churches." There is certainly a good case to be made for bringing religious groups together to discuss common interests on a wider basis than that of the Christian Faith. There is also a need for Christians to get together to face in common the issues that spring from their own dividedness. This need to associate together on a specifically Christian basis ought not to arise from a desire to emphasize exclusiveness, but more from the recognition that the Christian Faith poses its own special problems to Christians, which makes it imperative for them to seek a forum where their differences may be discussed on the basis of their common allegiance to Jesus Christ. In so far as Councils of Churches are intended to be that kind of forum, the insistence upon a Christian basis of membership is valid. Fundamentally it should be seen as a declaration of penitence, which declares our primary need to rediscover our own unity in Christ, for only when we are prepared to take this need seriously shall we be ready to undertake our mission in society. On the other hand, the insistence of this definition of the Church could be a retrograde step if it simply becomes a cosy Christian club. It ought to force the Council into accepting its wider responsibility to represent the Christian churches in inter-faith dialogue and fellowship wherever that is possible.

2:28-3:17). The Church is a community that is committed to an enacted creed. But that "creed," the confession of Faith in Jesus Christ, however expressed, is at the center.

The Ministry has its center at the same place. This was the claim of D. T. Jenkins in *The Nature of Catholicity*, and I must confess that I have not seen him answered. Writing generally from the Free Church position, specifically as a Congregationalist, he declares, "We are as ready, therefore, as traditional Catholicism is, to assert that apostolicity is the essential mark of catholicity, but our position is distinguished from theirs by the fact that we are compelled to insist that it is their *testimony* which constitutes the Apostles as Apostles. The testimony does not draw its authority from the fact that it is the Apostles who bear it, as traditional Catholic teaching seems to suggest, but the Apostles have authority only in so far as they forget themselves in being faithful witnesses to Jesus Christ. . . . It is not their faith or their zeal or their religious genius or any special charismata they possess, like the gift of the Spirit by the laying on of hands, and certainly not any accident of historical association, but their *testimony* which constitutes them Apostles."[4]

Two comments may be made regarding this passage.

First, there appears to have been a shift in the attitude to the episcopate between the time of the early Apologists and Irenaeus, almost a century later. The argument of Clement of Rome is that the apostles were witnesses of the resurrection and had received the gospel from our Lord himself. They then appointed the first fruits of their preaching as bishops, having first proved them, and the inference is that the faithful should accept the bishops who had been chosen for their faithfulness to the gospel.[5] The same intent may be gathered from Ignatius. Irenaeus, however, although he claimed that Polycarp, whom he had known before his martyrdom, had been instructed by the apostles, concentrated upon the actual historical line of descent, so that we might infer that *because* the Church had this succession of bishops, *therefore* it possessed the apostolic Faith.[6] This was probably a reasonable assumption to make at the time when

---

[4] D. T. Jenkins, *The Nature of Catholicity* (London: Faber and Faber, 1942), pp. 25f.

[5] *Ad. Cor.* 42.

[6] *Adv. Haer.* ii, iii.

Irenaeus was writing, but it would be less reliable as accretions crept into the liturgy and as the tradition then hardened. Only constant reference to the scriptural record would keep the Church and its Ministry true to the apostolic Faith.

Secondly, we need to think about what is implied in the word "testimony." Undoubtedly it does mean primarily the public profession of the saving work of Christ, and I recognize the protest that Jenkins makes against the emaciated theology of liberalism. On the other hand, I cannot be quite as disparaging. There is more to the gospel than morality, and the liberals often spoke as if the pure ethical teaching of Jesus could be skimmed from the doctrinal elaborations of Paul and other New Testament writers; and yet, as Forsyth constantly reminds us, we cannot ignore the fact that there is an ethical center to the Christian Faith because we are dealing with a *Holy* God. Orthodoxy of belief that disregards this, that refuses to face honestly the ethical nature of Christ's Spirit, is sterile. In its day liberalism was a protest against this kind of sterile creedalism. Jenkins himself surely recognizes this in *Tradition and the Spirit.* He says, "History proves that no fundamentalism arises quite so rapidly as confessional fundamentalism" (p. 134), and he points out that when that happens Protestantism falls into the very error that it is always so quick to criticize in the Catholic's attitude to the creeds.

Confession in word and confession in deed belong together and must be held together at all costs. As we recognize the constant failure to fulfill our public profession of Christ in deeds that adequately express his Spirit, it should force us to see how ill-placed and gauche are any pretensions on the part of the Church; the Church needs to understand itself as first among the penitents. Yet it must witness to that which it has known and experienced of the grace of God *in Christ* — its ethics come from Him.

The Minister is set within the same dilemma, for within the church his need of penitence and of God's mercy is greatest of all. Yet he must witness to the gospel: "Woe to me if I do not preach the gospel! For if I do this of my own will, I have a reward; but if not on my own will, I am entrusted with a commission" (I Cor. 9:16f.). The credentials of a Minister are centered in the gospel and in his call to proclaim it, and the authority which ratifies his Ministry is that which accompanies the manifest fruits of the Spirit.

II

EPISCOPACY?

In one of his less serious books Stephen Leacock described a meeting between the Reverend Edward Fareforth Furlong, Rector of the Episcopal Church of St. Asaph, and the Reverend Dr. MacTeague, Minister of the Presbyterian Church of St. Osoph. As he came face to face with Dr. MacTeague, we read, the good Rector "gave him the form of amiable 'good morning' that the episcopal church always extends to those in error."[7]

Perhaps the time has come when we owe it to our Anglican friends and others to address some words frankly and in love to them on the subject of episcopacy. I write as one who would certainly be prepared to accept a form of episcopacy for the sake of the Church's unity, but I have to admit that those who take this position in the Free Churches would probably be a minority, and the majority has had some cause for its misgivings. Even although Free Churchmen no longer become apoplectic at the mere mention of the word 'bishop,' it should not be assumed that all their criticisms are at rest.

My own position is sufficiently expressed in words that were recently uttered to Congregationalists in Britain, when the Chairman of the Congregational Union of England and Wales declared that "our duty is not to oppose the word *episcopacy,* however much it may have been misused in the past, but to share with our fellow Christians in the search, which is by no means a blind or unhopeful one, for its true meaning, and for the full and rich reality of a true episcopacy to be embodied in a united church."[8] The remarks of this section should be read against the background of this conviction. But however much I may disagree with traditional Free Church prejudices, I am quite unwilling to see the issues brushed aside; for one senses that Anglican writers have not really understood the deep-seated Free

---

[7] S. Leacock, *Arcadian Adventures with the Idle Rich* (London: John Lane the Bodley Head, 1952), p. 133.

[8] John Marsh, Chairman's Address, 1963, *Theme with Variations* (London: Independent Press), p. 25.

Church suspicion of episcopacy and all that the word implies.
Even Anglican writers who have done so much to revise our
concept of Ministry assume that the final form of the Church
must inevitably be episcopal. Every scheme of Christian unity
must come to terms with the historic episcopate, declares J. A. T.
Robinson, "for *despite* it the Church cannot be fully one, catholic, or apostolic."[9] Perhaps that is true, but if it is, it will have

---

[9] *The Historic Episcopate*, p. 21. Here I take issue with some Anglican writers with whom I am in fundamental agreement on so many other
aspects of the doctrine of Church and Ministry. For example, H. W.
Montefiore in the concluding chapter of *The Historic Episcopate* (p. 123)
declares, "All orders then are defective: but they are not equally defective. The church officer of the Seventh Day Adventists, the Presbyterian
minister and the Anglican priest are not all 'on the same level'. In the
first place, those ordained into the apostolic succession are given a spiritual grace and authorization from the Risen Christ through the church
which itself goes back in historical continuity to the Apostles of the primitive church and so to the historical Jesus Himself. They are ordained
into the form of ministry which gives full stature to the church." To me,
this statement seems to emanate less from biblical theology than from
certain *a priori* denominational criteria. My objections center in two main
questions.

First, who or what is the authoritative judge of "defective" orders? Is
not this kind of statement made with the presumption (and it *is* presumption) that a particular denominational viewpoint has the right and
competence to judge "defectiveness" as if that denomination were alone
the whole Church? I fear the enterprise not so much because oversensitive feelings among other Christians may be hurt, but I fear more for
the denomination that so presumes to know the mind of Christ and to
absolutize his will, for when one branch of the Church counts some
Ministries "in," and others "out," it virtually claims to be the whole
Church Catholic.

Secondly, does it not obscure our equal culpability before God for the
division of the Church? Canon O. C. Quick once made a wise remark
when he observed that "Perhaps God has concluded all under the sin
of schism that He may in the end have mercy upon all through the grace
of union" (*The Christian Sacraments*, p. 147). The solution of our ecumenical problem and the realization of the visible and organic unity of
the Church is not to be like Nanki-Poo, "a thing of shreds and patches,"
the acceptance of a little compromise here and a few formalities there;
it will be realized by churches that have been reborn through penitence.

Let me put the matter with some pointedness to the authors of *The
Historic Episcopate*: if within the renewal of the Church the "historic
episcopate" is seen to possess the fruits of the Spirit, if it has given evidence of its Christ-like humility and its participation in the redemptive
sacrifice of our Lord's own ministry, then the Holy Spirit, who is leading
the churches, will preserve it for the whole Church as one of the glories

to rest on firmer ground than the mere assumption that it is so. We should like to see the same biblical principles applied to the proof of this assertion that the Bishop of Woolwich has applied to the priority of Church over Ministry, and of the Kingdom over the Church.

Canon Anthony Hanson notices that Daniel Jenkins does not seem greatly impressed with the arguments for episcopacy from the experience of the Church of South India. Jenkins had commented somewhat tartly that "The fact that they [the Anglican Bishops] are encouraged to believe that they carry the official unity of the Church around with them wherever they go does often seem to make them reluctant to examine the possibility that they themselves may be hindrances to unity and barriers in the way of the free flow of experience and fellowship from one Christian community to another."[10] Precisely so. Canon Hanson suggests, "It is possible that Mr. Jenkins in his critique of episcopacy has concentrated too much on the bishops of the Church of England, and not enough on episcopacy as seen in other parts of the Anglican Communion, and even outside it."[11] This is true; there are other and very different kinds of "bishop" around the world. But where else is one to look for a picture of what a bishop purports to be than to the bishop who is near at hand? How he performs his pastoral office, how he expresses the unity of the Church, how he exercises his authority are in the end the test of what episcopacy is. I am no more impressed with episcopacy on the soil of Connecticut than I was on the soil of Surrey, and although from the opportunity of fairly wide ecumenical contacts I have, *laus deo,* seen episcopacy that is moving in its evangelical simplicity, I have no evidence to suggest that it depends on whether they are with or without the benefit of tactual consecration. If they belong to the gospel, they should reflect the gospel.

I suggest that the objections of Anglo-Saxon Free Churchmen to episcopacy are to be found partly in history and partly in ex-

---

of the Church reborn. But if not, then no purely historical considerations can possibly justify it as of the *esse, plene esse,* or even of the *bene esse* of the Church. There is at least an echo of the gospel in the thought that from the one who claims to have received most, the most must be expected.

[10] Daniel T. Jenkins, *The Protestant Ministry* (London: Faber and Faber, 1958), p. 63.

[11] *The Pioneer Ministry,* p. 170, n. 1.

perience, partly in psychological prejudice and partly in theological insight. On this subject a Free Churchman is likely to be
rather like Pope's natural man, "Chaos of thought and passion,
all confused," and I submit that he has to be heard with patience and understanding. It is little use adopting that most ir-
ritating Anglican habit of assuming that, despite all that can be
said against bishops, "Of course, the unity of the Church will demand that we must have bishops." Possibly it does, but the case
is not yet proven. Let us look at some of the objections.

(a) It is sometimes argued that the historic episcopate is the
symbol and guarantee of the Church's unity.

It *could* be, but we may honestly question whether it *is*. Admittedly, some of the oldest and largest forms of the Church have
the historic episcopate, the Roman Catholic Church, the ancient
Orthodox Churches of the East, the Nestorians and Monophy-
sites, and the Anglican Church, together with those in communion
with it. Unfortunately, there does not appear to be any mutual
recognition of Ministries between these branches of the Church.
Indeed, the authoritarian character of the churches tends to substantiate and perpetuate the differences in life and worship. As
the Free Church authors in *The Catholicity of Protestantism* put
the question, "There is therefore no difficulty in finding positive
statement about these [Church and Ministry] from the protestant
side. Can the same be said about the 'catholics'? Could any
positive statement be framed on the nature of the Church, or even
on the doctrines of the Sacraments and the Ministry which would
be agreed on by the Pope, representing the Roman Catholics, by
the Orthodox Eastern Churches, and by the Anglo-Catholic party
in the Church of England?"[12]

They are agreed on the nature of episcopacy, but the episcopate has not maintained the unity of the Church — indeed, as
between these churches it could be a major means of perpetuat-
ing separation.

(b) The history of episcopacy in the Anglican Church still
constitutes an offence to Anglo-Saxon Free Churchmen. The
story has to be faced and lived down. Modern Free Churchmen

---

[12] *The Catholicity of Protestantism* (London: Lutterworth Press, 1950),
ed. R. Newton Flew and Rupert E. Davies, pp. 30f. This book was prepared by representative English Free Church theologians in response to
a request by Lord Fisher when he was Archbishop of Canterbury.

may be less conscious of it than their forefathers, but it is difficult to excuse the expulsion of the Nonconformists in 1662, the lack of generosity in 1688, the episcopal opposition to the Enfranchisement Bill in 1828, and the ecclesiastical furor against the entry of Nonconformists to Oxford and Cambridge in 1870. The methods by which minority groups of Anglicans gained, or attempted to gain control in several American colonies before the Revolution — the Carolinas, Pennsylvania, New York State — makes somewhat bitter reading, and the fear of episcopal control was one important factor in the participation of at least the New England states in the war of the Revolution.

What I am saying is that to many "episcopacy" still means "prelacy" of a particularly arrogant kind. Whenever union questions are discussed, those who want none of it are still able to gain popular support by pointing to the Covenanters, or to the Pilgrims, and behind the story there is always the English bishop. The image of a bishop will have to change if it is to become acceptable to non-Anglican Protestantism, but more important than that, it will have to reflect the essentially pastoral character of the New Testament bishop.

(c) The suspicions are reinforced by the shifts and turns of the episcopal apologists.

Forgive us, but it has often seemed as if the Tractarians and their followers have been feverishly searching for a theology with which to maintain positions of privilege and power. The attitude of a Newman or a Manning, who accept the logic of their position and join the Church of Rome, deserves nothing but respect, but the attitude of a clergyman who retains his place in the established church while ignoring most of its Thirty-Nine Articles does not. During the past century we have been treated to a number of attempts to justify the ecclesiastical *status quo* in England, and the arguments have not been cumulative but have been strung up as alternatives in the hope that if one did not clinch the issue the next one would. J. H. Newman's famous *Essay on Development* (1846) was such a broadside that misfired, and when the appeal was made to the New Testament, no more could be proved for the episcopal system than for any other major polity.[13] The evidence provided by the science of New Testament

[13] Cf. J. B. Lightfoot, *St. Paul's Epistle to the Philippians* (1890), F. J. A. Hort, *The Christian Ecclesia* (1897), pp. 229-233, E. Hatch,

criticism was at best inconclusive,[14] and the summary expression of this inconclusiveness was reached by Canon B. H. Streeter's classic quotation from *Alice in Wonderland* — a conclusion which W. D. Davies has pointed out has been consistently ignored by Anglo-Catholic writers.[15] The appeal to history has presented certain flaws,[16] and although recent biblical theology seemed at first to offer some justification in A. M. Ramsay's *The Gospel and the Catholic Church* (1936), it too has been shown to offer certain grave objections.[17] Then a bold attempt to wed biblical criticism and theology to the historical thesis was made in K. E. Kirk's *The Apostolic Ministry,* and the theory of the *shaliach* began to brighten the episcopal horizon. It was obviously intended and expected by its authors to present the *coup de grace* to all opposition, after which there would be little for the rest of us to do but make humble submission. It was certainly not the fault of the former Bishop of Oxford and his colleagues that they proved to be tilting at a windmill, and with a very bent lance.

Let us admit that the arguments about the doctrines of the Church and Ministry from the various ecclesiastical camps have been going on for a very long time, but nothing in that history quite matches the shifts in the episcopal weathervane. The impression that a Free Churchman gets from this is that those who are arguing for bishops as *de jure divino* are not seriously concerned with biblical truth. He feels they are principally anxious to discover irrefutable evidence for a position that has already been taken or maintained for other reasons, so that where the opposing ecclesiologies cannot be blithely attacked, they may be blandly ignored.

The Organization of the Early Churches (1881), Charles Gore, *The Church and the Ministry* (1888). See also the comment made by Bishop Wescott quoted by J. H. Moulton, *The Christian Religion in the Study and the Street* (1919), p. 106.

[14] Cf. Vincent Taylor's comments in *The Expository Times* (1951), p. 271.

[15] W. D. Davies, *Christian Origins and Judaism,* p. 214f. The reference is to Streeter's *The Primitive Church,* p. ix. Commenting upon the many attempts to prove episcopacy, presbyterianism, and congregationalism from the New Testament, B. H. Streeter ironically observed that "in the classic words of *Alice in Wonderland,* 'Everyone has won, and all shall have prizes.' "

[16] Cf. *Supra,* ch. ii, n. 5.

[17] Cf. W. D. Davies, *Christian Origins and Judaism,* pp. 210ff.

Those who commit the ecumenical movement to some form of the Chicago-Lambeth Quadrilateral[18] will probably dismiss the foregoing paragraphs as typical Nonconformist prejudice. That it may be born of Nonconformist prejudice I do not deny, but it is not my intention to put the ecumenical clock back. Any historian must recognize that the proscriptions and disabilities were certainly not all on one side, as any Episcopal priest in Massachusetts or Connecticut will be pleased to tell you.

My contention is that even if we are dealing with something that is no more than a prejudice, we shall not get rid of it unless we are prepared to examine the hard truths at its core. The one thing that a Massachusetts Congregationalist and a Massachusetts Baptist (the few who were allowed in) would have agreed about in the eighteenth century was that they wanted no bishops on American soil! It was in many ways an irrational reaction, but no one looking at the history of the period could blame them for it. There is far less reason for their successors today to react against the word 'bishop,' but they do. I have commented previously on the stupidity of Free Churchmen who claim to have an ecclesiology based on the New Testament, reacting so negatively to the New Testament word 'bishop,'[19] but we get very near the heart of Free Church prejudice on this when we realize that we could be even more sarcastic about those who cling to the word but rob it of its New Testament content. This is the reason for the protest.

Most denominations have been trying to recognize that which is called *episcopē* in the New Testament. In America Methodism recognized bishops from the start; but since that time we have seen the development of Congregational Moderators and Baptist Superintendents in Britain, while in America we have not only Congregational and Baptist Superintendents but the Stated Clerks of Presbyterianism, Executive Ministers of State Societies among

[18] This was first promulgated by the House of Bishops in the General Convention of the Protestant Episcopal Church in the U.S.A. in 1886, and was accepted by the Lambeth Conference of Anglican bishops in 1888. The four points set down as mandatory for agreement in union discussions were (1) the Holy Scriptures as the Word of God; (2) the primitive creeds as the rule of faith, (3) the two sacraments ordained by Christ himself, and (4) the historic episcopate as the basis of governmental unity. The issue with Protestantism has always revolved around the fourth point.

[19] *The Ecumenical Review,* VIII (Jan. 1956), 185f.

Disciples and Presidents of State Synods among Lutherans. Most of these offices are but pale versions of the prelacy to be found in the "Catholic" churches, and they are certainly no clearer examples of the New Testament pattern; but each man who occupies one of these positions is called upon to deal not only with the administration of his area but also to act in some sense as *pastor pastorum.* I cite the trend not because these officers are closer to New Testament practice than are the bishops in Anglicanism, but because it may be a practical recognition of that which episcopacy at its best has sought to maintain, the "care of all the churches" that was at the heart of Paul's ministry and of the New Testament *episcopē.*

However, if a bishop is to be *pastor* to pastors, then he should make it clear that he regards himself in that way; for we are concerned with *Ministry,* and there can be no true Ministry in the Church that takes its pattern from secular lordship rather than from the Lordship of Jesus Christ who made himself "of no reputation." If this is true for Ministers generally, how much more true it should be for those who are called to minister to the Ministry itself. Show me your bishop and you should be showing me one who is apostolic not only in his concern for the Faith but also in the fervor of his evangelism, one who should be catholic not only in his loyalty to the Church's institutional structure but also in his compassion, one who is a servant not only in name but in the simplicity of his life.

Robert Harrison, one of the most implacable of the sixteenth-century Separatists, is hardly to be quoted for his views on episcopacy in this ecumenical age; nevertheless he very shrewdly observed that the theory of apostolic succession may be used in two ways — it might be used to substantiate the claim of an episcopal church to be the true Church, or it might be used to prove that it was descended from Antichrist! Writing of the Elizabethan bishops he asked:

> From whence haue they their calling, sendinge, and authoritie, such as pertaineth to a Minister? Hadde they not it from those which sitt the chayre of Antichrist? Yea, how manie are in all Christendome, which have been so rightlie ordeyned, but that their ordination haue come from the popishe Prelacie, within three or foure generations at the most? Now if a man take a griffe of a sowre fruite, and plante it, & then take a griffe of that new planted, & plant

that: and take of that agayne & plant it the thirde time, and so continewe vnto the hundreth time: will it lose its sowreness and gather sweetnesse? No more can an vnlawefull callinge bring foorth a lawfull, though it descende from one to another an hundred or a thousand times.[20]

The argument from apostolic succession was turned upside down!

I would not even begin to suggest that Harrison's argument could be accepted by Free Churchmen today, for to him the Anglican bishops were sufficiently tainted by reason of their consecration and tactual descent from the bishops of Rome. In the sixteenth century Reformers of all kinds were much more ready to throw that charge of "Antichrist" at Rome. But Harrison's argument is valid to this extent: the Elizabethan bishops had taken from Rome not only their episcopal consecration but also their prelatical arrogance. And that *does* belong to Antichrist. We would not wish to quarrel with the Anglican claim that their bishops have descended from the bishops of the Medieval Church by tactual succession, but we do raise questions about the kind of authority that was transmitted and the way it has been exercised. They had their ordination from the "popish prelacy," and this is the character that the succession has borne and by which too often it has been recognized. We have every hope that a true, apostolic succession could be possible through truly pastoral bishops, but we have the gravest objection to a non-apostolic succession of unholy prelacy.

We need the object-lesson of what a true bishop can be, for we have noted that often the claim to spiritual authority tends to produce claims to power of a very different quality, and the lordship of the Spirit becomes confused with lordship of a much more mundane variety. To point again to a British parallel, purple stocks, gaiter, and a seat in the House of Lords may be in themselves irrelevant, but they are apt to cast the shadow of "My Lord Prelate" rather than "my father in God."

Martin Luther accented the issue in the words he addressed to Pope Leo X: "You are the servant of servants, and, more than any man, in a most pitiable and perilous position." Then he went on to say, "In belief, trust not any who exalt you, but in those

---

[20] *A Little Treatise uppon the firste Verse of the 122. Psalm,* in *The Writings of Robert Harrison and Robert Browne,* ed. Albert A. Peel and Leland H. Carlson (London: Allen & Unwin, 1953), pp. 98f.

who humiliate you. For this is the judgment of God: 'He that cast down the mighty from their seat, and hath exalted the humble.' See how unlike Christ was to his successors, though all will have it that they are his vicars. I fear that in truth very many of them have been in too serious a sense his vicars, for a vicar represents a prince who is absent. . . . What indeed is such a vicar but antichrist and an idol? How much more rightly did the Apostles speak who call themselves the servants of a present Christ, not the vicars of an absent one."[21]

Hanson protests, with some justification, that we should not judge episcopacy by the earlier patterns of prelacy, and claims that we should look to the form that is emerging in the Church of South India. He cited the example of an Indian Christian, Congregationalist by tradition, who was asked by some Welsh ministers how, against the background of Congregationalism, he could accept bishops. The Indian said that in the Church of South India they did not regard their bishops as an administrator, a tyrant, or as a master, but as a "father in God." "This, surely," commented Hanson," is the true relation of a bishop to his flock, personal, not legal." [22] We agree, and if the bishop maintains this relationship in the Church of South India, then this most significant ecumenical experiment may do a great deal to break down the prejudices of Freechurchmen. Be assured that we are watching the results with interest; and it is to be hoped that we shall be able to watch them with growing sympathy.

Meanwhile our concern is with the *spirit* of episcopacy rather than with its form or with its name. In the famous sermon delivered in Cambridge in 1946, Archbishop Geoffrey Fisher made the suggestion that the British Free Churches might experimentally try episcopacy "on their own ground first" by taking the system into their own forms of polity.[23] In response, is it too much to ask the episcopal churches that as an earnest of their concern for the Church they should get rid of some of the trappings of their bishops and put more gospel content into the office? Only when it reflects Christ can other churches begin to regard it as a necessary aspect of the Ministry within His Church.

Admittedly this has been a digression, but I believe it is a di-

[21] *Concerning Christian Liberty,* in *Luther's Primary Works,* pp. 253f.
[22] *The Pioneer Ministry,* p. 169.
[23] "A Step Forward in Church Relations" (Church Assembly, Westminster, 1946), pp. 10, 11.

gression that is germane not only to the ecumenical discussion but also to our subject. I have been encouraged to write in these terms by finding the sentiments reflected in the words of a perceptive Anglican addressed to those of his own communion,[24] but as one who is committed to the ecumenical vision, I should be the more hesitant to raise the issue were I less convinced than I am that the New Testament *episcopē* is not only of the *bene esse* or the *plene esse* of the Church, but of its *esse*. We cannot avoid being concerned about the meaning of *episcopē* in the New Testament if we are concerned about ministry, for the *episcopos* in the early Church was above all things else a Minister to the Church. We cannot ignore the fact that he had his place in the Church and was given authority. It is therefore all the more necessary that we should comprehend the nature of the authority which he held and from whence it was derived. It would be tragic if our present-day ecumenical concern succeeded in regaining for the Church only a *form* of religion that denied its real power. That was a warning, you will remember, which was addressed to one who aspired to be a bishop (II Tim. 3:5).

The more we are prepared to walk along the ecumenical road to unity and the more we are prepared to acknowledge the place of *episcopē* within the Church, so much the more must we insist that its character is determined by Jesus Christ the Head of the Church. For if this is part of the essential Ministry, its character must reflect His character, and its rule must reflect His compassion.

III

"THE WORK OF MINISTRY"

In any study of the Ministry the most embarrassing contrast is that which exists between the ideal and the actual, and this is obviously true about the work in a parish. Any clergyman will tell you what the actual work of the Ministry is, how his time is eaten up by routine administrative chores and by the constant necessity of showing his face at the right place and the right time. He will probably complain with a good deal of justification that all these things prevent him from being a Minister in anything but a very superficial sense, and that the way in which our church-

---

[24] W. J. Phythian-Adams, *The Way of At-one-ment,* pp. 108f.

es are organized forces him more and more into being a professional administrator and little else. The Niebuhr-Williams-Gustafson
study presumably reflects the real feelings of real people about
their vocations.

(a) This is perhaps one of the most pressing problems that the
Church faces in our affluent Western society — how to keep the
ever increasing pressures towards institutionalism and bureauc-
racy in her own life under the control of Christ's Spirit,[25] and
hence how to free its Ministers to be Ministers in deed as well as
name. From here on I suppose we might launch into a full-scale
diatribe against the trend, or write off the Church as a total loss
to capitalism (or the welfare state) and begin to scout the horizon
for more adequate instruments of the Kingdom. There is always
the possibility that the institutional Church will become so idola-
trous that it is rejected by God, for we should remember that
Paul felt it necessary to warn the Church at Corinth of what had
happened to Israel (I Cor. 10).

I do not think, however, that we should assume too hastily
that this is so just because it looks that way to us. The "real
work" of a Minister is to lead members of the Church into a
deepening understanding of their reconciliation with God and
to prepare them for the task of witnessing to it, and although
we are given some clues in the New Testament of how this may
be done through preaching, the sacraments, and pastoral care,
there is little to determine in detail how a Minister is to accom-
plish his task. I certainly could not defend the scatterbrained
way in which some Ministers have to divide their time and interest in irrelevancies, and yet equally I believe that the mundane
affairs of good administration and effective organization can be,
and perhaps must be, ways in which a Minister serves the Church
and leads it deeper into the truth about God. Perhaps it is not
altogether what is done, but how it is done which is the real
ministry.

Recently there was an interesting parallel related to academic
life offered in the British magazine *Punch*.[26] Professors and dons
during term time are apt to groan at the amount of committee

[25] Cf. Walter G. Muelder's chapter on 'Problems of Church Bureauc-
racy' in *Institutionalism and Church Unity,* ed. Nils Ehrenstrom and
Walter G. Muelder (New York: Association Press, 1963).
[26] Stephen Toulmin, "It's a Don's Life," *Punch,* Sept. 25, 1963.

work, hack writing and bread-and-butter teaching they are forced to do, claiming — here, too, with some justification — that it keeps them from their "real work" of scholarly research. The author maintained that British universities should learn from the realism of their American counterparts, for "no good is done by maintaining the pretence that all teachers required in an age of general higher education either should be, or are capable of being original scholars or scientists."[27] One could argue, of course, that once the possibility of being recognized by one's peers as a scholar is removed, the level of genuinely creative teaching at university level is bound to drop, but that is a side issue for our purpose. The main point which the writer is making is that teaching can be a vocation in itself.

Something similar may be said about the Ministry. Here it is the teaching function that suffers — and how it suffers in the American parish! However, the way in which a pastor tackles the routine of administration probably brings him nearer to the members of his congregation and the problems they too face each day, than any other function of his Ministry. Even if he cannot get them to the church house for a regular Bible Study — and let us hope that he does — there should be a Christian style of engaging in the monotonous chores that does not constantly gripe about my "real job." The protest against the claims of organization may have to be made and made forcibly during a Ministry, and perhaps there is no place in the Church's life where we need more the services of the *pastor pastorum* in order to say it, but let us recognize that ministry is also a way of life in any set of circumstances. We cannot escape our involvement in every-day affairs, or in the sheer "busyness" of life — it is part of the twentieth century and of the life of those to whom we minister. We can deplore it on general grounds, and we should seek to change it, but as soon as we make our protest too personal, we fall into the trap of claiming to be "different."

I hope Ministers will read that last paragraph, but I hope that no lay church officers will think that it justifies the often irresponsible way in which churches use their Minister's time and effort. When they take their Minister away from the teaching and pastoral task that is his special call, they are usurping the place of Christ, for as we have seen, a Minister is primarily the servant

[27] *Ibid.*, p. 444.

of Christ and only in a derivative way the servant of the Church. As Bernard Lord Manning said in his Charge to a Church, "At your hands indeed he receives his commission; but it is Christ's commission, not yours; and it comes from Christ, not you. When your minister speaks, mark whose word it is he speaks. You do not hear from him an echo of your own voice."[28] And, we would add, you should not seek to impose on him the pattern of your own life, for he cannot be truly a Minister to you unless his first obedience is to Jesus Christ.

(b) A Minister must start with people where they are and not where he expects them to be. It is one of the most difficult lessons for a young man to learn, because having come out of college and seminary he thinks he *knows* what should be done and how it should be done. Anything else is, naturally, intolerable! Robert Browne was about thirty years of age when he wrote his *Treatise of Reformation without tarrying for Anie,* and the impatience and perfectionism of Separatism have always seemed to me to be the typical faults of youth's enthusiasms. A young Minister ought to enter his first parish full of new ideas and insights, but only experience and his own deepening and continuing study can tell him which of them are good, which of them might be good in a different set of circumstances, and which of them are best forgotten! It is in the vitality of our own religious quest that we learn over the years to separate the wheat from the chaff in our own thinking. We have been fortunate in having, perhaps, a dynamic professor in Existentialist Philosophy, or Christian Ethics, or the Theology of Karl Barth, and we come out full of the ideas that we culled from his seminar and equipped with the papers he generously graded *A* minus. We are fully prepared to give this congregation the benefits of our erudition, but we find that they are not too interested in these abstractions. Instead they seem preoccupied with such questions as "Why can't I get on with my husband?" "Is our school budget too high?" and "Why did Tommy Jones die on his ninth birthday?" These are, of course, the same problems, but they are set in concrete situations, and the Minister has to take his congregation from where the members are at this moment.

English parishes do not have softball teams or bowling alleys, but they often have tennis clubs. When I arrived in the church

---

[28] *A Layman in the Ministry,* p. 153.

that I was to serve in 1945, I was ready to be more than a little bit superior about church tennis clubs. I liked the game, but it was certainly not the "real work" of the Ministry. One day I was visited by a young man, recently demobilized from the Navy, who said that he wanted to become a member of the church. He had not been brought up in a Christian home, and the thought would probably never had entered his head, but he said, "I have played tennis with the members of the Christ Church tennis club, and there is a spirit in it that I have not met anywhere else. I want to know more about Christ, and to become a Christian."

This is by no means an excuse for wasting time, money, and energy on secondary activities such as tennis clubs, but it is a claim that they *can* be instruments for extending the Kingdom, and it is even more a claim that the Minister has to begin with people where they are and not where he is, or thinks he is.

This is as true of the congregation corporately as it is of individuals, for if a statesman must learn that he cannot go much faster than his constituency, a Minister has to learn that people can be led but not driven. Many of the excellent changes that he knows should be made in the church's life may have to wait, for as soon as he tries to force the issue, he will be tempted to assume an authority that is contrary to the Spirit of the great Head of the Church. Some things are imperatives because of the gospel, but many other things are simply desirable, and a Minister must be prepared to wait for these things in the knowledge that our God is a God of infinite patience.

This will not please those who see the Church more in political terms than in terms of the New Testament. A Minister may be accused of compromising his principles, and only he and his Lord can tell whether his unwillingness to force the issue is due to pastoral concern or weakness. One of the most difficult decisions that a Minister has to make is that of deciding when to act and when to refrain from acting, and the difference between moral weakness and moral strength runs along the edge of these decisions. Sometimes in history fidelity to the gospel has turned Ministers into exiles from their congregations, but there are times when the course of fidelity runs differently, as pastors in East Germany remind us.

What we are saying is that the ethical decisions of a Minister in his congregation are very much the same as the ethical decisions which the Church herself has to make within modern society.

We cannot slavishly follow a book of rules, but we *are* given the example of a Minis er who spoke out when others found it expedient to be silent, and when others armed themselves with swords, He went to the cross with His eyes open to the consequences. Yet He was not simply contrary for the sake of being contrary, for the circumstances helped to determine the course of action, and His final consideration was always God's will for the world. That is ministry, and that is the pattern for a Minister within his congregation.

(c) A Minister has to deal with people *now*. It is trite but true. One of the things that impresses us most about Jesus is that he always had time for people in their *present* need; he did not ignore the woman with the hemorrhage because he was already engaged on the case of Jairus' daughter, nor did he neglect the thief on the cross because his own needs were too pressing. He always had time for people. This is one of the authentic marks of ministry. To listen to people and to show concern for them at a time when it is inconvenient and unwelcome is another of the hard lessons that a Minister has to learn, for it is natural to think that our own interests and even our professional duties are of first importance to us. Our Lord shows us that our primary duty is with other people in their need *now*.

There will be times when a Minister is harrassed by trivial anxieties and petty worries foisted on him, but that which is trivial to us very rarely seems trivial to the one who has come to us. It is hard to recognize this fact when a request for help breaks into the important work of sermon preparation, but this is ministry — this is the stuff of immediate human events in which we are called to work. We recognize it in time of bereavement when an immediate word can be worth more than a long treatise on immortality a few months hence, but the principle is true for all phases of our work. Our concern is with people, the growth of the soul here and now.

(d) T. W. Manson emphasized that all ministry begins with the ministry of our Lord, and this has been one of the major themes of our study. While it is dangerous to press the similarities too far, it means that what is true of our Lord's ministry must also in some sense be true of our derived Ministries.

The theologians — particularly John Calvin in the fifteenth chapter of his second book of the *Institutes* — described the Ministry of Christ in the figures of Prophet, Priest, and King, and the New Testament seems ready to apply these terms also to the Church.[29] In a limited sense they are also applicable to the Ministry.

It is to be prophetic. That is, it has the responsibility of interpreting the Word of God within the contemporary situation and of revealing its living relevance to God's people. This much the Ministry has always understood as one of its prime tasks; but there is another sense too in which the Ministry is to be prophetic, for it is also a witness to the eschatological Kingdom of God, and it proclaims the triumph of its King.

It is priestly — not because it performs the priestly rites of a cultus, but as it reflects the high priestly vocation of Christ himself. Its priesthood is not a reversion to the claims and rights of Old Testament priesthood, but is centered in the atoning work of the One who was both High Priest and Victim for the reconciliation of man to God. It lives in the Spirit of his acted intercession for mankind, and in the power of that Spirit offers its life as an oblation and as joyful sacrifice.

It is kingly, but not in the sense in which it has too often tried to assert royal prerogatives over the world and to wring acknowledgement from men of its lordship within the natural order. Its claim to kingship is valid only as it denies all forms of secular power and authority, and is content to be entirely dependent upon its King. It reflects the royal priesthood of the kingdom, which makes no claims to any kind of superiority, accepts no title to power, and is content to be a servant. This is true ministry — and its character will determine what its work is, and how that work will be accomplished.

IV

THE FULLNESS OF THE CHURCH

1. Why Leaders?

God has set a problem in the middle of society. If he had given to all men precisely equal ability and equal opportunity,

---

[29] The Church is certainly regarded as a prophetic community, i.e., it witnesses to the reality of the eschatological Kingdom of God, and it utters God's Word to contemporary society. It is also described both as a kingdom and as priestly (Rev. 1:6, 5:10), and even as a "royal priesthood" (I Pet. 2:9).

there would have been no problem, and we might have achieved an absolute equality of democratic mediocrity. It would have been fair (in a limited sense) but dull. But the Creator in his wisdom has given us differing gifts and many situations in which to live them out, and at once we are presented with problems to solve: we have to resolve the relation between the demands of natural leadership to be obeyed and our corporate responsibility for the common good, between the claims of executive authority and those of legislative power. These problems and differences extend throughout the whole of society from the highest posts in government to those of the family, and in every form of society from the most advanced to the most primitive. By allowing these "inequalities" of nature, of capacity, race, and sex, the Creator undoubtedly gave us problems, but he also opened out to us incomparable possibilities of fun, excitement, and achievement. In fact, it is in the very conquest of these problems that mankind, whether as the race or as an individual, attains maturity; the circumstances of inequality become the very spurs and incentives to push forward and upward.

Why should it be any different in the Church? A concept of unity in the Church that implies a flat uniformity of worship and practice would seem to be a denial of the superabundant creativity and life that the redeeming God has put within the Church. Whatever else St. Paul's use of the metaphor of the Body may mean, it certainly means that all the limbs of the body are needed and must work in relationship to each other and to the Head, "so that if one member suffers, they all suffer with it; and if one member rejoices, they all rejoice with it" (I Cor. 12:26). There is unity of purpose and of interest, but diversity of gifts and ability. Here too, as in secular society, the leadership is dependent upon gifts and ability. Here too, as in secular society, the leadership is dependent upon gifts that have been given. Whatever we are called to do in the Church or in society is not of our deserving but of God's choice, not so much the sign of his favor as a seal of our responsibility to him. Kings, Presidents, and politicians may lose sight of these facts and may be tempted to claim honor and authority as if they had it by right, but in the Church there is no excuse for that arrogance, for within the Church the leaders are called "Ministers" — servants.

2. *The Calling of Ministers*: *to Bring in the Church in Its Fullness*

The passage in Ephesians 4 is so well known that it is difficult to grasp the dynamic conception of the Church that is implicit within it. The work of the Ministry is "to equip God's people for work in his service, to the building up of the body of Christ. So shall we all at last attain to the unity inherent in our faith and our knowledge of the Son of God — to mature manhood, measured by nothing less than the full stature of Christ" (Eph. 4:12f., NEB). Space travel is becoming so common that cosmonauts may become blasé even about the incredible vistas of space that are opened up to them. Perhaps that is what has happened to our understanding of Paul's letter to the Ephesians. The apostle is saying that we do not achieve spiritual manhood until we reach a stature that is full and complete — a stature that is full and complete even when measured in terms of Jesus Christ himself *and this is our destiny in the Church*. In the first chapter of the same epistle the author, writing of our Lord, expresses a similar thought. He says that God "put everything in subjection beneath his [Christ's] feet, and appointed him as supreme head to the church, which is his body and as such holds within it the fullness of him who himself receives the entire fullness of God" (Eph. 1:23, NEB). Or again, in the third chapter, he prays of the Christians in Ephesus that "with deep roots and firm foundation, may you be strong to grasp, with all God's people, what is the breadth and length and depth of the love of Christ, and to know it, though it is beyond knowledge. So may you attain to fullness of being, the fullness of God himself" (3:17ff., NEB).

The thought of the writer seems to be that the Church is to be the school where we are to experience and to grow into the very fulness of God in Christ; it is to be an experience of dynamic spiritual growth. Could you find any concept which is more different from one of flat uniformity in life and worship? Does any form of conventional piety, however elaborate and ornate or simple and austere, do justice to what we would expect from "fullness of Christ"? We are not concerned here with the question whether this or that form of the Church is more satisfying to us intellectually, aesthetically, emotionally, or even spiritually, but with what form of the Church could express the fulness that was in Jesus Christ. The ecumenical concept of the Church is not concerned with uniformity but with fulness — plenitude. It demands not this or that special insight into the gospel, but all the true insights that have ever been stimulated by the Holy Spirit, and all the true insights that ever will be stimulated within those who are moved to faith by the redemptive incarnation of Christ. Unity must have this dynamic understanding of the Church as its goal if it is to be true to the gospel, and nothing short of this is worthy of our ecumenical enterprise.

One of my first duties at the Ecumenical Institute was to join a party of students at the Christmas Liturgy of the Russian Orthodox Church in Geneva. It was all extremely foreign to me, and yet I could not help being strangely moved by the intense devotion of the worshippers. Candles, incense, ikons are difficult for an Anglo-Saxon Protestant to accept as a part of worship, and when they are linked to a liturgical form in Old Slavonic, one cannot help wondering what the seventeenth-century founders of New England would have made of it. And yet it was borne in upon me throughout this strange and exotic service that these people were truly worshipping the same Christ whom I worshipped.

A few days later in the little chapel at Bossey we joined in a celebration of the Lord's Supper according to the form of the Disciples of Christ. It was simple, plain, and some might even call it barren, although the warmth in the preaching was certainly no less than the warmth of those who had kissed the ikons. And when I reflected upon those two celebrations of the Holy Supper, beyond all questions of their similarity (and they *were* from a common source), or of their obvious differences (and no two services could have been more dissimilar), I found myself declaring that both must have their place within the Holy Catholic Church. It is not a case of either this or that, nor is it a case of simplifying one or making the other a little more rich in form, but it is a case of both belonging to Christ.

Insofar as Ministers are Ministers of the Church, they are called to work for the unity of the Church in its fullness, for if they are sent to lead the Church deeper into the realization of its own mission and ministry, they must lead it into a truer understanding of its own nature in Christ.

3. *A Minister Should Represent the Church in Its Unity and Its Fullness*

A Minister of Christ cannot be anything but a Minister of the whole Church. P. T. Forsyth declared that the Ministry "does not only show the unity that is there, it creates a unity that was not there, between God and man, between members, and between Churches. It is not only the symbol of the unity of the Church but its source."[30] Yes and No. A Minister can by his preaching and Ministry help bring into being the unity of alienated personalities, divided congregations, and even separated denominations — although when we reflect upon the careers of such men as John R. Mott or Joseph Oldham, we realize that "Ministry" here must mean something much wider than the specifically ordained leadership of a church.

We also know, however, that Forsyth's statement is too enthusiastic, and his words confuse the theological ideal with the ecclesiastical actuality. It is equally true that a Minister not only demonstrates the disunity in the Church that is there, but he can also create disunity. Our denominational ordinations reveal the fact of our disunity in its most unseemly form, because those who should represent the Church in its wholeness are made the agents of the partial, the competing, and the schismatic.

There used to be a time in England when the denomination of a Christian Minister could be guessed from the style of his neckwear. The Baptist pastor wore a black tie, the Congregationalist a white tie, the Wesleyan a tall clerical collar; clergymen of the Anglican Church sported clerical collars, the heights of which were in inverse proportion to their favored theological position — "high church," low collar, etc. — while Roman Catholic priests added the distinction of buttons on the stock. Such distinctions are now out of fashion; but whether we are Ministers in twentieth-century America or in Anthony Trollope's England, we are walking symbols of the Church's disunity, because as Ministers we are called to represent the whole gospel to the whole Church. But in fact we are the servants of a denominational view of the Church that implies a stunted view of the gospel.

We are called to be witnesses to the fulness of Christ, and our ordination should proclaim it.

4. *The Fullness of Christ Belongs to the Whole Church*

It does not belong to the Ministry, although Ministers partake of it; it is not their exclusive possession although they witness to

[30] *The Church and the Sacraments,* pp. 134f.

it. It belongs to the whole Church in which Ministers and laymen participate, and neither one can reach its intended spiritual goal without the other. This is perhaps the most important truth about the Church in the Reformation doctrine of the priesthood of all believers. So often this is interpreted in terms of a layman's rights, instead of in terms of the responsibilities of all church members, and yet this is to fall straightway into the besetting sin of all clericalism and would simply put the layman today where the priest was yesterday. But at a far deeper level what Protestants affirm in this doctrine is that the Christian community itself is a priestly community. There is a place for all ministries within its corporate ministry. Only the Church in its fullness can be big enough to inherit the fullness of Christ.

V

MINISTRY AND MISSION

This brings us inevitably to a consideration of the Minister in relation to the Church's mission. The credentials of a Minister are not primarily to be found in his professional competence, his innate ability, or his personal piety. In any congregation there may be many who are more gifted or more pious than the Minister, for although the gifts of nature and of the Spirit are to be used in the work of the Ministry, God's call reaches far beyond them. A Minister is called primarily to witness to the apostolic Faith, and to lead the Church into its own corporate witness to that Faith. We see this in the call of St. Peter. There is nothing in the New Testament to suggest that Peter was the most able of the disciples, or the most spiritual, but the context of the events described in Matthew sixteen is that of *faith*. Peter deserved the primacy for his unequivocal confession of Jesus as the Christ, the Son of the living God, and this is caught up after the resurrection in the reaffirmation of his leadership in the new apostolic mission.[31]

So it is with the Ministry. A Minister is to lead the Church into its apostolic witness. As the ordained servant of the Church he points the Church to our Lord's own ministry, and he points also to the world's need which beckons the Church to its own

[31] John 21, cf. Luke 5:1-11.

ministry. He is like a finger-post on the way — he is there to guide us, to point the way ahead by reminding pilgrims of the way by which they have come. The Ministry is, to use Anthony Hanson's apt term, a "pioneer Ministry," but we would stress that it is a pioneer Ministry only that the Church may become the pioneer Community.

A Minister is inevitably concerned with the members of his congregation and with the life of the institutional church and parish. A good deal of his time and effort will be spent doing things that affect the life of the parish and the worship in the sanctuary. He can very easily become preoccupied with these affairs so that they become the center of his interest and the test of his success or failure. And yet these are only means to the end that this same congregation will go out into the world to praise God by witnessing to his grace. A Minister is occupied primarily (and often, it seems, almost exclusively) with "the elect": he tries to confirm their faith, perfect their hope, and stimulate their love. But this ministry is exercised only that this same community of the "elect" may recognize that it is elected to service, to be witness (martyr) to God's salvation in Jesus Christ. Most of a Minister's speaking — the Puritans used to call it "holy conversation" — will be about the holy things of a holy God, and yet this is not for the sake of establishing his own or his members' piety, but in order to help them comprehend the miracle of God's Holiness stepping down into the world's mud that he might reconcile this world to himself.

If all ministry centers in the incarnate and redemptive ministry of Jesus Christ, then we cannot confine Ministers within the narrow ecclesiastical affairs of parochial life. If we think of a Minister as one whose holiness is sheltered so that he may dole out pure spiritual nectar to the weary and wounded warriors in the Church's front line, then we encourage a false opposition between the ordained man and his parishioners. It leads straight into sacerdotalism.

I am sure the New England Puritans were right when they insisted, against some of their European colleagues, that the Minister was not only to be pastor to a parish but that he must also be an evangelist. In such men as John Eliot and Thomas Shepard they carried this conception of Ministry into effect in some of the first missions to the American Indians, and the same concept of Ministry echoes through the work of Jonathan Edwards in the

Great Awakening. Certainly they often interpreted their evangelical mission in a very narrow and pietistic way, but the main point is that their Ministry carried a responsibility to the world outside the Church. The same protest is made today in those Ministers who, to make their witness, have taken up work in factories and workshops.

There is always a danger that a Minister may become so involved in these "secular" pursuits that he begins to ignore or slight his own special vocation, but essentially the protest is sound — it is a protest against the convention which tries to keep a Minister's vocation and that of the Christian layman entirely separate, it is protest against the idea that evangelism can be made the exclusive task of laymen any more than it can be the exclusive task of Ministers. The mission of the Church is the vocation of every Christian.

Aside from all the obvious dangers of the worker-priest movement, it sprang from true insights and a deeply Christian and compassionate concern. Those who entered the movement did not wish their Ministry to become enmeshed and confined within the silken threads of an ecclesiastical cocoon. They recognized that our responsibility as *Christians* does not cease when we accept the vocation to become Ministers to God's people. The ministry of the Church is for this world and the people in it, and the Church's Ministers cannot lead the Church into this vocation unless they share in it. Our Lord came as a witness to the Kingdom of God, and if our Ministry is dependent upon his ministry, the *motif* of witness to the world is at its heart.

This is why Ministry is still necessary within the Church — not because we wish to defend a privileged order or professional caste, but because that which this vocation *ought* to represent carries us to the very center of the Christian gospel and to the Church's own vocation. Like so many things in Christian history, the Ministry fails not because it is useless and irrelevant, but because it has been made the excuse for pride and privilege, things that are contrary to its own nature.

In 1656 Richard Baxter complained to his fellow Ministers about the determined attempts that had been made in Parliament to overthrow the public Ministry. He said, "I think it is no time now to stand upon our credit . . . . It rather beseems us to fall down at the feet of our offended Lord, and to justify Him in his judgments, and freely and penitently to confess our trans-

gressions, and to resolve upon a speedy and thorough reformation";[32] and Baxter set his own hand to the work by writing
what is perhaps the classic treatise on the work of a Protestant
Minister, *The Reformed Pastor*.

It is not bad advice to the rest of us. But perhaps we need
fewer books on the subject and more reformed pastors.

[32] In the Preface to *The Reformed Pastor* (London: James Nisbet,
1860), p. 4.

chapter eight

Postscript and Preface

I

THE MINISTER IN THE WORLD

Our book is already finished. But there are immediate implications in the realms of practice and theology at which we can only hint. Therefore this is a postcript to the previous chapters and a preface to areas that need to be more fully explored. The fundamental thesis has been that a Minister is called to identify himself completely with the ministry of the whole Church, and that this should mean not his separation from the life and calling of other Christians but more complete identity with and involvement in the total mission of the Church.

That sounds fine, but it still has to be reduced to practical terms. It simply makes more acute the actual dilemma in which a sensitively-minded Minister will find himself, for how *can* he "identify" himself with the secular context in which his church members live their lives? How can he identify himself with them in the ethical ambiguities and frustrations of making a living within the secular world? They work in banks, factories, markets, where day by day Christian standards may be called into question and compromised; while he works in "the church." Their life is so obviously centered in secular society, and his seems to be so

obviously set within an entirely different sphere. There appears
to be a great gulf fixed between his normal experience and that
of the men and women to whom he is called to minister. He
suspects that more often than not there is this unspoken criticism
in the minds of even his most loyal members, and there is something in this situation which can take the fire from his prophetic
utterance, forcing him to remain silent when he knows he ought
to speak.

I wonder, however, whether this criticism would still stand if
laymen really understood the pressures of the Ministry in the
Church. How realistic is it? If we were to recognize that the
institutional forms of the Church are no different from those of
the society around it, we should perhaps more readily see that
most Ministers are subject to the same kind of frustrations, and
open to many temptations similar to those faced in business or
commerce. The problems may be different in detail, but the
opportunities for a man to compromise his principles are present
in the parish just as they are in the wholesale or retail business.
I suggest that we have vastly overemphasized the distinction between the setting of the Ministry and other forms of work. Can
God use the very faults of the churches, as fallible human institutions, to make us realize that Ministers are engaged in
the struggle with the "world" no less than others? Can we
accept the situation in which the temptation to compromise is
always possible without falling into the faithlessness that regards
the compromise as inevitable? These are questions which Ministers need to ponder deeply.

Even apart from these fundamental questions, when we consider
the life of an ordinary Protestant Minister, is it so very different
from that of the members in his congregation? Some might make
out a good case for suggesting that it ought to be, but is it? Consider for a moment the following areas of human existence which
many Ministers share with their "lay" brethren.

(a) *Most Ministers are involved in family life.* A married
Minister faces the problems of educating his children, of working out an equitable distribution of his time between the claims
of his wife and family and the claims of his job (the church),
of encouraging the growth of his children towards emotional
and spiritual maturity, and of raising them to be responsible
Christian citizens in modern society. He has to face the moral
issues related to the proper place of sex within the life of

himself and his wife, and he shares in the task of helping his children to understand the issues in the context of a Christian home. He too, as he faces the possibility of accepting a more lucrative post, has to set the claims of the job he is doing against the needs of his family; he will have to examine again the place of money and ambition in his life, and the relation of these things to the faith he professes. All these matters are no more foreign to him than they are to any other man who is a husband and a father; and yet, although they bring their own inevitable anxieties and heart-searching, they *can* become the opportunity for a ministry to be exercised in and through the home.

When I was first ordained, I argued that a Minister's home life was his own private affair, and I cherished the illusion that it should be a little haven of retreat and refreshment where a Minister might retire from the stresses of the parish to relax or lick his wounds. I found that it was much more. In fact, it *must* be much more, if the home is to be a Christian home, for a Minister's home is no more a private, fortified castle than any Christian home should be. It is the place where the things we profess publicly should first appear in practice.

Martin Luther was probably the first to give us the pattern of a Protestant parsonage, and I cannot imagine Luther with his Catherine, surrounded by their children, and with a table crowded with guests, ever considering their home life to be a "retreat" from the work of the Ministry. I understand that for a Jew the center of religion is the home rather than the synagogue; so too I sense that for Luther the home was the very temple of that practical worship which must be lived out day by day. Here too the Minister can be a Minister — not prissily or selfconsciously but gratefully and from a full heart; for in no other place can he show better the meaning of the preached Word.

For most adult men and women the home is where they can most truly *live*. Daily work so easily becomes humdrum, drab, or bitter, but in the midst of our families most of us come alive, and if we do not, then we know that it is one of the first signs that something is very wrong. I am suggesting that Ministers should not underestimate the extent of their real identity with the "laity" in the joys, frustrations, anxieties, and happiness of home life. A Christian home can demonstrate the meaning of a benediction.

(b) *The Minister has a job to do.* It is going to be difficult to say much under this heading without being misunderstood, for in our present society the various forms of Ministry in the Church are almost entirely cast within the professional mold. This ought to raise fundamental questions about commonly accepted patterns of the Ministry, because the very tasks and capacities that enable a clergyman to identify himself to some extent with other professional men tends to cut him off from the industrial worker and the laborer. You see an example of the dilemma particularly in Britain, where even the "educated accent" prevents real identification with the bad grammar and harsh accents of the majority of the "working classes."

Perhaps this "professional" aspect of the Ministry is one of the reasons why the inhabitants of suburbia find churches more congenial than those who dwell in the industrial and downtown areas: the modern Minister's occupation and way of life identify him most closely with the accepted *métiers* and *milieu* of middle class suburbia. This remains one of the biggest problems of "integration" for the Church, and it is one that we have hardly begun to face. No Christian can remain content with a pattern of the Ministry that virtually makes a Minister conform so much to one class pattern that he cannot properly be "at one" with those who do not fit the pattern themselves. There have been some attempts to come to grips with this problem by means of inner city parishes and community projects, but I am sure that the churches will have to develop a much more flexible approach to new forms of Ministry needed in the Church of Jesus Christ. I even cherish the hope that if the members of suburban churches could be introduced through a teaching Ministry to a more biblical understanding of the Church, they would not be content to allow their Ministers to become clerical replicas of themselves. They might even want him to venture into a secular, "dirty" job for part of his time, realizing that he cannot truly be a pastor to them unless he can be a pastor to all men.

At the same time I do not believe that the answer to our present dilemma is to close down all our suburban churches and kick the Ministers into factories, although in a world of revolution that may well be done for us in the providence of God. There *are* professional aspects to the Ministry, and not all of them are to be hastily discarded. It might not help us much if we were to gain the "common touch" at the expense of high standards in training, competence, and integrity, and I suggest that these can be points at which a Minister's work may bring him into relationship with others through mutual respect. A Minister should be much more than a professional man; but if he neglects the professional aspects of the Ministry, if he is slack in his study, inefficient in his administration and incompetent in the exercise of his public skills, he will not be likely to fulfill a true ministry in any sense of the term. The chances are that if he is insensitive to his responsibilities at this level, his own spiritual life needs attention. We gladly concede that there should be more to the running of a church office than sound administrative practice and efficient mimeographing, but nevertheless these routine matters have to receive proper attention.

We have hinted at this already,[1] and this is a place where we can easily be misunderstood. Many Ministers will protest that their biggest problem is the fact that lay people try to reduce the Ministry to precisely these terms, and feel that they should be set free. I agree — but they should be set free to exercise *ministry,* and not in order to assume the role of executive vice president. Meanwhile, in the present situation of the Church, Ministers have the responsibility to fulfill certain professional, administrative, and often routine functions; and of equal importance to the question *why* they should have these functions, there is also a question about the manner in which these duties are to be approached. I suggest that they *can* be a means of identification with members of the congregation, for the majority of the people in our pews spend their lives in just this kind of work and routine. Without in the least condoning the lack of Christian perception that is content to interpret the work of the Ministry in professional terms, I nevertheless would ask Ministers to look for those features within the suburban captivity of our churches which reflect our identity with the life of others, and which can therefore help us still to perform a ministry to men. If we are prepared to look for the opportunities of ministry within our present situation, we shall be the more ready to understand our vocation when the Church is forced to return to a "tentmaking ministry" in the factory or on the farm. For thirty years our Lord did the routine job of a carpenter and it was a part of his ministry.

(c) *A Minister is a citizen living in secular society.* The real

_____
[1] *Supra,* pp. 42, 208ff.

point of contact between the Minister and the members of his church is not the "secular" character of the tasks he may perform, but the Christian witness he bears as he goes about the world doing them. For the Minister lives in the world — he lives in the town and on a street and not behind the walls of a monastery. True, he can raise real but intangible barriers to the world, as any psychopath may do, and this tendency may be a psychological hazard to which the profession is prone. But there is no need for it. He *can* be open to the world if he will, and perhaps if he were more open, he would realize that he shares a commitment to witness with all his fellow members in the Christian community. This is the task in which all Christians should feel as one because this is the mission to which they are all committed. It belongs to us all, and it belongs to us all the time: we do not shed it when we file away last Sunday's sermon, or when we give up our place on the Church Council. A Minister should personify this commitment whether he is occupied with ecclesiastical detail on church premises, attending a convention, or taking his son to a football game. In his own total response to life in the world he can not only recognize his identity with other Christians, but he can also exercise a true ministry to them.

He is a citizen. More specifically, he is a *Christian* citizen, and this has less to do with supporting ecclesiastically sponsored programs than with the way he exercises responsibility to society. As a Christian citizen he too has to try to relate what he believes about Jesus Christ to the issues of political liberty, social and economic justice, and world responsibility. A few misguided people may be tempted to identify Christian witness in these matters with support of a particular political party, but to a Christian citizen the motives and the reasons behind personal decision are far more important. If, despite all a pastor preaches about the brotherhood of man and the Fatherhood of God, his attitude to racial justice or world peace or economic justice is dominated by fear and self-interest, what is his congregation to think? His status as a citizen is a point of identity with all other men, and they will look to him not so much (we hope) to discover *which* way he will vote but how he relates his Christian faith to his decision.

Even as clergymen, Ministers are in the world almost all the time, doing many of the things that are done by other people. They travel, they stay in hotels, they eat in restaurants, they meet strangers in the course of casual acquaintance. When a Minister is outside the area of his usual stamping ground, his great temptation is not so much to forget that he is a Minister but to forget that he is a Christian. My plea here has nothing to do with putting up the front of being a Minister, although it may be mistaken as that. Ministry, true Ministry, is simply representative Christian commitment. The temptation when we are "off duty" is to allow ourselves to become lost in the anonymous mass of humanity where nobody knows who we are, nobody cares what we represent, and where the standards are certainly not those of our Lord. I submit that whether we are "off duty" or not we still represent the Christian's commitment to Jesus Christ and to the Church's mission. Perhaps nothing supports the jibe that Ministers are simply "paid to be Christian" more than the fact that so often they seem to act that way. Put a few pertinent questions to yourself: would you voluntarily visit a hospital or a prison when you are on vacation? How "open" are you to the loneliness and the confidence of others when you are on a train journey or in a strange hotel? Or how do your conversation and actions measure up to your preaching when you are away from home? This is not something for Ministers only, but a Minister should be representative. We are all called to be witnesses to Jesus Christ, Ministers and laymen alike, and as far as I can see, this is a job in which we should not expect double pay for overtime.

(d) *A Minister is involved with money.* We must revert to that jibe that a Minister is "paid to be a Christian." Perhaps it would be truer to say that a Minister is one who is paid (a modest stipend) so that he is free to express the Church's mission and concern. But he *is* paid, and there is no escape for the Minister in his involvement with money, his own and other people's. He cannot avoid "the root of all evil" any more than his neighbours in modern society can, and in this fact he cannot help sharing with them in all the temptations, the anxieties, and the potential for good or evil that money, or the lack of it, brings to all of us. It represents temptation — anything to do with the world and its standards involves temptation — but a Minister cannot truly be a Minister unless he stands in the place where temptations are possible.

The use of money raises ethical problems that the Minister cannot shirk. We recognize money as a stewardship and we recognize that different men have different needs, but when we have said all that can be said about the remuneration that ought to be given to those who bear greater responsibilities, can we feel entirely comfortable about the fact that while some men grow relatively wealthy in the service of the Church, others struggle in penury all their lives? If there is in the Reformation traditions essentially a single order of ministry, can we accept the artificial orders created by wealth or the lack of it? I have never understood the logic whereby cultures have exchanged the false values of a stratified aristocratic society for the even falser values of a stratified plutocratic society, and by the same token I find it difficult to justify in the Church the exchange of an ecclesiastical hierarchy for an economic hierarchy. I am not pleading for a rigid egalitarianism — we do have different needs, different capabilities, different responsibilities, and perhaps they should be recognized by differences in remuneration — but surely our Lord expects his Church to watch the disparity carefully. Undoubtedly money can do good, and yet we always need to be conscious of the fact that it can be the price of betrayal. No man can be the conscience for another in this, but in the end we must all face the carpenter of Nazareth.

This simply illustrates the problem that the use of money raises for the Minister, but it is a problem that he cannot evade, for it is part of the essential dilemma of the Church, the dilemma of being at once both in the world but not of the world. The Roman Catholic Church has made a distinction between the religious orders and the "secular" priests who serve in parishes. The monastic ideal can be defended at many points, particularly when it is undertaken, as in the Protestant community at Taizé, for the specific purpose of *disponibilité* in evangelism, but it involves an inevitable separation *from* the world. Protestant Ministers are called in the best sense to be truly "secular."

A French pastor once pointed out to me that monasticism actually removes the individual from the three most pressing areas that try the temper (in both senses) and the patience of Christians in the world — the responsibility of marriage and the family (the vow of chastity), the stewardship of wealth and possessions (the vow of poverty), and the necessity to make decisions (the vow of obedience). Since the time of Luther, the Protestant Minister in a congregation or parish has deliberately *not* been removed from these responsibilities, and insofar as he is not, he shares in a very real way in the ambiguity and the mission of all Christians within the context of the secular. This is essential to his calling, for it reflects the redemptive incarnation by which our Lord himself became a Man among men.

II

"SIMUL JUSTUS ET PECCATOR"

We have spoken of the "ambiguity" of living as a Christian in the world. We might have called it the "hypocrisy." We are all "hypocrites" — actors playing parts to which we only approximate. Indeed, there is a sense in which civil society depends on the pretense of people acting better than they know themselves to be. Our common life would very soon end in chaos if everyone went out and actually committed murder every time he felt like it, or if we were completely frank and honest in expressing our true opinion of our friends and acquaintances. The kind of honesty that claims to be "cruel for your own good" is more often than not sadistically destructive. We *must* all "pretend" to be good citizens when at heart we know ourselves to be far from the ideal. We are trying with varying degrees of success to be loyal followers of Jesus Christ, when we know ourselves to be even further from the ideal than is the citizen from his. The real hypocrisy enters in when we pretend *to God and ourselves* what we are not. We must keep the two levels of "pretense" distinct in our minds. Christians must pretend [*pretendere* — to stretch forth] to be like Jesus Christ — *imitatio Christi,* the imitation of Christ — but the pretense that the world rightly derides is when we take a lower standard and try to represent ourselves as actually fulfilling all that Christ demands of us.

The sceptic reproaches the Christian as a hypocrite not because Christian pretense is any different from that which he puts on in striving to be a model citizen, but because church people so often seem to accept a form of piety as a substitute for the real goodness they claim to follow. They deliberately confuse a standard less than the best with the best, and their association with the church appears to be a claim that they have already achieved what the Christian Faith implies rather than an open confession that they are sinners. "Churchiness" and respectability are no substitute for the real thing, and the sceptic knows it. Christians often seem to be trying to persuade the world that they are, and that is the basic hypocrisy.

This temptation will always be one to which religious people are prone, for it arises from the challenge that religion makes to the compromises within which people are set. But we must not evade it or the challenge which faith makes to the compromises within which *we* are set. Our problem is to live within a society where we are constantly tempted to lower our standards and distrust our Faith, and either to run away from the challenge on the one hand or to fall into the basic hypocrisy of representing ourselves as sinless on the other. It would be so much easier if we *could* escape from the worldliness of this world, but we dare not. To avoid living in this world by enclosing ourselves within either the sectarian purity of the "gathered church" of the saints, or within the cloistered innocence of the monastic community, is no answer. To do this is ultimately to abdicate our Lord's authority over the world he came to redeem. For all their obvious "ambiguity" and the problems they present, perhaps ultimately the careers of such men as the Capuchin friar Père Joseph,[2] and the Puritan dissenter Oliver Cromwell, have more to commend them in the sight of God than those of the anchorite or the separatist, who for the sake of their own salvation hide away in a cave or a holy conventicle and commit the world to the devil.

Ambiguity — hypocrisy if you will — is written into the very nature of the Christian's vocation in this world, for he is called to represent Jesus Christ, and he is not Jesus Christ. And the one who bears this burden of compromise and the temptation to disloyalty most is the one who, by the very nature of the call placed upon him, must be the most representative — the Minister. Yet God calls him to go into the area where betrayal is

---

[2] I have deliberately chosen two men, one from the cloister and the other from the conventicle, who were forced to relate their religious separatism to the life of this world. François du Tremblay, "Père Joseph," was a Capuchin friar and the right-hand man of Cardinal Richelieu in the diplomacy of the Thirty Years War. There is an excellent study of his life by Aldous Huxley, *Grey Eminence: A Study in Religion and Politics* (New York and London: Harper, 1941). For a study of Oliver Cromwell's life from a similar perspective, I may perhaps refer the reader to my own biography, *The Lord Protector: Religion and Politics in the Life of Oliver Cromwell* (London: Lutterworth, 1955).

a constant temptation. The prime danger is, of course, in refusing to recognize that the compromises exist or that they can
have a hold upon us. The tragedy of Albert Svensson in Olov
Hartman's novel *Holy Masquerade*[3] is not that he was a dishonest
minister when his wife was an honest pagan, that he was a
hypocrite whereas she was not — in her identification with the
Virgin even Klara recognizes that a Christian is called to play
a part that is far bigger, better, purer than he (or she)
actually is — but it was in the fact that Svensson would not
admit his own compromises. In the final issue he cannot regard
Klara's profession of belief in Jesus Christ as anything but in-
sanity, because it would have called into question all the religious
conventions by which he had lived and excused himself. So
he ends by justifying wholesale evil in the name of good. This is
where the involuntary hypocrisy of Peter in the court of the
high priest is exchanged for the part of Judas in the garden.

There is only one way to prevent our denials of our Lord from
falling into that kind of intransigence, and that is to recognize
them before God for what they are — to see that as Ministers
we represent the Christian also *in his sinfulness*. If we stand
primus inter pares (first among equals) within the congregation
of the saints, we also stand before our God as first among
sinners. Our weakness and our sin may cause us to fall, not
once but many times, and we stand first in our need of grace.
Svensson was right to claim that God's grace is sufficient to
cover all our faults and sins; but not when we refuse to call our
sin by its proper name, not when we hide it behind our "good"
intentions and our "pure" motives, not when we try to justify
our priestly forms of expediency as holy sacrifices. To take
refuge in Svensson's claim upon God's mercy without facing the
unpleasant facts about oneself is to rely upon the "cheap grace"
that Bonhoeffer called the deadly enemy of the Church.[4]

"Simul justus et peccator" — Luther held that a Christian is
both justified and a sinner. A Christian must never lose the
consciousness that he is always both. To wallow in the sense
of our sinfulness and to forget that we are justified is to reveal
lack of faith in God's grace and in Christ's redeeming work, but
that has not been the great temptation of the Church. The

---

[3] Olov Hartman, *Holy Masquerade,* trans. Karl A. Olsson (Grand
Rapids, Mich.: Eerdmans, 1963).

[4] *The Cost of Discipleship* (London: S.C.M., 1948).

predominant note of church people in their overture to the world has been the certainty of their own salvation, without any corresponding recognition that they are sinners under grace. This is when the salvation that the Christian claims will seem to be a lie. And it will be a lie if he refuses to be penitent, to recognize his sinful compromises for what they are, or if by some clever alchemy of self-justification he represents them as new gold from the gospel. At the deepest level Ministers represent Christians in their constant need of penitence. They do represent those who serve the Lord, but only as they constantly stand under judgment and under grace. Within this tension they live, representative of the fact that God's grace is sufficient for all men, even for such as they.

III

WHAT NOW OF THE CHURCH?

In 1831 Ferdinand Christian Baur published his study of the "Christ-party in the Corinthian Church," an event which may be said to have marked the beginning of the scientific criticism of the Bible. It opened the battle between biblical critic and fundamentalist which raged throughout the nineteenth century, and the echoes are still heard today. Some of the views of the critics have been rejected, but many are accepted today as a theological commonplace. And yet the theology of our century has not remained satisfied with the theoretical constructions which the critics put forward to take the place of the traditional answers. Although twentieth-century theologians have accepted many of the critics' historical and literary disclosures, they saw that beyond all the human frailties and partial insights of the biblical writers there was a persistent residuum that could not be explained away. Many theologians have been forced to acknowledge that in the Bible there is still the revealed Word of God; and it has been the particular contribution of biblical theology in this century, while gladly accepting the critics' valid discoveries, to re-assert the Christ, the Word of God, who is revealed to us through the pages of the Bible.

This is no place to argue the issues afresh, neither is it my intention to do so, but I mention it because it may illustrate a significant parallel with regard to our understanding of the Church. In our day sociology has cast a cold eye upon the institutional forms of the Church very much in the same way as the textual and literary critics have looked upon Scripture. Insofar as the observations are accurate and the analyses just, it seems to me that Christians must accept the findings not only with a good grace but also with real gratitude. There is no more justification for the modern churchman to be dishonest or blind about the nature of the institutional church in the twentieth century than there was for the nineteenth-century churchman to resist facing the truth about the nature of the Bible. It is just as possible to be an ecclesiological "fundamentalist" as it is to be a biblical "fundamentalist." The situation is precisely similar, and if today the tendency to call for heresy hunts is a little less open and vocal, it is nonetheless to be repudiated. Whatever truth there is in the sociological analysis of the Church must be faced and accepted gladly.

But without prejudging the ultimate issue, it also appears to me that underneath all the criticisms of the Church there is still a core of truth that cannot be explained away. It is much smaller, granted, than the denominations and many ecclesiastics are prepared to recognize, but it is still a reality. For despite the manifold signs of human sin, despite the wickedness of its bloody history, despite its pride, its faltering witness and its constant denial of its Lord, there is within this community of faith that which God calls his own, that which he uses as the agent and apostle of redemption.

This may be interpreted by the more radical brethren as an oblique attempt to justify the *status quo,* or to salvage something from the wreck of our hopes, or as mere wishful thinking, or even as a bland attempt to make ecclesiastical reaction theologically respectable. That is certainly not the intention. What there is of gold in the residue has nothing to do with the practical objectives of the denominations, the traditional form of the parish, the cozy-club fellowships of Woodland Boulevard, or with bricks and mortar. It has to do with that intangible Something within the Christian community which, in the midst of all pretensions, hypocrisies, and weaknesses, still faithfully witnesses in every age to the incredible truth that in love God's Word became flesh and dwelt among us — visibly *flesh.* Perhaps we must look toward a theology that, having regarded the Church's true image without illusion, can still assert that the Church is integral to God's plan of salvation for the world. And

Christian theology needs to make that assertion, not because it is tied to the present forms of the Church, but because it must acknowledge God's grace. We must affirm the Church because our ultimate concern is not with the Church, but with the very nature of the God whom we worship, with the certainty of his promises and with the assurance of his living presence in our midst.

IV

A Man Set Apart

What we have just said about the Church must also be said about the Ministry. Ordination and all that it implies must be open to any criticism from any source that can carry the endorsement of the gospel, for a distinct and separated Ministry of the ordained can be justified only insofar as it maintains and exemplifies the gospel of Jesus Christ. But insofar as it does maintain that gospel, it cannot be lightly discarded.

When we have uttered our most devastating criticisms, something persists. When, during the course of church history, strictures upon contemporary Ministry have been embodied in forms that have sought to express the will of Jesus Christ, then the pattern of Ministry appears, because all Ministry finds its source and justification in His ministry. It has been our intent to show that Minsters are given by God to the Church to remind the Church that it is the Minister of God's Kingdom within the world; by God's grace the Ministers are to exemplify that vocation in their own service of the Church and prepare the people of God for their own call to witness. From this perspective there cannot be any fundamental division between the Church's members and the Church's Ministers, for ordination exists to expound the Church's own essential nature.

Yet there is an element of difference between those who are ordained and those who are not which cannot be entirely explained away. A Minister *is* "separated," set apart "by prayer and the laying on of hands" in order that he may give himself wholly to the preaching and teaching of God's Word, to the administration of the sacraments and public worship, and to the pastoral care and service of God's people. Just as the Church itself is set apart to minister within the world, looking indeed towards the time when the Holy City of God will be made manifest and there will be no longer any need for a distinct and separate "temple" (Rev. 21:22), so the Ministry is set apart to recall the Church to our Lord's total claim upon it, looking towards the time when these distinctions will disappear and the one messianic Ministry will embrace us all. In the exercise of his own vocation a Minister should help the Church to understand the ambiguity of its own existence in the world, and the paradox of its own set-apartness for service. For we are living "in between the times" and these distinctions are not permanent, but are means to the end that God has for his creation. We are looking to the time, and beyond time, when Christ shall be all in all. It is within the context of this eschatological hope that the differences between Ministry and laity, Church and society must be seen, and it is also within this same context that I suggest they must be recognized and accepted: the Kingdom of God has not yet come in its fulness.

Many Protestants will probably feel uneasy at this suggestion, and rightly so, for it could easily be used to justify sacerdotalism and claims to clerical status that are foreign to the gospel. That is not the intention, for we recognize that nothing was more distinctive of Reformation theology than its attack on the false barriers between the sacred and the secular in the Church of the sixteenth century — barriers that were expressed most rigidly in the distinctions that had developed between the clergy and the laity in the later Middle Ages. This authentic note of the Reformation has reappeared in our own day in the thought of Dietrich Bonhoeffer.

It is because clerical "separateness" is understood to be part of the more inclusive question of the relation between the sacred and the secular that it has become a debatable issue in our century, and for this same reason I turn briefly to the relation of the sacred to the secular in the hope that it may offer some light on how we may understand the set-apartness of the Ministry within the Church.

As we have observed, there *is* an interpenetration of the sacred into the secular and of the secular into the sacred which is to be expected, and even welcomed. The sacred properly enters into the secular when it gives a man a sense of serving God within his daily work, and the secular may properly enter into the sacred when it causes the Church to take the ordinary stuff of life seriously, to keep the holy offices and pious expressions of Christian people close to reality. There is, however, a kind of interpenetration that is false and blaphemous, for blasphemy enters in when one *invades* the other, as if it were a territory to be conquered and ravished.

Let me illustrate the issue boldly in an area that seems to have become something of an obsession with the modern generation. Sex is certainly as much a part of God's plan as is the eucharist, and yet we are rightly scandalized by the idea of consciously or deliberately allowing sexual ideas to invade divine worship. It is not that one is "purer" than the other, but that it represents an invasion of the sacred that threatens to humiliate and destroy it; and there is a passage where Bonhoeffer reminds us that it is just as false to allow scruples to invade and destroy our act of self-giving to the one we love. There is a time and a place for everything: God calls for mutual respect between the sacred and the secular.

If we keep this sense of mutual respect in mind, I believe it can help us to understand a Minister's separateness. He is separated for the service of God, and yet he can fulfill this service only by respecting and serving those from whom, in a sense, he has been set apart. There would be no false clericalism in the Church if we were to remember the apostolic injunction to be "in honor preferring one another." Moreover, if the Minister has respect for the proper place of the holy and the profane duties within his own life, he will not be likely to fall into the error of so stressing the former that he ceases to be a man living among men. Ministry ceases when we become angels.

This is perhaps another way of saying that we Ministers have to make the insights of the incarnation as central to our own living as they are to the gospel we proclaim. It is in the Word made flesh that God showed us, not only his amazing love for men, but also his amazing respect for the material matter out of which they were made. In our Lord's incarnation not merely humanity, but also the flesh, the human circumstances, the temporal relationships, and every condition of secular life was given its own dignity. Where that inherent worth had been twisted or perverted, his life redeemed it, for the incarnation was essentially redemptive, it was undertaken so that man should be reconciled to God, to his neighbour, to his world, to himself.

This is the ministry into which the Church and its Ministers are called. It is the ministry of reconciliation that derives its authority and its character from the redemptive work of Christ. Its essence is hidden in the One who, although he possessed the divine nature from the beginning, yet "did not think to snatch at equality with God, but made himself nothing, assuming the nature of a slave." This is the ministry which defines the nature of all Ministry, to which we must always return.

Appendix

It has been my intention to include at the end of this volume a chapter on the contribution of the Fourth World Conference of Faith and Order (Montreal, July, 1963) to our thinking on the Ministry. There were several reasons which suggested that Montreal might provide us with a new "breakthrough" in our ecumenical approach to this subject. We had been stimulated by the new concern about the laity and by the biblical emphasis upon the Church as the people of God; we had been forced to review our attitudes to episcopacy as reunion discussions all over the world forced the issue into the foreground, and as we were promised the increasing participation of Eastern Orthodox Churches in the World Council of Churches. Moreover, this was the first time for many years that a major ecumenical conference had put the Ministry on its agenda, and against the background of biblical theology and ecumenical realities, it was hoped that the occasion might force us to deepen our insights and clarify our objectives on this subject.

The title of Section III, charged with discussing the nature of the Ministry, was "The Redemptive Work of Christ and the Ministry of the Church." It was not the most concise of titles, but there was evidence that sound ecumenical thinking had gone into its formulation. It appeared to recognize that the nature of the Christian Ministry must be brought into primary relationship with the reconciling work of Christ, and by relating the redemptive work of our Lord to the Ministry "of the Church," it seemed to imply that any discussion of particular Ministries would have to begin in the total ministry of the whole Church. However, our hopes about new light on the nature of the Ministry proved to be as disappointed as our assumptions about the title proved to be unwarranted; and I would maintain that these two facts are not unrelated.

Dr. Paul S. Minear, whose labors over the past few years have been generously given to the preparation of Montreal, said that in comparison with the Faith and Order conferences of the past, "We have failed." Section III shared in the general failure. Its Report was probably no better and no worse than the others, but there was no new understanding of the problems raised, and little new insight into the way ahead. Good things were said during the debate, biblical language was used in the drafting, ecumenical sentiments were expressed all the time, but there was no clear consensus, no sense of having been led into fresh truth. Although at the end there was some agreement on the issue that must be raised in further discussion of the Ministry, those who took part had reached an impasse in their own treatment of the subject and left feeling not a little frustrated.

There has been considerable soul-searching since Montreal. Any survey of the reasons why it did not produce the clear word of prophecy must begin with the recognition that "the clear word of prophecy" is not the only valid criterion for "success" in ecumenical conferences. Nevertheless, frustration and sense of failure remain, and we can find many material reasons for it — the theological and ecumenical unpreparedness of some delegates, the inappropriateness of the Winter Stadium for the plenary sessions, the incredible heat and humidity of Montreal in July, and the pressure of having to begin drafting reports before the real discussion had started — all of which Patrick Roger aptly summarized as "chat under a hot tin roof"!

Doubtless these were material factors, but there is a sense in which the failure of the Montreal conference reflects the very success of the ecumenical movement over the past few decades. For the first time a conference almost representative of the whole Christian world found itself face to face with the problems posed by the world in its totality. The Eastern Orthodox were present and vocal in unprecedented numbers, and although Roman Catholicism was not officially represented, we welcomed a large number of Roman Catholic observers and were grateful for their presence. The Protestant-Catholic issue is now permanently on the agenda of the ecumenical movement. Moreover, Protestantism itself has widened its horizon to include every shade from Pentecostalists to Bultmannian theology. It is unrealistic and unkind to expect those who are participating in this kind of international conference for the first time to react as if they had been through every ecumenical encounter since Stockholm 1925 or Lausanne 1927. A time for personal adjustment to the ecumenical encounter is always necessary, and although our predecessors in the movement reached conclusions in their work, every participant has to retrace their steps in his own personal pilgrimage.

In past years that could happen during the course of the conference and still the conference would say something new and constructive. This was in part due to the fact that the area of concern was relatively limited; but perhaps it was even more due to the fact that leadership was vested in a small group of "professionals" (often unpaid) who were intensely committed to the ecumenical idea, who had been with the movement from the beginning, who knew every aspect of it thoroughly and who gave massive preparation to each new step of the way. The careers of such men as John R. Mott, J. H. Oldham, and William Temple reveal how far they shaped the course of the movement, and the extent to which their leadership was recognized as fully competent and informed on the points at issue.

The leadership today is certainly no less competent and committed, but the World Council of Churches must now tackle problems in a dozen different fields where previously attention might be concentrated upon one. A small staff under the continuous pressure of dividing its time between many urgent problems cannot give the kind of thorough attention to a single subject as J. H. Oldham gave, for example, to the Oxford Conference on "Church, Community and State" in 1938. It was therefore impossible at Montreal for delegates, many of whom were still finding their ecumenical sea legs, to discuss responsibly subjects that they sensed deserved far deeper and more comprehensive study than even the "experts" have been able to give.

This is one of the new ecumenical realities with which we have to live. The World Council of Churches *is* recognized by its constituent churches as the agency for the resolution of many problems that they must now face together: the very success of the ecumenical movement now imposes on the W.C.C. the variety and vastness of its crowded agenda. The Rev. Patrick Roger, Executive Secretary of the Faith and Order Department, put the issue sharply in two questions he raised after Montreal: "How far does this kind of pressure that we experience not only in Montreal but in so much modern ecumenical work reflect truly the pressure under which the whole Christian Church must live today? How far is the pressure on our hearts and minds and nerves and tongues a necessary part of the discipline which God is laying on his people all over the world in the second half of the twentieth century?"

True — and if Montreal has made the churches face this reality, it may be regarded as a very fruitful success.

This appears to be far from the work of Section III and "The Redemptive Work of Christ and the Ministry of the Church," but it is a necessary background to it, because the difficulties we experienced in that Section arose from the explosion of ecumenical responsibility in recent years. Basically they arose among those who had been active in the ecumenical movement itself, but whose interests led them to concentrate upon one or another aspect of the problem without seeing the subject under discussion in its wholeness.

Far from the members of this Section being uninformed, there was almost a plethora of talent. Many were serious theologians who had written with insight and erudition on the Church, or the Ministry, or the redemptive work of Christ; others had been made enthusiastic by the new thinking on the laity and were fully occupied within that branch of the Church's work; others again had been active in serious efforts of church reunion in which the nature of the Ministry and the place of episcopacy had loomed large. The chairman was Professor J. D. McCaughey, a theologian, who had taken a leading part in the union negotiations in Australia, and the staff advisor was Bishop Lesslie Newbigin, who as a Reformed theologian, a writer on the doctrine of the Church, and bishop in the Church of South India personified almost all these concerns.

Yet the Section reached an impasse, and the significant fact is that the divisions   which cut across denominational boundaries — were to be found among those who were committed to the ecumenical movement and were active in it. This was perhaps the deepest frustration. Those who had been stimulated by the "lay" concern and by the interpretation of the Church as the people of God, expected that the Section would endorse a thoroughgoing definition of the Church in those terms, but they had not related these insights to the place of particular ministries in the Bible. On the other hand, those who had come to a new appreciation of the "historic episcopate" seemed to expect the Section to recognize episcopacy as possibly of the *esse,* probably of the *bene esse,* and certainly of the *plene esse* of the Church. They were less ready to consider the nature of the authority that the New Testament bishop exercised. I have no doubt that at times our new friends from the Orthodox Churches in Russia and Rumania must have been completely mystified by what was going on, although they valiantly wrestled with the issues and often made very constructive contributions.

This was the major cleavage, but it led to others. Many members of the Section — possibly a majority — thought that we would follow the sequence suggested by our title and discuss first the relationship of Christ's work to the ministry of the whole Church, and then proceed to consider the work of ordained Ministries. At this point there was a sharp division of opinion on procedure between many in the Section and its leadership. The Section was instructed to discuss the Ministry, i.e., the ordained Ministry, and this was the specific assignment.

In my view this was regrettable, not only because a review of our Lord's ministry in relation to the whole Church would have put our discussion of ordained Ministry within its necessary perspective, but also because it would have reminded us of the source and nature of episcopal authority in the New Testament. In other words, it would have held the two halves of our interest together, and it could have been the means of correcting the enthusiasms of those who saw part of the ecumenical picture with regard to the Ministry, but who tended to be somewhat myopic about the rest. Furthermore, the exclusion of all questions related to the ministry of the whole people of God began as an irritation, but by the third day had become a major frustration. It led some seriously to question the form of authority that was being exhibited through the World Council itself: was this to be regarded as a taste of episcopal authority? Was the World Council of Churches moving from the position where it had been willing to lead, to one where it was beginning to *insist?* Some members learned a great deal about the possibilities in episcopacy within the first three days of Montreal, and although the situation improved after it had reached its low point, the lessons will remain for a long time.

In respect to the work of Section III the Fourth World Conference of Faith and Order offers the following lessons:

(a) A dichotomy in thought does appear to have developed between the concerns of the Lay Department of the World Council of Churches and the concerns of Faith and Order. This was suggested some time ago by Henrik Kraemer (*A Theology of the Laity* (1958), p. 10), and although it has been questioned (*Laity,* No. 15, pp. 14f.) it was made very evident at Montreal. Even if the staff in the Departments share no such misunderstanding, a split has certainly developed in the way in which their separate emphases are understood within the constituency. And that is just as bad. However, a review of the concerns of these departments in recent years reveals an odd fact, which may or may not be significant. Whereas the interests of the Laity Department seem to have forced it into fundamental bibilical and theological study, the Faith and Order Department appears to have been preoccupied with the essentially *practical* issues of reunion, in which, of course, the question how to reconcile episcopal and non-episcopal churches occupies a good deal of the floor space. I wish to point no moral, but it would seem that if the servants of the ecumenical movement are not to develop schizoid tendencies, a thorough ongoing study of the Church and its Ministry is called for in which both departments can be involved.

(b) A question is raised. Is the appeal to episcopacy (I was tempted to say "of" episcopacy) in church union negotiations essentially historical, theological, biblical, or pragmatic? We notice that the idea is entertained with a good deal of affability by church administrators. I write as a Freechurchman who is by no means frightened by the New Testament concept of a bishop, but who is scared stiff by what can happen when episcopal authority is confused with coercive power. Faith and Order must examine the nature of the episcopate in the New Testament.

(c) That in turn raises the question of authority and its character in the Church. The nature of ecclesiastical authority and its relationship to the redemptive ministry of our Lord is a primary study in this field, for no treatment will be adequate until it goes back to the source — Jesus Christ.

(d) Finally, a practical point of some importance, and one

that is directly related to the "ecclesiological nature" of the World Council of Churches and the way in which it regards itself. Is its own function to be interpreted essentially in terms of ministry, service? If so, then the Council itself, and its accredited representatives, will have to remember that it cannot help being an example of what "ministry" could mean within the Church that it seeks to realize and fulfill.

INDEX OF SUBJECTS AND PROPER NAMES

Sacrament, 128, 138f., 149, 186
Sacrifice, 140f.
Sadolet, Cardinal, 115
Salvation,
 a vocation, 144
Scriptures, 169f., 174, 196; cf. Bible
Shaliach, 49f., 202
Shepard, Thomas, 219
Socinus, 190
Sociology, 16, 18, 234f.
Spurgeon, Charles H., 74
State, 16, 59
Streeter, B. H., 46, 48 note 4, 70, 202

Tavard, George, 27
Taylor, Graham, 67
Taylor, Vincent, 71
Temple, William, 243

Unity, 91, 92, 93, 95, 98, 107, 108,

136, 158f., 197, 198, 199, 207, 214, 215, 216; cf. Ecumenism

Vatican Council, 27, 28, 179
Vocation, 19, 66, 130, 142, 144, 146; cf. Call, Election

Waltz, H. H., 30
Weber, H. R., 30
Weber, Max, 142, 146f.
Wells, H. G., 84
Wesley, John, 55, 192
Williams, Daniel D., 33
Williams, Roger, 180
Word of God, 14, 19, 105, 149, 169, 172, 173, 186, 213, 234, 238
World, 18, 223f.
World Council of Churches, 25, 31, 184, 185, 243f.
 department of the laity, 30, 128
 Faith and Order, 128, 184, 241f.